Organic Finance

Modern finance science is profoundly broken and damaging, morally and culturally. It has no choice but to change its theory and pedagogy – but the question is how and in what ways?

We urgently need to see the world from a very different, kinder, gentler and more caring paradigm. In truth, the planet is bio-diverse, and so is society, with a huge tapestry of faiths, customs, beliefs and practices in finance. A holistic approach is urgently needed. This book builds a new un-anthropocentric moral and sustainable finance from the ground up, helping students, professionals and scientists to reconstruct the knowledge and connect it to indigenous beliefs and timeless wisdom. An interdisciplinary, nontechnical approach is adopted. Respect for all living beings, the protection of forests, soil and soul, and the importance of trust, culture and relationships are critical to building harmonious communities.

Examples and techniques to re-engineer finance science are offered throughout the book.

Atul K. Shah (PhD – LSE) FCA is a world-renowned writer, broadcaster, award-winning researcher and editor, and author of six research monographs, including *Inclusive and Sustainable Finance*, *Jainism and Ethical Finance* and *Reinventing Accounting and Finance Education*. He is based at City St. George's, University of London, and has taught at the London School of Economics, University of Maryland, University of Bristol, University of Essex, among other universities. www.atulkshah.co.uk

"The discipline of finance needs a complete overhaul to remove its ethical, cultural and political bankruptcy and denial. Professor Atul Shah weaves together an alternative narrative grounded in the wisdom of many contented communities and cultures of the world which knew how to put finance in its place as a servant of society, never its master. He has dedicated several decades to this project. I welcome this plural, grounded and holistic narrative, and call upon educators and scholars to embrace it and transform their research and teaching, as without timeless wisdoms, we are doomed to fail our planet."
Professor Lord Prem Sikka, House of Lords, UK

"Atul Shah shows us that another finance is possible and already among us: meaningful, inclusive, diverse, and more-than-human, but also often marginalised, dismissed, and unheard. We all need to listen."
Professor Hendrik Vollmer, *Warwick Business School, Editor of* Handbook of Accounting in Society *and Associate Editor of* European Accounting Review

"Professor Shah has produced a once in a lifetime book. He takes us on one of the most extraordinary explorations of the intellectual, cultural and significant insights to be found throughout the cultures of the world which fundamentally challenge just about everything conventional economics teaches."
Martin Palmer, *BBC Broadcaster, Founder of FaithInvest and Author of over 20 books*

"Reading Atul Shah, you realise that classical and modern economics has excluded as 'externalities' almost everything that really matters to us and our lives. Here is the prospect of a compassionate economics that talks about what really matters and exposes indigenous beliefs which have long been hiding in plain sight."
Brian Eno, *Multi-Award-Winning Musician, Artist and Political Activist*

"Culture, Faith and Ethics in Finance have become divorced from the discipline for far too long and resulted in great social disruption. In this book, Professor Atul K. Shah makes a bold and multi-cultural effort to connect the knowledges, and show how so many organic practices in finance have been hiding in plain sight and are prescient and helpful to our modern predicament. I hope this book will spawn a whole new constructive literature on multi-cultural finance."
Charles Richard Baker, *Professor of Accounting, Adelphi University*

"Homo Economicus is a fiction created to support a world view. Today, finally, he is at least ailing and perhaps expiring. What replaces him will define the future of our species. Modern finance has removed the reality of history, culture and context from its science and education methods to perpetuate the myth of Homo Economicus. This is unsustainable. There always was another way, that more accurately reflected who we are, and what truly enriches us. Professor Shah's plural perspective draws from heritage and wisdom traditions which resource for those concerned with the state of our planet today – a beacon of light in a very dark world."

Professor Christine Cooper, *Editor*, Critical Perspectives on Accounting Journal

"*Organic Finance* is both a critique and a manifesto for change. Its witty, provocative and accessible style should appeal to finance professionals, policymakers, and educators. Using deep insights and practical examples, the book inspires a hopeful vision of financial systems founded on care, equity, and sustainability and seeks to civilise finance. For India, this magisterial work is highly relevant to how finance actually operates on the ground – our western textbooks urgently need to change to adapt such organic science."

Professor R Narayanaswamy, *Professor of Finance and Accounting (Emeritus), Indian Institute of Management, Bangalore*

"The failure of modern public financial management stems from a technocratic global policy mechanism (blunt instruments) that assumes one size fits all - China should respond the same way as a small Pacific Island. What is necessary is to understand the culture and context and build from the ground up instead of an arrogant and ignorant top-down approach. We need a new inclusive paradigm which multiplies trust and social capital and Professor Shah shows how. We have no choice but to take heed."

Professor Khalid Hamid, *International Director, CIPFA (Public Accountability)*

"We need all hands to address our sustainability and inclusivity challenges. Yet too many well-intended people remain hampered by assorted business fictions and myths. Professor Atul Shah offers a provocative fix through a reconceptualization of financial practices holistically grounded in cultural sensitivity and an ethic of environmental stewardship."

Professor Daniel T. Ostas, *JD, PhD, Chair of Business Ethics, University of Oklahoma*

"The depersonalised, rapacious values of modern Finance are central and dominant in ordering our lives. *Organic Finance* is timely in exposing the socially divisive and ecologically damaging effects of financial nihilism. And, crucially, it presents a communitarian, holistic alternative based upon tried and tested indigenous practices."

Professor Hugh Willmott, *Bayes Business School; Cardiff Business School*

"'Finance buries its morality under equations and calculations, helping to destroy the planet whilst profiting from its inequality and environmental catastrophe.' The boldness with which Professor Shah challenges this truth and constructs a new organic theory is highly laudable. In India, there are millions of family businesses motivated by faith and spirituality that operate organically and are contended to grow without debt and serve their customers honorably. Greed is constrained by relationships, principles and values and the need to pass the business on to future generations. This science deserves to be globalised, and *Organic Finance* is a timely blueprint."

Professor Devendra Jain, *Flame University, Pune, India*

"Professor Shah's new book is prescient in trying times, exposing how Empire is deeply woven into the equations of Finance. He shows that a timeless indigenous way is needed to protect our culture, ethics and environment and prevent selfish finance from depleting humanity."

Dr Anton Lewis, *Associate Professor of Accounting, Governors State University, USA Author of* Counting Black and White Beans: Critical Race Theory in Accounting, Accounting Fables and Tales of Race and Racism in the Borderlands of Business

"Atul Shah re-examines modern finance thinking through an eco-centric lens to surface and address crucial silences and deficiencies in current theories and practices. Provocative reading for a planet in deep crisis."

Professor Rajib Doogar, *University of Washington*

"This is a truly inspiring book that serves as a beacon of hope. Drawing on multiple cultures and beliefs, Professor Atul Shah identifies how business and society can reshape and reorganise to move into a postcapitalist era to heal mother earth."

Professor Alpa Dhanani, *Cardiff Business School*

deeply understand the nature and limits of money, and replenish trust and relationships."

Russell Napier, *Founder, Library of Mistakes*

"New paradigms do not arise often. Finance in particular has seen little innovation outside the confines of neo-classical economics that articulates, more often than not, a view devoid of wider humanistic concepts. Professor Shah discusses with aptness a multi-cultural organic conceptualisation of finance that speaks to wider environmental and ethical issues of our time. The book will not disappoint those seeking a broader perspective of the field."

Professor Alnoor Bhimani, *London School of Economics*

"This is a timely contribution, rich with original ideas to rethink the purpose, meaning and teaching of finance – to decolonize it from its destructive and exploitative relations to humanity and ecology. It opens a new strand of literature which enables indigenous cultures to speak about their own rich heritage of finance wisdom in a positive and constructive way, which the dominant western paradigm has ignored to devastating effect for far too long."

Professor Afshin Mehrpouya, *University of Edinburgh, Chair in Accounting, Sustainability and Governance*

"Leadership and Finance are often at odds. Culture and belief bring the much needed balance to the scale and encourage purposeful entrepreneurship, with a strong spirit of selfless service to nature and society. I salute this research innovation which has the potential to change global professional training in finance, and root it in ethics and values."

Margreeth Kloppenburg, *Chair of the Board Faculty Ethics, Culture and Behavior of the Royal Netherlands institute of Chartered of Accountants*

"Finance is a siloed and broken science which excludes diverse wisdom and perspectives. Atul Shah boldly and authoritatively shatters these fences to reveal profound pearls of wisdom hiding in plain sight. Being committed educators and students for an ecologically and socially just future for everyone, we have no choice but to engage and transform our curricula so that we become part of the solution to the unsustainable Anthropocene."

Professor Chandana Alawattage, *Adam Smith Business School, University of Glasgow*

"*Organic Finance* reinterprets money as a catalyst for inclusive and sustainable development, challenging conventional economic beliefs. It offers a culturally grounded, empathetic strategy for transforming money to benefit the world and its inhabitants, contesting the greed-driven, materialistic underpinnings of contemporary society. A novel strategy for the ethical reconfiguration of the financial system."

Dr. Malay Patel, *Expert in Strategic Management and Cultural Philosophy*

"Atul K. Shah shakes up neoliberal and neocolonial ideologies with a bold vision of finance in the service of human and ecological flourishing. A gift of indigenous wisdom – inspiring and liberating!"
Dr. Melanie Barbato, *Senior Lecturer, Pacific Theological College, Fiji, Author of* Jain Approaches to Plurality: Identity as Dialogue

"As a mathematician I have come to understand the beauty and elegance of equations when it comes to finance, but the abstraction is not the reality and we forget it to our peril. This multi-cultural narrative captures the breadth and depth of personal and corporate finance in ways which radically reignite our hopes for sustainable finance. It opens a wide new field of enquiry."
Professor Janette Rutterford, *Open University*

"Atul K. Shah's *Organic Finance* is a necessary intervention in today's global discourse on finance. With his bold critique of mainstream economic paradigms and incisive exploration of alternative wisdoms, Shah reimagines finance not as an imperialistic tool of greed, but as a communal force for sustainability and ethical growth. I see striking parallels between Shah's call for financial pluralism and the innovations of historical merchant families, who balanced profit, trust, and social responsibility across generations. This is a timely manifesto for scholars, educators, and leaders seeking a humane and inclusive future through business."
Sudev Sheth, PhD, *Author of* Bankrolling Empire: Family Fortunes and Political Transformation in Mughal India

"Professor Shah offers a new paradigm and language through theory that is pluralistic, wholesome, organic and creative, drawn from the profound wisdom of nature, faith traditions and indigenous cultures. He enriches the understanding of finance far beyond its current models and formulae. His powerful inter-disciplinary approach, aligned with his critiques of finance from his economics training at the world-renowned London School of Economics, are impeccable and game changing. His understanding of, and challenges to, mainstream equations and technocracy open up a large ocean of diverse possibilities and deeper wisdoms."
Dr Lynne Sedgmore, CBE, *author of* Presence Activism

"We live in a tempestuous, awful era; it is one in which our planet is under grave threat from climate change, 25,000 people including 10,000 children die of hunger every day and in 2021 Global hunger numbers rose to as many as 828 million (UN estimates). Blameless men, women and children are being killed by the sophisticated (and extremely expensive) weapons of war. There seems to be something completely rotten and soulless at the heart of our political and economic systems. We urgently need to find kinder, more intelligent alternatives which cherish human life and nature. Atul Shah's new book sets out such an alternative. This makes it an important intellectual

Organic Finance

Building a New Sustainable and Inclusive Framework from the Ground Up

Atul K. Shah

Routledge
Taylor & Francis Group
LONDON AND NEW YORK

Designed cover image: Bhavik Haria

First published 2025
by Routledge
4 Park Square, Milton Park, Abingdon, Oxon OX14 4RN

and by Routledge
605 Third Avenue, New York, NY 10158

Routledge is an imprint of the Taylor & Francis Group, an informa business

© 2025 Atul K. Shah

The right of Atul K. Shah to be identified as author of this work has been asserted in accordance with sections 77 and 78 of the Copyright, Designs and Patents Act 1988.

All rights reserved. No part of this book may be reprinted or reproduced or utilised in any form or by any electronic, mechanical, or other means, now known or hereafter invented, including photocopying and recording, or in any information storage or retrieval system, without permission in writing from the publishers.

Trademark notice: Product or corporate names may be trademarks or registered trademarks, and are used only for identification and explanation without intent to infringe.

British Library Cataloguing-in-Publication Data
A catalogue record for this book is available from the British Library

ISBN: 978-1-032-87802-7 (hbk)
ISBN: 978-1-032-86964-3 (pbk)
ISBN: 978-1-003-53453-2 (ebk)

DOI: 10.4324/9781003534532

Typeset in Sabon
by Taylor & Francis Books

Printed and bound in Great Britain by
TJ Books, Padstow, Cornwall

This book is dedicated to my parents Keshavji Rupshi Shah and Savita Shah, and to my wife Nina, who has long suffered the anguish that comes from living with books everywhere, and someone who is often found dreaming rather than listening. To Jaina and Meerav, you are the living batons of our beautiful wisdom tradition, and long may you spread its light through your character, leadership and example. Thanks to my publishers at Routledge, especially Rebecca Marsh and Kristina Abbots, without whose support the dissemination would have been challenging.

Tree-Ky Business

Why is it that a tree never moves?
Why is it that it never goes to visit
Other trees?
Does it not want to branch out and network?

Why do trees never go into business?
They have a ready market for their fruit.
Birds could be charged for parking or overnight stay.
On a hot day,
Trees could easily profit from selling their shade.

It puzzles me why it is that trees,
Have no ambition in life!
They seem to be over-content with their lot,
And have no interest in exploiting their resources,
Or making something of their strengths.

Rarely do trees present a statement about their performance,
Or congratulate themselves for the quality of their products.

Do they really STAND for something?
I have never seen a tree write a poem,
Or sing a song.

Trees are lousy customers –
They never buy anything!
In fact, they never visit our stores,
And ignore our advertising!

Have you ever seen a tree drive a car
Or purchase an airline ticket?

They never listen to orders,
So we can't even give them any
Jobs!

Tell me how have trees contributed to economic growth?
All they produce is more seeds and trees,
As if there weren't enough already!

Trees are practically useless,
And harbour plenty of insects!
They have no sense of urgency about anything,
And their silence is so deafening!
LET'S CHOP THEM ALL!

Atul K. Shah

Contents

Foreword 1   xiv
LYNNE SEDGMORE CBE
Foreword 2   xiv
MARTIN PALMER

1   Evil Finance   1
2   Soil and Soul   49
3   Seed   73
4   Eco-System of Finance Beliefs   101
5   Inner Growth   134
6   Forests of Hope   158

Index   181

Foreword 1

What the world needs now, more than ever, are thinkers, challengers, influencers and paradigm shifters who can combine and synthesize mainstream and alternative views into a new perspective that genuinely inspires and transforms.

I have known Professor Atul K. Shah for the past twenty years. I have witnessed his genuine dedication to serving society and his continual academic, economics, and spiritual inquiry. He is a true polymath and an exceptional lecturer and communicator. His wise and powerful contributions to politics, academia, civil society, the media, financial institutions, select committees, and to conferences all over the world are prolific. I am inspired by all his previous books, blogs and academic writings. Atul is a regular commentator on ethics within his profession and his work has been profiled in the *Financial Times, The Guardian, Forbes*, Economia, BBC Radio broadcasts, the World Service and Channel 4, and he also writes a weekly editorial for iGlobalNews.

Professor Shah's forensic and perceptive challenges are vital, as well as inspiring. Atul is a Jain, one of the oldest living cultures of the world, and he is continually inspired and nourished by this prescient science. He has touched, changed and enriched many lives, including mine. I never tire of saying how the Jain values of tolerance, non-violence, duty, resilience, interdependence, and *Anekanta* (or many sidedness) are desperately needed in the world today. For me, Jains are financial and green pioneers, steeped in an ancient faith tradition and wisdom that is highly relevant to today. Jains are also one of the world's most successful business diasporas with hundreds of years of experience in commerce and accounting. That knowledge and heritage has today been submerged by secular modernity, but it desperately needs to resurface, given our dark times. I am so grateful that the indigenous voice of Professor Shah is able to speak so eloquently and authoritatively to the all-powerful discipline of finance in a modern contemporary language. This is no mean feat. He is providing profound intellectual leadership in a desert of materialism, learned ignorance, and selfishness.

Modern scholars acknowledge Atul's "significant creativity, self-sacrifice and legacy" based on his personal leadership in shaping global innovation in western Jain wisdom through Anglo-American engagement, and as the founder of the Young Jains global organisation and founding editor of *Jain Spirit* magazine. His is a rare, wise and courageous voice infused with an intelligent synthesis of both modern and ancient wisdom and is able to connect to a very diverse global audience through his plural upbringing.

Atul has devoted many decades of his professional life to challenging and naming greed, corruption, shortsightedness and outdated economic theories within all aspects of the financial sector. His Routledge books *Jainism and Ethical Finance, Reinventing Accounting and Finance Education* and *Inclusive and Sustainable Finance*, meticulously researched and articulated, are lighthouses of hope. In this latest book he goes straight to the heart of reforming the theory and science of finance, reminding us that finance should be the servant of society not its master. His innovative, inclusive and sustainable theory of finance is a profound contribution to radical thinking and reframing of our broken global financial systems. This is a project few would dare to write, given the profound narrowness of our contemporary banking and finance greed merchants. Finance experts have lost the skills to tap into timeless wisdom altogether.

I particularly like the way this book reveals and explains how finance professionals deny the existential crises the world is facing, and how these experts are immersed in anthropocentric thinking. This is the only paradigm and language they know, but they need to learn new and inclusive ways of understanding and acting. A huge part of the problem is an inability to move beyond a secular/non-secular dualism, alongside a blinkered denial of the importance of culture and diversity. This requires a move beyond universal theories and equations, removing the blinders of abstraction.

Professor Shah offers a new paradigm and language through theory that is pluralistic, wholesome, organic and creative, drawn from the profound wisdom of nature, faith traditions and indigenous cultures. He enriches the understanding of finance far beyond its current models and formulae. His powerful inter-disciplinary approach, aligned with his critiques of finance from his economics training at the world-renowned London School of Economics, are impeccable and game changing. His understanding of, and challenges to, mainstream equations and technocracy open up a large ocean of diverse possibilities and deeper wisdoms.

Importantly, the treasures in this book are highly accessible for the non-financial reader, as well as inspirational for experienced financial experts. I hope that students training in finance and economics will read this book and build on its creative sustainable vision, through new teaching and research. I know that the general reader deeply disturbed by modern finance and yet unable to find the language to critique it will be empowered and uplifted by this work. I yearn for the economic system to be shaken and transformed based on the insight and proposals threaded throughout this powerful, wise and groundbreaking book.

Dr Lynne Sedgmore CBE, author of *Presence Activism*

Foreword 2

I really don't even know how to begin this because, well frankly, Professor Shah has produced a once in a lifetime book. He takes us on one of the most extraordinary explorations of the intellectual, cultural and significant insights to be found throughout the cultures of the world which fundamentally challenge just about everything conventional economics teaches. Here you will find a range of reading, knowledge and reflection which is truly universal in its scale, depth and intensity. He takes wisdom, insights and inspiration from around the intellectual world, ranging from profound philosophers to home-spun wisdom and weaves for us all a journey of discovery.

Professor Shah comes at the problems of a monolithic world view called economics which has destroyed civilisations; wreaked the natural world; distorted relationships between peoples and cultures and which is so arrogant it hasn't even seemed to notice this was happening. Drawing upon his own heritage of Jainism and therefore not just Indian culture but that extraordinary pool of wisdom and insight known as Vedic – covering Hinduism, Buddhism, Jainism and influencing other cultures such as Sikhism and Zoroastrianism, he can summon up both history and culture to form the advance guard of his thorough critique of western materialist culture – if that word is applicable here.

As someone coming from what has been described as the grandmother faiths of western capitalism, Marxism and modernity, bastard grandchildren in almost all cases – I find myself as a critical Christian from a socialist family, welcomed into the fold. Shah is not proposing that western cultures and eastern cultures are irreconcilable. Far from it. In many cases it has needed eastern cultures and beliefs to reawaken a sense of the sacred in nature; reawaken a sense that values are not add-ons to the advertising market but arise from core beliefs. It has also taken Christianity and the best of western culture to challenge ancient views on women, power and faith that had encrusted other faiths – and had also done so to Christianity. And it is the beliefs of modern shareholder capitalism that he helps us uncover with their implicit imperialism, colonialism, sexism and cultural indifference which lies at the overriding assumption that materialist culture is reality while everything else is so relative as to be insignificant.

I have known Professor Shah for over 30 years. We first met when I was working as HRH The Prince Philip, Duke of Edinburgh's religious advisor on the environment. Prince Philip and I had launched an engagement between the major conservation and environmental organisations of the world – he was President of WWF International and I had run the world's first multi-faith education centre, focusing on how different faiths understood our place in both nature and in the built environment. Together Prince Philip and I challenged the secular world to stop ignoring the faiths. When we started in 1986 there was no major environmental or UN programme that worked with the faiths. Yet the faiths are the largest sector of civil society and run over 50% of schools, a third of all universities and almost half of all medical facilities worldwide. They are also trusted in ways that no government, no NGO, no UN programme is trusted. And perhaps it was because of this that the materialist secular world simply ignored the faiths or attacked them as being out-dated and irrelevant at best, evil and malignant at worst. The faiths are a threat to those who would place humanity at the centre of all meaning; financial success as the crowning glory of human endeavour and selfishness – with a little philanthropy when possible – as the height of human nature. Yet this secular arrogance persists to this day and warps most of what "world leaders' think is reality.

In this frankly brilliant book, Shah demolishes all these assumptions.

But what he also does – which so many critics of the current economic cultural scene fail to do – is offer alternatives. Alternatives that for centuries – even millennia – have worked, faults and all, but have managed to help communities thrive. He draws upon ancient writers and beliefs – from Buddha through Greek thought to the mystics of the great faiths – in order to challenge us to be better and to think bigger. He also asks us to question such fundamental building blocks as the very way we educate. Like me, he is inspired by great educational thinkers such as Paulo Freire and his seminal book *Pedagogy of the Oppressed*. For Shah, the very values and assumptions of the western educational model harbour within them the seeds of destruction, of cultural arrogance and ignorance and the failure to help children discover for themselves their own inner light and wonder.

This book doesn't just demolish. It offers both the old, and the contemporary, roots for new life to flourish on this dangerously exploited planet. He asks us to pull down the idols we have created which venerate greed as good; personal triumph as more important than community success; which reveres those who stop at nothing for personal gain. In their places he offers us wisdom from political thinkers; poets; religious teachers; village life and the arts with which to reconstruct a better more wonderful world. It has often been noted that, in western culture, two of the most powerful images of human life both died at the age of 33: Alexander the Great and Jesus. For those of us from a western culture with wonderful spiritual insights, wisdom and practices, he asks us to choose. Do we go with the World Conqueror, who destroyed ancient cultures and imposed his own – or with the gentle teacher of a small occupied country?

I am sure that this book will offer encouragement to many from the marginal cultures and belief systems of the world whose scholars always find themselves on the defensive, forced to adopt a western model to get published or promoted. Many of these cultures have long histories and traditions of experience in finance but lack the framework and language to express these positively, authoritatively and constructively. I am confident that it will help to shape a radical shift in finance teaching and training by making culture and ethics central and making the equations build and value trust and social cohesion, rather than destroy them. Finance scholars can now take responsibility for their science and help build a truly sustainable future. After all, what other realistic option do we have?

Thank you as always, my dear friend Atul, for helping me see my culture as one with riches as well as with scars and curses. Thank you for offering to help us all do the same with our own cultures. And thank you for not letting us rest on our laurels but through your encyclopaedic reading and experiences, offer us the delight of diversity as the antidote to crushing uniformity.

Martin Palmer, Founder of Faith Invest, BBC broadcaster and author of over 20 books

1 Evil Finance

The discipline of finance is supremely powerful and profoundly broken, morally and culturally.[1] It is an ideology steeped in scientific jargon which mystifies and distances itself from reality or morbidity, and has converted money, which is a means to an end, to an end in itself. This fiction (Bay & McGoun, 2018; Graeber, 2014; Lagoarde-Segot, 2018; Muniesa, 2024) has been the cause of vast inequality in society, and a significant disrespect and attack on animals and nature, fuelling human arrogance and irresponsibility. Unlike an oil spill or a flooding incident, the ingredients of finance and their impact on the global climate catastrophe are not visible to the naked eye, yet they have lasting and irreversible planetary ramifications. Scientists rarely agree on anything, but they have confirmed that over the last four hundred years, we have been living in the Anthropocene (Lewis & Maslin, 2015), a time when one species, the human, has done *irreversible* damage to the planet and our ecosystem, through its greed, fossil fuel extraction and pollution, over-consumption and violence on an unprecedented scale. Simply put, we have come to trash our homeland beyond repair. Even human cultures which have lived with a light footprint, without greed for money or possessions, and instead preserving and nurturing life in farms and forests, have been decimated. At the very least, we need to face the role of our science and knowledge in this calamity, instead of perpetuating the falsehood. This book takes on the catharsis, and showcases sustainable finance knowledge and wisdom which has long been hiding in plain sight.

Many ordinary people feel overwhelmed and overpowered by finance, often losing their health and well-being in the process. Our institutions and markets for money have been a primary cause of this catastrophe, yet they continue to survive and capture human life and society like a noose (Fleming, 2017b; Renner et al., 2021; Rich, 2013). Culture and ethics, so central to human adaptation to money, have been removed from the science by experts obsessed by a universal objectivity, a materialistic *Homo Economicus* (Cohen, 2014) and narrow specialisation. Finance has created defensive silos to protect itself from challenge and critique, and these have become self-perpetuating, converting many abstractions into 'scientific truths' (Keasey & Hudson, 2007). Volatility, greed and insecurity have been hard-wired into the culture and hubris of deal-making, having significant reverberations in wider society (Ho, 2009).

DOI: 10.4324/9781003534532-1

Technocracy and abstraction have helped build a wall around the scientific critique and at the same time enhanced accounting and finance's power and reach globally. The French philosopher Frédéric Bastiat, presciently observed:

> When plunder becomes a way of life for a group of men in a society, over the course of time they create for themselves a legal system that authorizes it and a moral code that glorifies it.
>
> (Bastiat, n.d.)

We could add 'And a knowledge system and institutions that legitimate and authorise plunder in the name of science' – that is effectively what economic science has done to the world and continues to do. Leading experts are today condemning the science and practices of finance (and economics) for its fictions, contradictions and siloed thinking (Bay & Schinckus, 2012; Brooks et al., 2019; McGoun, 1997; Shaxson, 2019) and encouraging much more diversity in its theories and imagination (Lagoarde-Segot, 2015). They are also calling for significant ethical reforms and renewal, where morality, sustainability and the care of society and the environment are made central to the knowledge base (Boatright, 2010; Christophers et al., 2017; Keasey & Hudson, 2007). In particular, there is a growing demand for greater inter-disciplinarity, accountability and responsibility in the finance science, given its significant economic and political influence (Ardalan, 2023; Borch & Wosnitzer, 2020). At the end of his seminal study of the 5,000-year-old history of debt and finance, Graeber surmises:

> What I would like best of all, would be to see this book contribute ... to a broader moral reassessment of the very idea of debt, work, money, growth and 'the economy' itself.
>
> (p. 398)

This book takes up this call and helps shape a plural, non-technical, moral and responsible finance which is exactly the opposite of modern financial training and hubris – caring, nurturing and replenishing of culture, trust, social relationships and environmental capital. To enable this, even the language and framing of finance had to be redrawn (Shah, 2022a). It is a theory designed to help us see what role finance could serve if we are to live in harmony with all living beings – a new wholesome, organic and creative approach to finance. The ideas in the book are inclusive and holistic, drawing from the deep well of wisdom that comes from nature, faith traditions and indigenous cultures.

The approach adopted is plural rather than singular, absolutist or universalist – its aim is to enrich the understanding of finance far beyond its models and formulae. It attempts to view finance from the ground up, giving soil, nature, trees and animals a proxy voice. The existing culture and belief systems of different cultures and communities all over the world, many of which are pro-social and respectful of nature, are acknowledged and shared. Readers concerned about the corruption of finance should find significant hope and discover in the pages the possibilities for rewriting the code, practices, markets and institutions of finance such that they *serve* the planet and abandon the bullying and extraction from nature and society. In this sense, it is a deliberately hopeful book, idealistic even, designed to show how and why a better world is possible and practical too.

Expropriation and exploitation can be replaced by shared growth in community, health and wisdom, far beyond the constraining mortal and material world which modern finance is consumed by (Monbiot, 2023; Rajan, 2019). There is a growing realisation that empire was not just a physical attack by European countries on various continents and nations, but it was also a subliminal attack on hundreds and thousands of human cultures and traditions, whose knowledge and social systems were deemed backward, uncivilised and illegitimate (Fanon et al., 2004; Fenelon & Alford, 2020; Kingston, 2015; Mbembe, 2019; Randazzo & Richter, 2021; Taylor, 1997; Williams, 2012). The abstraction that has become so common and elusive today is but an extension of empire, a way of subjugating cultures and eliminating critique by hiding behind a technocratic tower of babel. At a deeper level, empire was an attack on the beliefs, souls and heritages of many cultures of the world which lived in harmony with their land, animals and forests. We now know that many of these cultures were prescient and understood that human life could never be sustained at the expense of plants, animals and nature. They lived a communitarian life, where cooperation was the norm, and worked together to achieve common ends, where greed and selfishness were seen as vices rather than virtues.

The unique contribution of this book lies in the demolition of many myths and taboos cultivated by the discipline of finance. For a long time 'ethical finance' was seen as an oxymoron. Similarly, culture and finance were divorced, even when significant materialistic behavioural assumptions were made in the modelling of finance theory, including the invention of *Homo Economicus*.[2] Money is a social and cultural construct, and influences culture, and is also influenced by it (Dodd, 2014). Positivism encouraged a science free from ethical values or 'bias' allowing human society to be choked in the name of objectivity, evidence or neutrality. It encouraged supreme irresponsibility in finance.

Human violence, animals and the environment are still absent from most textbooks, and racism and faith are completely excluded. The silences and ignorances in finance are legendary (Gendron & Smith-Lacroix, 2013; Lagoarde-Segot, 2020; Newell, 2013; Rich, 2013). Greed and selfishness are celebrated as virtues, and diversity and indigenous wisdom have no place in the highly instrumental equations and calculations. There is no such thing as community in this utopian economics. The abstraction of reality has been normalised, and a new technocratic 'reality' counter-imposed on finance students and society at large. As an example, one belief is that if the equations say that everyone is greedy and selfish, then surely it must be true … The eminent social scientist Bruno Latour (Latour, 2014) eloquently shows how economists would rather protect capitalism at any cost then to allow the planet to die, such is the absurdity of the science. This book instead exposes a caring and constructive finance where money is used to serve society, and cultures of compassion and respect for all life are rejuvenated.

Finance Fictions and Silences Galore

A fictional new species called *Homo Economicus* was created to enable scientific justification of universal human and environmental exploitation (Çalışkan, 2022; Cohen, 2014; Fleming, 2017b). The knowledge we are seeking today was and continues to be actively buried by modernity and neo-liberalism (Shah, 2022a; 2022b). It is deemed pagan, heathen, black and native something which will take society backwards, when it is much of European philosophy and culture which have been so damaging. We have to find ways to uncover what we have lost, or reveal truths that are hiding in plain sight, by removing the empire mindset and allowing cultures to speak their own truths on their own terms, without any prejudice from the scientist (Fenelon & Alford, 2020; Poyser & Daugaard, 2023). Such diverse wisdoms are revealed very well in *The Dawn of Everything* written by an anthropologist and an archaeologist (Graeber and Wengrow, 2022), who show in detail how different and advanced many non-colonialist cultures were, with greed and materialism seen as vices rather than progress.

Tax is a cost to be minimised in finance, and there is little ethical discussion on this (Murphy, 2015, is an exception). In fact, the equations encourage tax avoidance and reward companies for doing so. Reflections on the long-term consequences for the public sector, which explain how corporations cannot survive without infrastructure like roads, energy, education, legal protection of private property, and healthcare, are deleted by senior professors and from the professional exams. The giant Big 4 global professional accounting firms have highly profitable tax practices which specialise in such advice (Brooks, 2014; Brooks, 2018; Mazzucato & Collington, 2024). The recent tax haven scandals like Panama Papers or Paradise Papers, expose lawyers, bankers and accountants directly involved in the design of these schemes, but finance textbooks remain silent.

Another significant silence in finance is about the whole economies of fossil fuels, war, armaments and aggression, which are state funded or subsidised to the tune of trillions of dollars every year, and the beneficiaries are private corporations (Beck, 1992; Eckersley, 1958; LaMothe, 2023; Said, 2014; Thompson, 2017). This finance is actively destabilizing, and just as the fossil fuel industry directly attacks nature and pollutes the environment, it cannot operate without stock market, bond and debt finance from international banks. The chains of finance, and the purposes behind them, are submerged in the name of profits, efficiency and wealth creation.

Furthermore, an economy of war leads to a culture of fear and anxiety, with violence towards animals and nature becoming normalised – this has significant social and political consequences which are simply ignored by finance science. We need a theory which recognises the importance of purpose and motive, and the planetary sustainability implications of big money. If this means that our structures of markets and institutions need to be redrawn, we should not avoid this challenge. The fundamentalism in the textbooks of corporate finance is so extreme that the value-maximising equations are assumed to apply irrespective of product, industry or service. There is an abject subliminal attack on context which includes culture and industry. Bibliometric analysis of an emerging 'cultural finance' literature shows that even here, there is little time for deeper philosophical reflection on money and its cultural construction (Goodell et al., 2023). Most of the studies are quantitative, assuming that culture can be measured and its impact quantified – the discipline is using known and familiar tools to analyse its own ruinous assumptions, with predictable results.

Whilst wealth creation and maximisation is encouraged in the equations, the serious personal and psychological consequences of wealth are simply ignored by economists. In fact, money is celebrated as the key to happiness and fulfilment, when in truth, it rarely achieves either. For young, eager economics students, this philosophy is turned into a belief system, doing even more damage to society (Gerlach, 2017). Research shows that it causes Affluenza, where instead of providing security, wealth often multiplies distrust and insecurity (James, 2007). Wealth can often become a disease. Marriages and families routinely break up, and addictions like drugs, alcohol, possessiveness and sex take over, ruining mental health and well-being. With rising inequality, we have rising mental health crises – there is a direct correlation with the growth in materialist culture (Hertz, 2020). Far from giving contentment and joy, wealth becomes a burden and a source of loneliness and restlessness. Whilst surplus wealth increases inequality in society, the pain suffered by the majority as a result of this greed is ignored or blamed on the poor.

Through financial markets, the future can be discounted to the present, and there is no reflexivity about the nature of time, nor of any inter-generational inequity that may result from this (Durand, 2017). A garage startup is so clever that it can turn people into billionaires overnight – where did that money come from, and who loses to the garage? Stock and financial markets are assumed to be free, highly competitive and efficient, and regulation and monitoring are seen as taboos which imposed costs on the firms and investors. Decades of financial crashes have made no dent on the 'theory' of finance. Financial valuation is a key to progress, and captures the whole truth about a corporation would you believe – the stock market value of a corporation is assumed to fully capture its overall worth to nature and society!

Finance has changed the meaning and significance of money to suits its own theories, instead of trying to be realistic. Even religion and belief have been removed from the science, when in reality, religion was key to the birth and growth of capitalism (Friedman, 2022). At heart, finance and economics are nothing but a human belief system (Sahlins, 2013). Globalisation and financialisation were commonly seen as beneficial and advances for the free movement of capital, even though labour could not move freely, and social and environmental harm could be exacerbated at a planetary level by multinational corporations (Fleming, 2015). The large corporation is celebrated in Finance as a 'great' development when in reality, it is seriously undermining our democracies through political capture (Bakan, 2020). As to the exponential compounding of interest and the sheer unsustainability of this financial method, as entropy is a law of nature, there is total silence in the finance textbooks, and instead a legitimation of the beauty of compounding (Renner et al., 2021).

False Pedagogy: The Detachment of Meaning, Purpose and Responsibility

Another major ignorance in finance is about narrative and stories. The seminal book by Graeber (Graeber, 2014) examining the 5,000-year history of finance is full of true stories uncovered by anthropologists, with examples of how different cultures, nations and traditions adopted money at different times. It exposes the vast global diversity of the culture and practice of finance, from kings needing money to pay soldiers to defend their territories or collect taxes, to villagers never wanting to be paid back in full, such that the relationship stays open and mutuality is reinforced. Modern economic and finance science and education has abandoned narrative altogether, and instead supplemented a counter-narrative of science and scientism, using equations to create *Homo Economicus* and force a particular rationality into the science. This has led to hubris and significant financial debacles over centuries, with the last five decades among the worst (Reinhard & Rogoff, 2011). *Financial Times* editor Gillian Tett exposes the central role of culture and relationships in finance, and shows how an anthropological perspective can enrich our understanding of it (Tett, 2021).

The simple fact that different industries have very different needs for finance and attitudes towards it is ignored by this imposition of an objectivist, supernatural corporate finance. Pluralism has been deliberately and actively suppressed by universalism and technocracy. If narratives are taught in the classroom, they can encourage students to find meaning and purpose, and also share their own stories and experiences, making the subject come alive. Instead, there is an abject murder of narrative and meaning in contemporary finance training. True stories can travel inter-generationally, and be used to remind learners about the importance of morality in finance and its sustainable qualities of reputation, honour and trustworthiness. This in turn can inspire better reflection and prevent relapses in morality during times of plenty, preventing the growth of greed, and instead encouraging the sharing of wealth. This is how the Jains have become successful in finance, and retained this in spite of challenges and adversities. They have learnt to value their own reputation and honour, and not to abuse or exploit it.

There is an active state of cognitive and emotional dissonance cultivated in finance, which enables professionals to further distance their consciences from their expert decisions and actions (Ho, 2009). Expropriation of the state is glorified as if it were scientific and efficient, but, in reality, finance has become a curse on society (Mbembe, 2019; Murphy, 2015; Shaxson, 2019). Finance education has increasingly shaped a culture of expropriation which is deeply enshrined in the DNA of these giant corporations and financial institutions. It completely ignores the fact that the modern corporation is supremely powerful, yet entirely undemocratic and very difficult to control or regulate (Baars & Spicer, 2017). The damaging effects to society and environment of such behaviour is very well documented (Bakan, 2004; Fleming, 2014; Monbiot, 2000). This explains why discussions of culture and morality are so problematic for these organisations and their secular theorists.

The networking and collusion between bankers and finance traders to manipulate markets, minimise taxes, fuel war and state expenditure, rob the public purse, influence politicians and ensure they are bailed out during major financial crises, is absent from finance science, in spite of the overwhelming evidence (Bullough, 2018; Luyendijk, 2015; Prins, 2014; Tett, 2010). This is a very human (irrational or rational?) act on which the silence in the finance textbooks or courses, even in behavioural finance analyses, speaks volumes about the real factors which lead to significant wealth transfers. Markets and prices have often been manipulated by collusion, benefiting a few at the expense of the many (Finel-Honigman, 2010; Prins, 2014). Research shows that cultures and networks do influence finance behaviour, for good or bad, depending on the motives and moral or religious restraints (Shiller, 2013).

The climate emergency means that every scientist needs to take responsibility for their science, and 'feel' the pain inflicted by it on nature, animals and society (Dryzek et al., 2011; Newell & Paterson, 1967; Obeng-Odoom, 2020; Sedgmore, 2024). It is an existential reality, not just a remote possibility. It is not enough to separate the knowledge from the underlying values and beliefs, as the dangers to humanity are serious and lasting. A wide range of scholars, including Nobel Laureates have critiqued the science of economics and its foundational beliefs, and yet there is steep resistance to change or to taking responsibility for their equations and theorems (Choat et al., 2024; Naylor & Thayer, 2022). Elite Universities and institutions are the biggest resistors to change, and they regularly produce PhD students armed with the same baggage, amplifying the technocratic hold on the discipline (Kvangraven & Kesar, 2023). Both knowledge and pedagogy in finance have become a big part of the problem instead of helping with the solution. They thrive on complexity, making it increasingly difficult for lay people and experts to critique the financial frameworks. Experts have become increasingly unaccountable and divorced from truth and representational faithfulness.

Eminent education theorist Etienne Wenger (2000) explains that learning is such a profound part of society and its ability to shape meaning and identity, that it cannot be separated from knowledge and theories of economic and social life. In finance, there has been a segregation of knowledge and pedagogy, with an undeclared and subconscious assumption that meaning, context and identity are irrelevant to expertise. An 'objective' knowledge system has come to dominate the professions and institutions. This causes a deeply fractious yet powerful knowledge system which is *imposed on society*. Such a practice dislocates and disrupts social norms and meaning-making, distancing finance practice from morality, imagination and identity. When we bring aesthetics and nature into our personal development, we become much more whole and wiser (Brady, 2018). The method and content of training in finance has itself been deeply violent and unsustainable, and a means of giving credibility to anthropocentrism, deep inequality and paranoid materialism in social life.

Equations Hide and Corrupt the Truth: Empire *Subjugated and Othered* Indigenous Culture, Animals and the Environment

'Native' was a generalised reference to all colonised peoples, as if they were one and the same. It was a 'sub-species' not human or humane, and worthy of control and 'civilization' (Akala, 2019). Just as other species have been deemed resources for production and consumption, so was the native. Even worse, the native had no culture or belief system of any worth, and the colonialists suppressed their dignity and self-esteem deliberately and pro-actively through their words and deeds (Fanon et al., 2004). The shadow of this prejudice still prevails today and has been embedded into the fabric of the social and economic sciences today – native theories of culture and finance are made inferior and invisible. Culture has no standard meaning or definition – this makes it tricky to write about, but that does not negate its relevance to financial decisions. It is about what gives people belief, meaning, purpose and a sense of belonging and community. It often influences ethics and norms, languages, communications and behaviour in ways which have significant economic implications for organisations and society.

The universalism of modern finance and economic sciences embraces this profound cultural ignorance and prejudice, hidden behind its calculations (Banerjee, 2022; Kvangraven & Kesar, 2023; Osterhammel et al., 2021; Sultana, 2023). All natives were deemed worthy of white settler domination and superiority, slavery and apartheid being some of the most extreme examples of cultural superiority exercised through brute force (Sanghera, 2021). Any attempt to rebel against these deep indignities was crushed by unfathomable violence. The 'Third World' is the latest redefinition of the native, putting colonised nations into another box of inferiority. Economics and finance have ingrained a violent and abrasive counter-culture of selfishness and materialism, and the depth and breadth of the nuances of many indigenous cultures have been removed, turning them into a 'sub-species'.

War, conquest and violence were historical reasons how money was created, and why states needed finance to pay soldiers and armies for both protection and aggression (Graeber, 2014). Even today, America, the biggest military superpower on the planet, is also a global epicentre for finance with the dollar as a reserve currency. The fact that it is deeply indebted with a multi-trillion-dollar budget deficit is somehow overlooked. The record of history shows us that the enforcement of debt really depends on who has the gun – it is rarely 'rational' and this can also mean that whole nations can become subverted and corrupted by financial power. The 2008 global financial crash started in the USA. We urgently need to talk about what a peaceful and non-violent finance looks like, and model our science and education along these lines.[3]

Historians of empire (see e.g. Andrews, 2022) have shown that many colonial subjects actually had unique cultures and values, were deeply respectful of animals and nature, and did not seek plunder and conquest for their own enrichment, nor to suppress the culture and beliefs of other people. Research on postcolonialism exposes the damaging intellectual prejudices of empire, which sustained and legitimated settler occupation and institutional structures (Beliso-De Jesús & Pierre, 2020; Meghji, 2021; Osterhammel et al., 2021). The entire enrichment of Europe and the Americas came from conquest and expropriation and even after decolonisation, European intellectuals today dominate the social sciences. The residues of empire, control our systems and languages of finance, truth and equity.

The Nobel Laureate Jean-Paul Sartre succinctly wrote about the deep madness of Empire and the need to reform its psychological madness: 'To shoot down a European is to kill two birds with one stone – to destroy an oppressor and the man he oppresses at the same time: there remains a dead man and a free man' (Fanon et al., 2004). He saw colonialism as a deeper mental evil which harms the oppressors turning their lives into madness and vice. These words came from a European intellectual and Nobel Laureate, who was angered by his own people and their deep narcissism and plunder. He surmised: 'Everything will be done (by colonialists) to wipe out their (native) traditions, substitute our language for theirs and to destroy their culture, without giving them ours (p .13).' Edward Said (Said, 1995; 2014) exposes the depth of this intellectual cruelty in a variety of western disciplines, showing how power and knowledge are combined to diminish the Orient and the Third World. He foresaw the dangers of specialisation as a removal of context and an act of laziness and irresponsible social science. This is especially true in the powerful field of economics. Some even call empire and colonisation a disease (Crichlow, 2018). For a vast number of cultures all over the world, there was and still remains a strong spirit of contentment instead of greed, and a desire to build village communities and respect the land, honouring the sun, soil and rain for the harvest (Fenelon & Alford, 2020; Harrison, 2015). In many ways, theirs was an advanced culture, where finance was put in its place, and not allowed to overwhelm conduct and character.[4]

In stark contrast, the social sciences were founded during the empire, when most intellectuals were convinced of white cultural superiority and their duty to subjugate and colonise Africa and the Orient (Bhambra, 2023). This view gave the leaders and intellectuals the moral authority to conquer and plunder. Science rose to the challenge of justifying this prejudice through its authoritative institutions of knowledge and education – universities and the professions. Said (1995) shows that knowledge always finds a way of serving power and authority, but intellectuals ought to resist such temptations. In finance, the removal of politics from the discipline has made it even easier for experts to deny responsibility and accountability for the outcomes of their science. Decolonising and reparatory social science have become a new movement, yet to reach the technocratic discipline of finance.

We are today left with a residual knowledge system which is based on divide and rule, where animals, environment and even people are 'intellectually' divided so that they can then be exploited legitimately (Burrell et al., 2022; Beliso-De Jesús & Pierre, 2020; Niiniluoto, 2020). Even in fields like sociology, cultural arrogance is deeply woven into the way society is classified. Human diversity, cultural richness and even the possibility of superiority *against* white culture, were altogether dismissed (Sheridan & Longboat, 2006; Sultana, 2023). The one word 'native' summarises the deep prejudice and ignorance towards hundreds of millions of people subjugated by settlers. Individualism and greed have today become universal mantras, central to the disciplines of economics, finance and accounting (Shah, 2018). There has been an abject plunder of compassionate ethics and morality by these professions. The vast research on post-colonialism and empire's cultural demolition has been completely dismissed and ignored by these siloed commercial disciplines. Borders within science are convenient tools for giving credibility to exploitation when for many cultures, there was no separation between theory and practice (Naude, 2019).

If knowledge is a key to power, then the fight over truth and knowledge[5] in an era where humans want to claim superiority in spite of the Anthropocene, is very deep and at the same time unavoidable. We (especially Europeans) ought to take blame for our own actions before we can change our common future.[6] For many intellectuals, this is deeply discomforting and painful, and they would rather rush straight to solutions, then to look at how and why we got here in the first place. In fact, so obsessed has finance become about its own selfish and materialist logic that it has forgotten to even notice the vast diversity of its practice all over the world and see that there are cultures and communities where finance operates on different norms and principles, and is practiced in a sustainable way (Møller et al., 2023). Intellectuals have become desensitised and detached from the pain their models and theories cause to society and nature, and virtually *created Homo Economicus* to fulfil their science, rather than the other way round (Çalışkan, 2022). Animals and nature have a long history and experience of living contentedly and embracing biodiversity, without ever attending a university class. In this book, we will draw from this heritage to showcase what a sustainable finance can look and feel like.

Wisdom of 'Marginalised and Damaged' Indigenous Cultures

Readers of this book will discover in the pages a variety of wisdoms about finance which they did not know existed. This is because so much of this knowledge is buried deep in other disciplines like sociology, psychology, environmental science, agriculture, anthropology – subjects which have been completely fenced off by modern day finance experts. The references and bibliography will help unveil this knowledge and open possibilities for new inter-disciplinary ethical finance research and education. Furthermore, some of the oldest indigenous cultures of the world and faith philosophies have significant knowledge about the nature and limits of money, which will be unearthed in these pages and related to our contemporary challenges in creative new ways.

Indigenous cultures often operated outside the money economy, and developed their own systems of finance and exchange (Alex & Ichumbaki, 2024; DePuy et al., 2022; Hamilton, 2016). Debt and borrowing were linked to justice and honour, and there was generally a very conservative attitude to debt. Mutuality and sharing were the norms, and this also helped them to manage risk and cultivate trust and reputation. Attitudes to animals and the land were very different – while in some cultures, animals were statements of wealth, in others, land was revered and worshipped as the source of food, with rivers often having holy or sacred value (Mehta et al., 2019), like the Ganges or the Nile. There was a much greater respect for nature and its bounty, and no hurry to maximise growth and get the highest produce from land or animals.

Here is an example of how one highly intelligent Native American leader saw European culture, in words written by a French aristocrat in the early seventeenth century:

> They (Europeans) think it unaccountable that one man should have more than another, and that the rich should have more respect than the poor. In short, they say the name of savages, which we bestow upon them, would fit ourselves better, since there is nothing in our actions that bears an appearance of wisdom.
> (Graeber and Wengrow, 2022, p. 52)

The Native Americans truly had a very rich culture indeed, in contrast to the Europeans of that time. What the above quote shows is the vast possibilities of social innovation that can come from engaging with different cultures and beliefs, instead of sticking to one obsessively. Even worse in finance, diversity is demolished altogether by the equations.

In many cultures, working animals were a primary source of income, and cared for with the highest compassion (Ng, 2019; Turner & D'Silva, 2006). Children in these families, fell in love with these animals and saw them as kin from the time of birth. Life in many ways was much more raw, and there were no 'jobs', with work, leisure, festivals and music all interspersed in everyday life, without any borders called weekends, or 9–5. They did not need *science* to tell them what food to forage, or how to plant and grow – knowledge was passed inter-generationally through tradition and trade. It was also developed through trial and error and shared in the communities and through faith networks. These traditions were the antidote to weapons of mass destruction like machine guns or bombs – they shared non-violent knowledge selflessly. We forget that these cultures lived and prospered locally and relatively peacefully for hundreds and even thousands of years (Graeber & Wengrow, 2022), and that wisdom has been bypassed by 'modernity' and the enlightenment vision of a so-called *rigorous* scientific method. The *externalities* of empire buried the *possibility* of better knowledges and wisdoms – many cultures and societies had developed their own truths about life and its purpose and meaning.

One of the distinctive features of many indigenous living communities is wholeness (Fenelon & Alford, 2020). Members of such groups embrace interdependence and understand what it means to be connected and to share through relationships of trust and mutuality, with faith and belief playing a central role (Sacks, 2003). In fact, many of these traditions were born in forest cultures, where nature was abundant, and still they chose to protect it. When anthropologist David Graeber and archaeologist David Wengrow came together to write a new history of humanity (Graeber and Wengrow, 2022), they discovered that many ancient civilisations were far more socially and economically advanced than Europe. Furthermore, even ideas now seen as central to the European Enlightenment actually originated from European encounters with such rich and diverse indigenous cultures. When cultures and traditions have stability and peace, they have the significant power to carry knowledge and experiences over many, many generations, which is priceless in its wisdom. I have discovered this personally from my upbringing, and decades of study, dialogues, enquiry and travels about my own Jain culture, which is based on non-violence towards all living beings. In stark contrast, contemporary finance science sees all tradition as dogmatic and regressive, and not worthy of any study whatsoever.

Wholesome habits of living and learning are cultivated among young people from childhood and help shape their whole character and outlook on life, including their values and beliefs (Abrudan et al., 2021; Constanza, 2013). For them, the 'otherness' of inequality, animals or climate change is simply non-existent – the young think and live in a very inclusive way. This knowledge cannot be put in a textbook nor a formula, but it exists in all parts of the world. Often the wisdom that comes from being and belonging completely changes the outlook on money and finance in ways which are deeper and more profound than any particular scientific theory or epistemology. Modernity needs to find ways of understanding and respecting such cultures on their own terms, and see hope in them for renewal in terms of our planetary obligations and responsibilities (Sacks, 2010).

The pioneering education scholar Paolo Freire (2017) wrote a seminal book *Pedagogy of the Oppressed* where he criticised the poverty and violence caused as a result of standardised, factory-style education methods, which disempower and imprison the minds and critical-thinking within living communities all over the world. For him the foremost goal of education must be empowerment and freedom, rather than control by examination and constant grading and evaluation in support of the interests of the powerful. All education and knowledge is political, Freire believed – we need to apply it to empower people, and the removal of culture from finance education is the quickest way to disempower minorities of all kinds, let alone trees and animals.

Critical reflection and debate on the pedagogy of finance is absent. After the 2008 crash, when Shiller (2013) conducted a moral reflection, it was within very narrow parameters of secular professionalism, rather than the depth and breadth of institutional failures. He avoided the structural ethical problems of finance altogether. As this book is dedicated to a new organic and inclusive system of finance knowledge, Freire's breakthroughs help us in democratising finance knowledge and allow alternative perspectives grounded in different cultures to speak truth to power.

As a lecturer, professional accountant and scholar, I have been deeply concerned about these matters and have written a number of books whose findings reveal a different finance hiding in plain sight. Unlike the modern separation of the researcher from the science, I will demonstrate in this book how my upbringing as a Jain, one of the oldest living cultures of the world (Dundas, 2002; Shah & Rankin, 2017), has provided different insights and perspectives on finance. I have used my nurturing to ask fundamental questions from a fresh perspective, unravelling the possibilities and opportunities of a responsible and compassionate finance. Contemporary economists have buried similar wisdoms for decades and shown little interest in understanding it let alone modifying their science because of indigenous wisdom.

So far, I have written three books on this theme[7] – *Jainism and Ethical Finance* (with A. Rankin), *Reinventing Accounting and Finance Education: For a Caring, Inclusive and Sustainable Society* and *Inclusive and Sustainable Finance: Leadership, Ethics and Culture*. In *The Politics of Risk, Audit and Regulation: A Case Study of HBOS*, forensic analysis of the largest bankruptcy in British corporate history exposed the contemporary formulaic and performative approach to banking which was in denial of both history and culture. All these research monographs have been published globally by Routledge. In my last book *Inclusive and Sustainable Finance*, I extend this perspective by reconstructing the language of finance and making it more plural by drawing from various cultures and faith traditions. The chapter titles are very different from modern finance textbooks anywhere in the world – morality, tradition, community, experience and purpose. This is a rewriting of the core language and framework of finance and a recapturing of its fundamentals. This present book is a culmination of a decade of work on these research themes.

Challenging Anthropocentrism

In the Anthropocene, we humans have become the one species which have caused irreversible damage to our planet and ecosystem in a very short space of time – just four hundred years (Lewis & Maslin, 2015). No other species has done that, and we have millions of them on planet earth (Astrachan et al., 2020; Barrera & Amore, 2024; Boatright, 2010; Naude, 2019). Scientists rarely agree on anything, but the reality of the Anthropocene has been accepted by a large majority now. Whilst we have done irreversible harm to tens of thousands of animal species, and badly polluted air and water systems which are our life support mechanisms, we have also invented the atom bomb, which can destroy the whole of humanity. Our suicidal technologies of violence and self-harm are legendary, so climate change is not a serious worry – we are capable of easily extinguishing ourselves in the name of peace.[8] Human hypocrisy and aggression run very deep, and we are unwilling to face the urgent need for our ethical and cultural transformation.

Society has now become arrogant and selfish, and assumed animals and nature to be there to serve us, rather than for us to be a trustee, caring and protecting life on Earth. Our knowledge, institutions, wars, behaviours and technologies have directly harmed humans and all life on earth (Castree, 2021; Santos, 2016). Thousands of whole species have become extinct every year as a result of our actions. Our attack on nature has been relentless and unapologetic. In our thinking we have long treated nature as 'other' when we now know that all living beings are interdependent (LaMothe, 2023). There is an urgent need to reframe our thinking and sciences to be kinder and compassionate to all living beings, taking direct responsibility for our education, behaviours, institutions and technologies which have caused the Anthropocene. In order to do so, we have to undergo a moral and intellectual catharsis first. Examining and applying indigenous wisdom can really help reframe our thinking in finance.

In truth, it is a particular subset of humans responsible for this destruction – the groups which created a fossil fuel dependent planet, the genocide of indigenous cultures and wisdoms, large-scale industrialised agriculture (including mass slaughter of animals – Four billion killed every year for human 'food') and chemical-based food production. The 'recycling' of chemical waste from oil refining (e.g. plastics), has led to vast global pollution and species devastation, from the irresponsible pursuit of greed and profit. Institutions like banks and stock markets fuelled this global expansion of industrialisation, in the direction of West to East, with European culture and philosophy a primary driver for neo-liberal capitalism and a highly materialistic modernity (Moore, 2016). Globalisation and financialisation have exacerbated planetary plunder through the cold power of capital accumulation and free movement of money, displacing employment and breaking communities (Harvey, 1935; Montgomerie, 2008; Osterhammel et al., 2021; Samman et al., 2022). Corporations today actively destroy jobs making them meaningless and robotic all over the world in the name of efficiency, profit maximisation and resource expropriation (Fleming, 2015).

Prior to empire and industrialisation, life in most parts of the world was predominantly local and therefore the depth and scale of damage to animals and nature was much more limited (Graeber, 2014; Graeber & Wengrow, 2022). For many indigenous cultures and nations, land, animals and nature were sacred and worthy of care and protection (Møller et al., 2023; Sheridan & Longboat, 2006; Shiferaw et al., 2023). As an example, for many cultures, even the idea of land ownership was anathema – they felt it was the land which owned them and gave them responsibility for its care. Unfortunately, empire nations and mindsets subjugated such cultures and expropriated them in the name of 'civilisation'. Pristine non-material values and wisdoms were profoundly damaged if not devastated by European aggression, ignorance and sheer greed for wealth and power (Cowen, 2002; Osterhammel et al., 2021). Most of the disciplines of social science emerged during empire, including subjects like sociology or economics, so materialist conquest ideals became deep-rooted and authorised in the sciences as Bastiat has claimed (Bhambra, 2023).

Ethics and values which are critical to a sustainable future, have been plundered by the social sciences in the name of modernity and progress – some call this a *genocide* of culture, which can be more damaging than physical mass killing (Santos, 2016; Short, 2010). The modern industry of finance plays a major part in this cultural genocide. Just as empire was universalist in its attempt to subjugate natives, modern social science is obsessed by universal truth, especially in economics, where there can only be one theory of the firm, or of commercial objectives or even state management of the economy (Chang, 2011; Graeber, 2014). Technocracy and mathematics actively buried culture, diversity and pluralism, preventing its wider debate and analysis. This abstracted and surreal *monotheism* is profoundly damaging and supremely powerful at the same time. The same textbooks and teaching methods of economics, finance and accounting permeate the world of business education, evangelizing and spreading a mono-culture in the name of science (Choat et al., 2024; Hamilton, 2016). When values and assumptions are buried deeply, it is very difficult to resurface them and students find it impossible to critique what is being taught. In fact, they often get brainwashed into selfishness and materialism (Fleming, 2017a; Gerlach, 2017; Rifkin, 2001).

Most of today's educated people have become dehumanised, consumerised, individualised and materialised to such an extent that they have forgotten what it means to live in a community, to belong, to have roots and to be contented (Astrachan et al., 2020; Barrera & Amore, 2024; Burrell et al., 2022; de Bruin, 2015). Even the editor of the *Financial Times*, Gillian Tett, laments the breakdown of culture in finance, and the related lack of humanity, empathy and reflexivity (Tett, 2021). The late distinguished economist Herman Daly who was once Chief Economist at the World Bank, came up with the phrase *person-in-community* to reframe economic science and root it towards community, well-being and respect for nature – he was a pioneer in the whole field of ecological economics and understood the mainstream theory and equations fully and critiqued them with that knowledge (Daly & Cobb, 1994; Farley & Luzzati, 2023). In the field of accounting, there has been a large and growing critique of the mainstream, with an emphasis on the moral, cultural and environmental importance of accounting (Bebbington et al., 2020; Carnegie et al., 2024). Unfortunately, the discipline of finance has become distanced from accounting, refusing to learn from this vast body of critical research.

Professional elites often live and work in urban settings, far away from rural communities which are grounded and simple, without big ambitions for growth, progress or consumption, let alone wealth accumulation. Ethics and values are not something to be learnt at one time in the classroom or the professional courses – they are lifelong attributes which need to be nourished, reminded and reinvigorated (Barrera & Amore, 2024; Bell et al., 2021; Boatright, 2010; Naude, 2019). Human communities of tradition and belonging are often grounded, with members coming from diverse incomes and backgrounds, and have rituals of ethical renewal. The environmental grief that we are experiencing today should not be denied but accepted to help us transcend it and discover a non-dualistic perspective on life and nature preservation (Read, 2023).

Given the English language's dominance of business expertise, this filter becomes very 'culturally' selective as to who does the scholarship and how it is framed to appease international journal editors. All this alienates scholars and scholarship from deeper histories and wisdoms (Andrews, 2022). When such intellectuals hold positions of power and influence over public policy and professional education, the damage is multiplied. What is worse is the fact that the space for deeper debate about human purpose and meaning in a warming and unequal planet becomes very limited and captured.

Abstract and Impersonal: A Materialist 'Science'

It is very difficult to escape our dualistic and anthropocentric framing of the world, especially in the social sciences, which have been 'designed' to be humanistic and in the case of economics, deeply abstract, selfish and greedy. Finance, a relatively newer science, less than 80 years old, has grown in influence and reach globally in terms of both research and business education, shaping and reifying the core institutions such as financial markets and large global banks, fund managers, central banks and investment firms. So little is the reflexivity about the fundamental beliefs of finance and their scientific basis that it has come to assume that knowledge and evidence are sufficient to 'prove' the scientific claims – this is damaging and needs to be addressed if we are to meet the challenges of sustainability (Lagoarde-Segot, 2018; 2020).

Epistemology is confused as negating the need for Ontology. Numbers have been objectified and converted into facts, even when they are human constructs such as money, and these facts replace knowledge and deny any subjectivity or ethics and values underlying their creation. Belief, although deeply entrenched in the calculations of finance, has been removed from any critical or reflective analysis at the very time when humanity needs to fundamentally change its belief system to survive as a species. Graeber (2014) studied 5,000 years of human history, demonstrating that faith and finance have always been entwined, and that money and debt are cultural and political constructs, and definitely not factual or objective.

The combination of naturally violent belief combined with knowledge and institutional power has been lethal. Bay and McGoun (2018) take this even further and demonstrate that finance is an 'idea' which tries to construct the future, even when it can never be touched or felt – *it is platonic and religious in its nature*. It actively *prevents* us from living in the present, making us constantly mobile, hyper-real and restless (McGoun, 1997). The means of finance have been deliberately confused and constructed by experts so that society is unable to question them, they argue. Money is one example of this, but so are equities, bonds, derivatives, financial markets and even the nature of the corporation and its real worth or value (Coggan, 2012; Fleming & Spicer, 2007). Belief (or certain 'objectified' beliefs) have been given the authority of science, disabling critics from deeper questioning.

When a whole science is obsessed by 'apolitical' and *neutral* empirical evidence, and devoted to a technocracy which loves mathematical and statistical complexity, over time it becomes clever at suppressing and disguising belief and subjectivity, and abandons the big questions altogether (Brooks et al., 2019; Daly & Cobb, 1994; Shaxson, 2019). Numbers give the impression of exactitude and objectivity which can be attractive but also damaging if inaccurate or untrustworthy. They lead to a reduction, abstraction and commodification of the natural world which has serious environmental and human consequences.

The premiere academic journals of finance are all mainly edited in North America – examples include the *Journal of Finance, Journal of Financial Economics, Review of Financial Studies, Journal of Financial and Quantitative Analysis*, and the *Journal of Corporate Finance*. Whilst North America may have vast resources for financial research, its own track record in financial skills, literacy, inequality, racism, gun violence, animal and environmental atrocities, expropriation and outright fraud is significantly broken. We are forced to assume that the knowledge experts have no impact on the wider social and ecological realities – they must know the truth given their qualifications! The rest of the world has to toe into line, and follow the American theoretical models and research methods. The knowledge footprint of the American finance science is global and hugely influential. Even behavioural research is based primarily on WEIRD subjects – Western, Educated, Industrialised, Rich and Democratic. This is a very odd subset of people and significantly misrepresentative of global society, which in reality is much more diverse, culturally, linguistically and spiritually (Schulz et al., 2018). Drawing conclusions from this dataset and individualist, impersonal mindset can be damaging for our science and knowledge. A large number of global cultures and societies are pro-social and collectivist in contrast, for whom such analysis and related financial theories, are grossly unrepresentative and misleading.

Professions also have a significant influence on the practice of finance. Throughout the world today, we have millions of certified lecturers and professors, expert accountants, bankers, financial analysts and fund managers who play an influential role in the movement of money, its investment and speculation and the payment (or avoidance) of taxes.[9] These have very real and serious economic consequences (both good and bad) which are lasting. Furthermore, there is growing evidence that such behaviour is ruining their own lives and mental health, leading bankers and professionals into bullying, drug addiction and alcoholism, subverting work environments and whole cultures (Lewis, 1989, 2011; Luyendijk, 2015). Sedgmore (2024) calls for the growth of a 'presence activism' where climate anxiety is transformed into positive action – professionals can find a renewed sense of purpose.

Challengers of this paradigm are forced to embrace the language of economics to critique it in its own terms, something which becomes a trap and barrier. If, in addition, incentives for experts are designed to encourage this profound scientific fiction, and remove it from global and environmental accountability, then society has no way out except for a major scientific revolution. Belief systems are difficult to change, and even more so when they are suppressed and denied. Given that finance is a 'practical' construct, designed to facilitate smooth exchange, the ways in which we educate and train finance experts should also come under the microscope, as this will influence how they behave and shape financial products and practices. Modern finance science has conveniently ignored pedagogy just as it has bypassed ontology with a disregard and disrespect of the power and influence of finance practitioners.

Paradoxically, the more power we have given to money and finance, the more we have allowed it to corrupt our culture and education systems. This development parallels the ways in which even in the field of communications, the dominance of global commercial media corporations has meant that the medium has become the message and the truth has become obscured and even falsified by fake news (Zuboff, 2019). The more society has become materialised and financialised, the more it has eschewed culture and belief and replaced it instead with anonymity, distrust and transactional coldness. Scientists have amplified this dislocation by legitimating the fictitious objectivity of money.

All this has made it impossible for us to recover core values like kindness and selflessness, or even trust and community. Our language and terminology have been tarnished, and even when we care, we are forced to calculate rather than to love. As a result, there is significant and growing concern about the contemporary political and moral crises in science, which question its power, legitimacy, corruption and most importantly, the values and ethics of the scientists and the funding. There is a particular concern with quantitative research and the focus on singular analyses, when the truth may be more complex and multi-faceted, as exposed in the present climate crisis. Numbers conveniently divorce and obfuscate the diversity of context, which makes the resulting analysis unreliable (Boyle, 2010). Governments may prefer evidence-based research and policy, but what counts as evidence and how it is collected cannot be ignored.

States and policy-makers often choose policy to fit the evidence (data rigging) rather than the other way round – the rhetoric is highly politicised (Campbell-Stephens, 2021; Warren-Jones, 2017). While putting problems into a confined box may be convenient for scientists, it will not lead us any closer to the truth. In fact, some scientists argue that technocracy and quantification are designed to obfuscate the deep underlying flaws and challenges, deceitfully making complex problems appear solvable (Dryzek et al., 2011; Lagoarde-Segot, 2020; Veland et al., 2022). The discipline of finance and its leaders who police the science fall into this fiction – and very few experts are willing to challenge them and shout 'The emperor has no clothes' (Keasey & Hudson, 2007; Whitley, 1986). The hard reality of modern-day inequality, farmer suicides, pollution and climate change, is forcing us to face our economic assumptions, and for the scientists who have made a career out of a particular paradigm, this becomes very problematic.

What is most surprising is how significantly the global financial landscape is littered with failure, hubris, moral hazard, gambling, power-grabbing through inefficient mergers and acquisitions, financial booms and crashes, multi-billion-dollar bankruptcies and outright deception and fraud. If you were to read a finance textbook, there is little evidence or analysis of any of this, implying that it is an aberration at best, and makes no dent on the science. The simple fact that banks are publicly licenced to create money even when counterfeit printing of money is illegal, was denied until recently (Coggan, 2012; Pettifor, 2017). The moral, cultural and leadership failures are only charted by outsiders like investigative journalists, who have provided painstaking detail about the hubris and corruption prevalent in modern banking and finance, often led by certified professionals. The theory of efficient competitive markets and institutions is forced to prevail in spite of the evidence against it. This is a reification of the abstraction of the science from reality.

Globalisation, corporatisation and industrialisation have created major upheaval and turbulence (Stiglitz, 2019). Two significant developments, the mass production of oil and gas and its use in everyday life, including the growth in plastics and chemicals, have been at the heart of our deliberate poisoning of life on earth. The concept of factory production and economies of scale have turned animals into food machines for a growing humanity. They are seen as soul-less and incapable of pain or suffering, and instead of being reared locally in a free-range manner, they are now manufactured away from the grasslands and industrially slaughtered. While few human beings would have thought of and designed these global institutions of mass oil extraction or animal slaughter, we are all now suffering from its consequences. Finance has been key to the facilitation of this industrial-scale attack on our living ecosystem, and often steered itself away from blame. Its calculations and equations have buried the underlying ethics and values, resulting in this eco-cide.

Deep Control and Surveillance through Technology

The rise of 'surveillance capitalism' where a very small number of global technology firms come to dominate global finance, knowledge, information and consumption, raises very serious questions about free markets, democracy and individual freedom (Zuboff, 2019). This concentration of power has never before been experienced by the world, and through the control of social media, it is undermining human relationships and reciprocity, by controlling our knowledge and capturing human behaviour for deeply commercial ends. Like Big Brother, these monopolies (Google, Meta, Amazon and Microsoft) have used finance to grow beyond human control and accountability, breaking and disrupting our health, communities and societies in the process.

They are knowingly, deliberately and actively undermining our sustainability by disconnecting our bodies from our minds and spirits – our independence of thinking has become subverted by fake news and consumption influenced by digital algorithms. A new 'behavioural surplus' has been shaped by technology and expropriated by it, leading to an unsustainable downward spiral of culture and well-being. It has become imperialism and surveillance by stealth, creeping into our homes and lives with our permission, without us realizing the scale of the capture. Social media bullying, victimisation, computerised financial fraud, have become normalised all over the world, and are growing in size and scope. FinTech, the combination of finance and technology, not only attacks our ecosystem but undermines our humanity too. Greed and monopoly have emaciated us.

Zuboff is right in warning about the calamitous consequences of this in terms of very basic human needs like trust, relationships and community – profound 'organic' building blocks of society. Surveillance capitalism breaks down our families and society deliberately and actively, undermining the cohesion and social capital we need to survive and prosper in life. Without these qualities, we will be reduced to a deeply insecure society, constantly at war, with deep scars on our mental and physical health and wellbeing. Wholesale finance driven by materialism and concentration of power through the use of smart technology can end in breaking up human sustainability, irrespective of climate change. This raises very profound questions about the ideological framework of modern finance expertise which seems intoxicated by short-term greed. At the very least, there is an urgent need to remove the cognitive dissonance of experts from the widespread damage caused by high finance.

For Zuboff, technology has come to be the cold calculating arm of finance, concentrating commercial power and enabling deceit on a global scale. Technology has come to subvert living culture, without any guilt or punishment. It has unleashed serious counter-cultural forces which are disrupting human sustainability. The apolitical and intellectual capture of finance science needs to be shattered if we are serious about reform. Pointing fingers and challenging the status quo has become impossible – such is its commercial reach and seductive powers. The combination of finance, concentrated technological power, political capture and globalisation has become a critical force in our downward spiral as a living and responsible human species. At the very least, the academy ought to be bold to unpack its hidden politics and outright deception in the protection of public and planetary interests.

Money: Human Fiction Turned into Objective Fact

Money, the key ingredient of finance, is a fiction which society has created to help make life easier, and production and trade, harmonious. Scholars have shown how scientists and modernity have *converted money into a fact*, to suit their own calculations and models, which it is not. In the process, any notion of belief, trust or relationships has been bypassed completely. The sad truth is that the science of economics today is unwilling to expose this fiction as a cultural and social construct and not an objective, physical fact of life. The facticity of money has been deliberately constructed and reified by economic science.

In spite of the significant and growing cracks in this 'truth', far too many experts are steeped in denial mode, and earning a living from this fiction. Life has been commodified by money, and relationships have become unnecessary to the production and efficiency of money, and even eroded by the spread of money's reach into all aspects of social life. These stark facts will not be ignored in this book but instead be *reincarnated* and exposed as critical to the reform of finance knowledge. This deliberate *creation* of fiction is not different from the narratives of empire – a human sub-species had to be created to justify violence, piracy, slavery and superiority.

Research shows that whilst modernity is acknowledging a diversity of cultures, the discipline of finance still wants to keep the scientific hold on the definition and analysis, ignoring culture altogether. Deep down, there is a political battle over forms of knowledge and truth in the Anthropocene, and experts, especially in fields like economics and finance, do not want to acknowledge a diversity of ontologies, let alone the importance of wisdom to sustainable science (Sandel, 2013). The varieties of beliefs are irrelevant, and instead comparison is bordered within the epistemological realm.

Dimensions like ontology and spirituality are then deliberately subverted when it comes to cultural attitudes to the environment, even when it is human culture that we urgently need to reform in the face of our environmental crises. Wisdom, which is a holistic worldview including mind, body and spirit, is missing from our scientific literature because it challenges a rational, empiricist, specialist mindset. We are failing to be humble and compassionate in spite of the significant inequality and environmental exploitation. Our systems of knowledge have become a serious part of the problem and can therefore not easily become the solution, unless we understand fully where we have gone wrong.

Research on racism and knowledge production exposes painful truths about how non-white or indigenous cultures have been assumed to be uncivilised and unworthy of superior epistemological systems.[10] The recent move to decolonise the curriculum is exposing the deeper layers of prejudice which have also been conquered and subjugated by empire. This has meant that when it comes to such profound human crises as climate change, where we need pluralism and the wisdom from traditions and communities which have for thousands of years lived in harmony with nature, we have significant deep prejudices in our authorised systems of knowledge. In this book, we will overcome this 'censorship' by avoiding those editorial and often elitist gatekeepers and sharing a wide variety of indigenous perspectives who have no voice in the discipline of finance whatsoever. In the process what will become clear is that while the academic business world is looking into technocratic 'solutions' for climate change, the indigenous traditions have vast wisdom which is being ignored due to the deep epistemic prejudices.

Pain and grief are natural human emotions necessary to transformational work, and the present economic and environmental devastation requires experts to experience this suffering to enable them to work towards transformational wisdom. The divorce of knowledge from experience has been a major cause of the fractures we see today and continues to block sustainable reforms to shape inter-generational equity. For us to find a better way forward, we need to feel the pain and the anxiety that comes from our modern predicament. Theory needs to meet our hearts and spirits, and escape from its confinement in our brains. Reforms need to begin from within us, and nature can be a huge teacher and inspiration for this.

The Unsustainable *Commodification of All Life*

Neo-liberal capitalism and its global reach have ended up commodifying life – a human being is labour, and a cost, not a being with emotions, values and tradition. Nature and animals are now classified as land and property – they are 'entitled' to be owned and possessed by humans; relationships and trust have been replaced by money (Sandel, 2013). Now that we have currency, we do not need public trust and confidence to make it credible; when we look at history, money emerged as a result of trust and faith. Aspects of life which are priceless and wholesome have become tradable and saleable, diminishing the importance of the breadth and depth of nature and humanity, where culture and community are submerged by individualism and market-based consumerism.

Numbers impersonalise finance and abstract it from lived experiences, cultures and communities. This makes the discipline cold and calculating, while at the same time claiming to be objective, universal and scientific. The devastating human consequences of finance are brushed aside and ignored, and stock markets, banks and corporations celebrated as being good, even ideal for social progress, when the reality is otherwise. Graduates and professionals trained in this way become desensitised from the culture within their own organisations, let alone wider society, and become very instrumental and transactional, and are incentivised to act in this way. This means that leaders in finance who are in positions where they handle large amounts of 'other people's money', lack the ethical training, stewardship and conscience to bear this significant responsibility with honour, fairness and professionalism (Kay, 2015). Graeber (2014) argues that a world of numbers can only be held in place by weapons – 'the maintenance of systems of coercion constantly do the opposite: turn the products of human cooperation, creativity, devotion, love and trust back into numbers once again ... transforming the very foundations of our being' (p. 387). 'A debt is just the perversion of a promise. It is a promise corrupted by both math and violence,' Graeber concludes (p. 391). Finance has been party to our global cultural and spiritual genocide.

Financial markets and institutions have played a critical role in this commodification, allowing money to take over everyday life. The free movement of capital has led to a global scale of expropriation of nature and resources which the planet has never seen or experienced before (Ferguson & Petro, 2016). Some call this an extension or key instrument of the Anthropocene – the Capital-O-Scene (Moore, 2016). Underlying the globalisation of capital are a hidden set of materialistic values like profit and wealth maximisation which legitimate plunder in the name of entrepreneurship and success (Rifkin, 2001). Financial instruments like bonds, equities, foreign exchange, derivatives and futures contracts have enabled the trading of time, and abstract human constructs like interest rates and inflation, fuelling speculation and capital flight across borders with no loyalties to people and nature. Experts have created these innovations out of thin air, and then shaped whole infrastructures for trading and gambling in the future credibility and prices of abstract commodities. In spite of the growing demands for a more sustainable humanity, these structures and their sciences have proved incapable of fundamental change. Most reforms that are proposed liked ESG or Green Finance are tinkering at the edges of the ecological precipice.

In aiming to reform the science of finance, it is important to comprehend the breadth and depth of the challenge that is posed. Science has been largely understood as the pursuit of objective truth, free from belief and ideology, but in the case of finance, it has become deeply ideological, and fictitious, making society very vulnerable. Financial crashes and disasters on a national and global scale, have been consistent every decade over the last 50 years (Reinhard & Rogoff, 2011), and the man-made devastation they have caused has led to significant human dislocation and inequality. If one were to examine the pages of eminent finance journals today, there is little sign of any anxiety among the academics, who remain some of the highest paid professors anywhere in the world. In a recent leadership address by the President of the American Finance Association (Starks, 2023) (the supreme body in finance science), there was a hint in the title about the importance of values in finance, yet there was no reference to philosophy or morality in the entire paper. Instead, all the references were from within the finance discipline, showing that there is a deep furrowing of the 'safe literature and ideology', in spite of the challenges from outside. Finance academics have a bunker mentality in the face of calamity (Brooks & Schopohl, 2018) – the opposite of what society would expect from ethically minded and responsible scholars.

We have no choice but to go back to first principles in redrawing the knowledge map of finance, and acknowledging the vast diversity of its beliefs and practices all over the world. Instead of making people, morality, and culture peripheral to the science, we need to make them central to build an integral science from the ground up, replacing an empire-based top-down science. Faith, which has hitherto been excluded, needs to be reintroduced and respected for its moral convictions and conscience. Furthermore, it is a fact that prior to the creation of modern Universities, a lot of the debates about truth, freedom and justice happened within faith communities all over the world. In fact, eminent Universities like Oxford and Cambridge were created by Christian leaders. Nalanda University in India was a centre for deep scholarship for a variety of Asian cultures and traditions.

A holistic and wholesome approach is likely to be more relevant to everyday experiences of people than the current technocratic approaches. It also opens the possibilities for all kinds of people from different fields like psychology, sociology and politics, to speak meaningfully about finance and not be oppressed by its equations. It is a fact that finance disrupts and ruins lives, destroys whole towns and communities, and enables the slaughter of animals and rain forests on an industrial scale. While the textbooks of finance ignore this calamity, society suffers from its consequences. For policy makers, this approach will help them deepen the understanding of the causes of economic turmoil and anxiety on the planet.

The Enduring Value of Values: Sustainable, Organic and Communitarian Finance

For many cultures of the world, individualism and autonomy are alien concepts – their lives are deeply entwined with their families and communities, and they have no clearly distinctive and separate identity from these groups (Fenelon & Alford, 2020). This profoundly changes their attitudes to morality, trust and kinship, helping to ensure that money and materialism are not allowed to overwhelm life, and even when accumulated in excess of their needs, money is kept in its place. They have disciplines and principles about wealth which are quite sophisticated, and value non-material aspects of life such as relationships, reputation and honour very highly – in short, they have much to teach us about sustainable finance (Poyser & Daugaard, 2023). Community and divinity are also deep instinctive beliefs which professionals and experts in the West often find very difficult to understand or relate to, even when they are quick to negate or challenge their value. Our climate crisis demands that we act in communities and embrace the interdependence of all life. This creates a unique place for indigenous wisdom in our quest for sustainability.

Education research shows that a vast amount of learning happens in groups and communities, through lived experiences, cultures and traditions (Wenger, 2000). This is antithetical to modern technocratic and individualist approaches to learning, which deny such social and organisational methods of learning. Textbook finance training is an extreme example of this, as it sanctifies greed and individualism and rejects society and community. There is field and historical evidence that even in Finance, it is networks and groups who often achieve the most sustained success, and their knowledge is gained from outside the classroom or the professional exam curricula – although most of this evidence is about greed rather than equality (Burgis, 2024; Finel-Honigman, 2010; Luyendijk, 2015; Prins, 2014; Hoang, 2022).

Experiential learning is another example of shared field learning, but because it is subjective and intangible, finance science dismisses its relevance. It is well known that for most finance jobs, experience and networks are a very significant factor in the appointments process, especially when it comes to influential leadership positions. This success can be for purely expropriative motives, like Mafia gangs or financial market speculators, or it can be for purposeful and upliftment of enterprise, society and well-being through shared finance. Even the high-charged finance trading floor is a trade union, which often demands its own bonuses, is co-operatively competitive, with overflowing lunchtime city pubs in London or New York, facilitating the exchange of niche inside information (Luyendijk, 2015; MacKenzie, 2005).

Inter-cultural dialogues, beliefs and encounters often open deeper engagement with truth and help us understand our own culture and values better (Sacks, 2003; Barrera & Amore, 2024). In the process, we expose many of the assumptions which we thought were normal but instead are different in other societies. Meyer (2016) explains through case studies how easily managers can be misunderstood across cultures, and how hard it can be to build trust and persuade others. This research has the potential to create many creative and valuable insights about the nature and limits of finance. The subtle cultural neutrality assumed by finance demolishes the possibilities of any cultural dialogue or conflicts, let alone one between cultures. This denial of culture and human diversity also leads to a deeper obstruction of inter-cultural science and dialogue about the different ways in which people perceive and experience finance. Given our global interdependence, this omission is very serious and significant.

Warren Buffett is widely regarded as one of the world's most successful businessmen and entrepreneurs in the last 50 years. One of the central elements of his leadership has been the emphasis on people, culture, values and long-term vision. Cunningham (2014), has meticulously documented Buffett's business approach and sustained growth of the various businesses he acquired, and finds that the most important ingredient has been the focus on integrity and culture, which are intangible values and give lasting financial success. Prahlad (2019) demonstrates then when leaders place culture and ethics at the centre of their development vision, a lot of rural empowerment can be achieved, replenishing social capital rather than depleting it. When the present book discusses an organic approach, it echoes Buffett's philosophy and lack of greed or short-termist financial focus, and explains that in the long term, value is generated organically. The subtitle of the Cunningham book is *The Enduring Value of Values*.

Money is plural and *not* universal – its character and influence vary from country to country, and even between peoples and communities in the same country (Dodd, 2014). It is a cultural, social, political and economic construct, with diverse histories and characteristics. The urgency of the challenge to remodel finance is therefore very significant, and not to be taken lightly. The conventional theories of finance in terms of corporations, markets, interest rates and globalisation are extremely abstracted from the grassroots communities and natural world. Experts have gone for quantity and trumped quality, making us all 'rational servants' to the whims of the knowledge and institutions of finance. Contemporary finance science disables us from thinking differently and conceptualizing a world where finance is a servant of nature and society, not its master (Kay, 2015). Birds have never needed money to feed, fly or to sing, but we humans seem to be unable to cope without money and credit. We have allowed it to overwhelm our lives and economies. As a result, the best we can do when it comes to environment and society is to talk about ESG – a small tweak on the existing system, more cosmetic than substantive.

Furthermore, if our own academics and intellectuals are in charge of framing a very powerful science, from which they personally benefit through large salaries and consulting fees, they are the last people to do deep soul-searching about the very methods and framing of their science (Gendron & Smith-Lacroix, 2013). Given their hold on the discipline, radical critique, even when it is absolutely necessary given our existential crises becomes virtually impossible to publish in an authoritative way. The split between our personal ethics and knowledge outputs creates systemic hypocrisy and encourages deceit without remorse or reflexivity.

Shifting Paradigm

Philosophers of science like Kuhn explained that paradigms are what help scientists sharpen their focus by working with generally accepted assumptions and theories (Kuhn & Hacking, 2012). Kuhn also showed that it is very difficult to critique a scientific paradigm on its own terms and through its own experts, as they have developed a particular way of thinking and testing which they have been trained in and committed to for a long time. Paradigms only shift when enough people from outside this mindset critique the accepted theories through evidence, and even scientists within the conventional paradigm begin to see its weaknesses and explanatory failures. Once entrenched, paradigms are very difficult to shift – revolutions require a large and growing storm of intellectual protest. In the case of finance, the power and wealth that derives from following a greed mindset is worth challenging because of the expropriation and devastation it has caused to all living beings.

Philosopher of science Michael Strevens has written:

> Scientists seeking to make sense of the evidence cannot be neutral. They must take a stand on whether the instrument is relaying the truth or whether the theoretical assumptions hold. Having nothing further to guide them, they must go with whatever seems right. They must resort to educated guesswork, and that makes scientific reasoning irreducibly, unavoidably, essentially subjective.
>
> (Strevens, 2022, pp. 67–68)

In economics, politics and finance, the surge in positivism has led to the growth of an irresponsible attitude to science (Stiglitz, 2019). This has meant that the scientist, even the *social* scientist, has become detached from a caring attitude, taking the view that their job is to explain the reality rather than take a normative approach to building a better society. The ethics and values of the scientist have become submerged in the quest for 'objectivity'. Philosophers of positivist science have suggested that academics can detach themselves from reality and have no prior assumptions or biases when they engage in collecting and analysing social data – it is as if the *evidence* is neutral and objective. In contrast, there has been a huge growth in 'critical' social science (Banerjee, 2022; Borch, 2020), which rightly questions the fundamentals of our knowledge systems, but does not then go on to recraft a better science or knowledge which could help improve the world. In short, not only have humans attacked nature in an irreversible way, their knowledge systems and professionals also continue to do so without taking any responsibility or accountability for it (Cook, 2011). This is unsustainable.

Fortunately, there has also been a growing intellectual rebellion against neoliberal and neo-classical economics and finance, from the vantage of ethics, psychology, sociology, politics, environment, critical accounting, geography, anthropology, business and global studies. A large number of important journals have emerged such as *Economy and Society, Critical Perspectives on*

Accounting, Review of International Political Economy, Finance and Society, Socio-Economic Review, Economic Geography and *Critical Finance*. However, the shift in terms of the professional education and training curricula has been marginal at best, with a strong bias towards profit and wealth maximisation, and avoidance of larger public interest issues such as corporate scandals, market failures, fraud, money-laundering and an epidemic of tax avoidance. At universities, there is a shift in some institutions, but this depends on the academics and their leadership and drive to change the content of the teaching, and the degree of commercialisation. Business schools are significant cash-cows (Pettigrew & Starkey, 2016), so they will hardly ever become the hotbeds of critique and challenge to mainstream neo-liberalism. In the field of accounting, professions still have a high level of influence on the taught curricula at universities all over the world, and most students who study the subject are looking for vocational training rather than critique (West, 2003). In many parts of the world, an accounting education is a route to a good job in the corporate sector, and often costly to access for a majority of the people.

Graeber and Wengrow (2022) explain how when we examine diverse communities and societies, there are many examples where their cultures and organisation methods were far more advanced. There was a significant amount of social innovation and experimentation then we give credit for today in our Euro-centric social sciences. Our modern ideas of freedom, progress, prosperity and inequality are often very unsophisticated and loaded towards some ideal version of 'modernity' and liberation. Instead, belief and tradition often created unique harmony and social cohesion, with care and community central to social life, without the need for external formal institutions like the state or even democracy. Even knowledge was produced for local use, rather than international applause or competition. Graeber and Wengrow elaborate on the nuances of culture and show how diverse the meanings of happiness, love, or freedom really are. From such a perspective, a modern textbook in Corporate Finance reads so parochial, ideological, vacuous in creativity or imagination, irrational and an exercise in conceited myth-making using the modern power and institutions of finance.

Wholeness and Being

Philosophers of science are realizing that one of the fundamental problems of modernity is its dualism and obsession with objectivity – avoiding the simple fact that the observer cannot be separated from the observed (Wilber, 2002). The *symbol* of wealth – money – has come to 'represent' the material fact which is core to the science of economics. Whitehead (Whitehead, 1979) calls this 'the fallacy of misplaced concreteness' something which is particularly appropriate to finance, where abstraction of reality is the norm, and wholeness is avoided actively and deliberately, due to the paranoia with specialisation. Whitehead is very critical of this fallacy, and the damage that is caused to society in fields such as economics as a result of the discipline's power and influence. Eastern traditions emphasise a wholeness of knowledge that is beyond material measurement or dualism, which is possible to attain through elevations of personal consciousness where the mind truly becomes *enlightened* and loses its separateness from the Universe. There existed in history a vast variety of indigenous economics systems which did not require much abstraction, and still led to peace, fulfilment and prosperity (Graeber and Wengrow, 2022).

The more we invest in our empiricism and symbolic knowledge, the further we will go from understanding the deeper ontology of finance (Bay & Schinckus, 2012). Institutions like financial markets and banks created by such knowledge systems decimate society and nature through their partiality. It should be no surprise that inequality, social upheaval and environmental devastation continue to be endorsed by this flawed science. In taking a non-dualistic approach in this book, we are breaking away from the shackles of empiricism or positivism, and actively seeking new ways of making finance sustainable. Inter-disciplinarity is not simply about breaking silos between disciplines – it is also about acknowledging the 'wholeness' of knowledge and wisdom and finding ways to connect understandings as opposed to narrow abstraction and fictitious symbolism. It helps if we start from an acceptance of the unifying nature of truth and the flaws of materialist objectivity.

Reframing our knowledge and thinking is critical because it is the basis by which institutions like banking, bond or stock markets, and professions like accounting, law, banking and investment have been created. Whilst these institutions and professions may appear objective and neutral, ostensibly to protect public interest and ensure fairness and equality, their record in the last hundred years, has been a dismal corruption of the true knowledge of finance and its profound moral and ethical basis (Rifkin, 2001). They have become hidden chainsaws not only of rainforests, or through financing the killing of four hundred billion animals a year for meat, but they have directly attacked and undermined humanity through inequality and exploitation (Fleming, 2015). Workers are seen as labour costs to be minimised rather than human spirits, and replaced by automation and technology, in order to maximise profits and efficiency at the expense of living communities (Fleming, 2017b). Off-shoring and contracting have led to precarious family lives, where skills and income become increasingly redundant, and care and compassion are subject to financial priorities, rather than human values worthy of preservation.

Being human is more than collecting evidence, or analysing it or even theorizing science. The motion and materiality of finance is designed to keep us constantly moving, borrowing, owning and spending. However, life has to be much deeper than this – if death is guaranteed, then why were we even born? Wholeness is about uniting the mind, body and spirit, and feeling the oneness of this trinity. It comes before disciplines or even what we call knowledge today. Thinking and language also have their limitations as they dissect the truth and filter its communication. Sages and saints have transcended everyday life to experience deeper truths which make them peaceful, silent and deeply introspective. In our quest for a wholesome finance, we need to find ways to tap into this wisdom and intelligence, and respect its source. Basic phenomena like birth, life and death, the purpose and meaning of existence, are not divorced from finance but central to it.

Climate Change, Consciousness and Faith

Environmentalists keen to reform finance may discover in these pages a language and terminology which can help them make a convincing case for client earth. Parents and grandparents keen to leave a better planet for future generations will find hope in these chapters, and come to understand how we have come to be this way. Reframing taken for granted presumptions about life and behaviours will make it challenging for us to unlearn and relearn. Fortunately, we have a bank of wisdom sciences about living in harmony with the planet that we can draw upon. These traditions can be 'unforgotten' in our need to create a cool, harmonious and caring planet.

Faith traditions have some of the oldest living histories of beliefs, good and bad – they have tried to pacify humanity, and console it in times of significant risk, hardship and uncertainty. It is true that violence and war has often been fuelled by faith, with non-believers being castigated as heathens or kafirs, and the inquisitions or the Moghul invasions, leading to vast bloodshed and forced conversion. Not all religions of the world, or 'pagan' belief systems, have been cruel to others – faiths and beliefs have also been forces for good and instruments of peace and harmony in many parts of the world. In my own Jain tradition, the central philosophy of *Anekant*, embraces respect for different worldviews and beliefs, and is firmly non-absolutist (Rankin, 2010). Its spirit of *Ahimsa* or non-violence towards all living beings, embraces biodiversity at its very core – the depth of the philosophy was not developed in reaction to climate change. The modern-day misunderstanding and misrepresentation of faith cultures by the 'secular' social sciences profoundly diminishes indigenous intellectual wisdom, and the opportunities they give to help humanity out of its abyss.

Most of the modern day 'reactions' to climate change have been just that – repeat actions without any remorse, apology or even integrity. We have not even thought about 'defending' humanity in a trial against planet earth – we continue to assume our own immortality and the need for it. For far too many of us, our own preservation on this planet has to be secured, without any need to change our mindsets and behaviours. This is unsustainable and a mere extension of anthropocentrism. In reversing climate change and human greed, exploitation and violence on the planet, we need to look back in time toward ancient cultures who already saw this non-violence towards living beings as the right way to live. This science was not developed out of fear or a need for self-preservation, but instead a deeper honesty and sense of responsibility and accountability. It holds a vast reservoir of timeless truths which we can tap into, and this ocean is readily available.

An important dimension of knowledge and wisdom, spirituality, has itself been attacked consciously and sub-consciously by economic science. Adam Smith, the widely acknowledged and often mis-represented founding father of modern economics, was primarily a moral philosopher and saw morality as central to economics (Smith, 2023). He was deeply influenced by Christianity and principles of equity, democracy and fairness. In respecting land, animals, air, water and our ecosystem, the tools and language of contemporary science are limiting, and at times a key part of the problem. We need to find a way of transcending our existing awareness of truth, objectivity and empiricism, and break the boundaries of our scientific training to deeply reform the knowledge systems of finance.

Whilst the inner consciousness is not directly visible or tangible, its importance and acknowledgment is critical to the understanding of the organic theory propounded in this book (Wilber, 2002). Planetary pollution is not unrelated to mental pollution – the spread of materialism has prevented society from having a deeper purpose and meaning in life, increasing fear and insecurity and widening inequality. The counter-culture shaped by finance and economics has had a direct impact on human behaviour towards animals and nature, with the technologies of mass manufacturing and industrialisation multiplying the damage, sometimes exponentially. Alongside so-called economic progress, there has been a steep decline in mental health and well-being, especially among the 'first' world nations.

Research on consciousness shows that we are not just material robots, but beings with deeper capacities of learning, growth and reflection, which can help us transcend life and mundane existence (Verny, 2023). The body and the mind are interconnected and deeply entwined. Consciousness has the power to help souls go beyond dualisms and take us into the depths of knowledge which are beyond language or ego, and truth is seen in its whole, without any filters or prejudices. Even some fleeting experiences of this secret reservoir of spiritual knowledge will really help absorb the concepts and narratives that are illustrated in the book. If science is a profession committed to the pursuit of the highest truths, then limiting analysis to material prediction, observation and analysis will prevent us from experiencing the deeper nature of truth. The depths of our current economic and environmental crises simply cannot be resolved without engaging with human consciousness and transcendence. Whilst these are subjective phenomena, their wisdom avoids the traps of dualism, flawed objectivity and materialism. Meditation and reflexivity help leaders see and experience the joy and bounty of a non-material life, and reduce their fears and insecurities.

The pursuit of holistic truth and consciousness will help us cultivate and nurture the humility and awe that is needed to rebuild a whole and responsible science. The tools of rational thinking will be found wanting and limiting, and readers will need to go on a reflexive journey to understand the depths, limitations and meaning of money and finance. Spirituality does not mean an abandonment of reason but instead an acknowledgment that there are multiple layers of truth and understanding, and the spirit can help us experience the deeper nature of reality. Our material knowledge of the world is limiting and society needs to learn to transcend it. Such wisdom may not always be easy to communicate through language or reason, but this does not mean that spiritual science is irrelevant.

The growing field of environmental governance is raising deeper questions about pluralism and anthropocentrism (DePuy et al., 2022). Whilst many want the environment to be framed to serve human interests, there are emerging voices which are not afraid to challenge this perspective and give voice to hitherto marginalised groups such as small farmers or indigenous people who continue to live within their means and protect animals and the land. There are scientists who challenge the colonisation of the mind and are unafraid to seek wisdom where it has long been suppressed or marginalised. The ocean of biodiversity that is among faith traditions is also acknowledged and respected rather than ignored or insulted.

Epistemic *Non-violence*: Plural Frameworks for Life *and* Finance

The research method of this book is to shift from our traditional binaries and dualities, especially in relation to the non-human world but also in the denial of culture, belief and ideology when it comes to finance. As we have seen, money means different things to different people, and while entrepreneurs may prefer risk-taking and see risk as opportunity, others prefer public service jobs which give them meaning and purpose, and are content with the money they earn from this.

The vast variety of cultures, communities and beliefs globally also mean that there are plural understandings of money, and even some indigenous communities who live and work outside the money system. There are also cultures and beliefs which encourage greed, selfishness and materialism, and these ideologies need to be challenged as unsustainable. The diversity and pluralism of finance needs to be acknowledged and valued, and its understanding can help us negotiate our journey to an inclusive and sustainable future for *all* living beings.

This book tackles profound prejudices in the social sciences about race; philosophical and theoretical whiteness; religion and belief; indigenous culture and wisdom; the politics of knowledge; mono-theism in economics and the *othering* of nature; factory-based commercial systems of education and training; structural biases of knowledge production and pedagogy; bordered thinking; the attitudes to animals as food and resources; and above all, the privileged status of the human being as Master of the universe, who still needs to be saved in spite of everything he has done. I have been helped in this journey by my upbringing as a Jain and a strong belief in respect for all living beings, and the importance of pluralism (Shah, 2024). Respecting insects turns human power and arrogance into humility and responsibility. Jain wisdom has always been a very different and prescient ontological system, developed over thousands of years of meditation, scholarship and critical debates, art and story-telling (Dundas, 2002). The Jains have never separated knowledge from practice, and it's a deeply introspective and reflexive tradition, where humility is nurtured, and forgiveness is sought on a daily basis.

The chapters draw from a variety of ecological, spiritual and cultural insights about the nature of biodiversity on this planet, and the criticality of human trusteeship motivated by responsibility and compassion towards all living beings. It is an up-side down perspective of life on earth, and a direct challenge to human arrogance and aggression. The core finance duality and separation of animals and nature from the market fundamentalist and materialist ideology will be ruptured without any apology. Evidence from research in biology, environmental governance, indigenous wisdom and the profound Dharmic wisdoms of the world which never treated nature as 'other' will be pulled together to frame the perspectives for a new organic finance.

Radical contemporary research is challenging how modernity can speak about an 'ontological turn' as a result of the Anthropocene without engaging with the deep scholarship, wisdom and wholeness of knowledge and belief long held by indigenous cultures. The ontological pluralism in these chapters will help chart the possibilities of a new inclusive and respectful framework for finance which ought to be our mission. Readers unfamiliar with this pluralism should suspend belief and critique before casting judgement on what are very different ways of knowing and learning. Context and history matter deeply in shaping a new finance.

At the end of reading this book, you will develop a different framework of looking at finance, one which is not alien to everyone, and has at times and places been hiding in plain sight, but we have failed to see and learn from it. You may even be empowered to look at your own finance culture and tradition in a new light, giving you fresh ideas for framing your finance case studies and reshaping the teaching curriculum. Contemporary economics has disabled us from seeing the biodiversity of finance. This framework will be holistic in the sense that it will not separate man and nature, or man and society, or even money and market design. Similarly, culture will not be divorced from finance, nor will money from physical and mental health. Trust and relationships will no longer be ignored.

Horticulture combines human and soil cultures to enhance our understanding of plant life – we try to apply these types of ideas to finance. The indigenous knowledge of farmers in learning in harmony with the land will be unearthed in shaping a grounded science. Long-held concepts of finance, like the innate selfishness of individuals or the materialism of life will be challenged and reformed. Legal systems which give property rights to some in certain circumstances, and not to others, or encourage animal and environmental abuse will also be questioned. The perspective will be inter-disciplinary and holistic, ensuring that parts are consistent with the whole.

The findings will open new possibilities for rewriting the theories and models of finance, and ensuring their compatibility with a harmonious polity, environment and society. The resources in the book can help create a new teaching module, which can fit a variety of courses on sustainability or ethical and responsible business and enterprise. All too often, finance has become hyper-technical and thereby removed itself from outside challenge and critique. Readers from disciplines outside finance will be able to understand these jargon-free chapters and concepts and find empowerment and the knowledge tools to challenge contemporary institutions of finance and received professional wisdoms. The book should help open the discipline to wider trans-disciplinary challenges and critiques.

Nature is *Not* Dumb: It Sustains Life

The silence of nature or the inability of indigenous people to communicate their wisdom in the language of the colonialists has led to violent attack and destruction of the fabric of our ecosystem. Culture and spirituality are very complex and nuanced – they cannot be 'defended' in a dialogue with someone who is arrogant and determined to plunder. Nor can complex cultures be understood by people who have little culture and an obsession with power and wealth. Even translation has significant limitations and can be subverted by power inequalities. We are presently being forced to think very differently about our life's priorities, culture and desires, and give primacy to air quality, water, animals and nature in ways powerful people and institutions have not done for a long time.

This is all the more reason why we need to understand how we came to believe what we do today, and why without changing this belief system, our transformations will be very superficial. If compassionate and inclusive culture has been sequestered from finance, we need to find a way of bringing it back in, not from a side door, but from the bottom up. This is why this book has taken such a radical approach to developing a new grounded science of finance. The voices assumed to come from nature and indigenous wisdom are backed by evidence, but also come from the author's own meditations, heritage and Jain background.

Metaphors from nature such as soil, soul, seed, growth, forests and environment are used to help us develop an organic theory of finance. They are very helpful given our challenge to build a more holistic and environmentally harmonious ecosystem, where business and industry are a part of the solution rather than a cause of the catastrophe. While trees or rivers do not speak, their living practices have a lot to teach us if we allow them to convey their truth, and listen and observe through our varied senses. Poets, philosophers and artists have long written about this wisdom and awe of nature. In this book we draw from this heritage to craft a holistic understanding of finance.

This book is an attempt to transform the very belief system and harmful institutions of finance, given our profound existential challenges, through imagination and reflection. It embraces biodiversity and human cultures which revere nature, for the torchlight of transformational wisdom that is needed. Through the chapters, you will come to gain new ways of grounding finance and keeping it a means to peaceful cohesion with all living beings, not just humans, without allowing it to become an end in itself. The multi-disciplinary research perspective and bibliographic references will help the reader see the breadth and depth of knowledge which can help finance become more sustainable and less selfish and parochial. The present power and mastery of finance which has bred deep violence, mental anxiety and inequality will be replaced by awe, humility, responsibility and conscience. Nature does not have a language for greed or selfishness, and has always embraced death as a part of life. It also has no problem with diversity or difference, and sees coexistence and mutuality as the very science of life, not just something to be tolerated or accommodated.

To fully understand this book, mere reading and intellectual analysis will not be sufficient. It will help if readers can also spend time visiting and experiencing a rain forest, or an indigenous temple or gurudwara, and even try some meditation, mindfulness and reflection techniques to experience inner wisdom beyond the intellect. We need to apply creative ways to allow different cultures to speak their own finance truths. Animals and nature can inspire a deeper yearning for peace and truth which is selfless and borderless. Beautiful artistic spaces which take us back in time can help us to see and experience what is enduring, and the relevance of reforming our culture to embrace true sustainability. We need to suspend our usual rationalist scepticism when we try such an experience, even if we do so temporarily.

The rest of the book is organised in the following way:

Chapter 2 Soil and Soul

This chapter will introduce the concept of an organic theory of finance and why its need is urgent. The ground of finance in nature, culture and community has become lost and ignored in corporate finance, which assumes that markets are the best arbiter and corporations the best institution to deliver progress. Without spelling it out, the subconscious impression given is that culture and community are irrelevant or even a nuisance to a universalist science of finance. It will also cite evidence from existing grounded practices in different parts of the world, many of which are hiding in plain sight, using an inter-disciplinary lens. The separation and duality of thought and action is one of the core problems of euro-centric culture and science. Soil and soul are inseparable and deeply entwined. The chapter will then discuss the foundations for an ethical finance which involve the combination of faith, trust, relationships, community and culture. Understanding the nature and limits of money is critical to shaping a new grounded finance. The chapter will finally explain how these elements can be valued, supported and shaped to reform knowledge and society.

Chapter 3 Seed

Finance cannot grow by itself – it needs good grounding in culture, trust and relationships. These seeds cannot be taken for granted nor manufactured in an assembly line. They need to be nurtured and cultivated with patience, understanding and mutuality. Their presence in the form of morality also needs to be understood, respected and valued. Traditions and beliefs play an important role in the cultivation of sustainable enterprises. Risk needs to be experienced to be managed – it cannot be avoided or ignored, nor is it always a bad thing. It often gives birth to adventure and opportunity, with growth in the horizon. Exponential growth cannot be sustained by nature – compounding has its limits, and if we are not careful, reckless growth of people, chemicals and pollution will choke the planet. The fact that markets permit the discounting and financialisation of the future is deeply problematic for sustainability. The faith, resourcefulness and determination needed for successful enterprise will be discussed, and the role of culture and family in providing these and sustaining them will be explored.

Chapter 4 Ecosystem of Finance Beliefs

For finance to grow, soil and seed are insufficient. We need an environment which encourages risk, enterprise and opportunity for organisations which serve the needs of the planet. Death and decay are natural but often denied or eliminated from finance dialogue – a world of perpetual cash flows is modelled instead. Banks are powerful globalised creators of money, with little responsibility and accountability – the arrogance of wealth and its concentration is destroying civilisation. Their purpose and goals need to be redirected for the common good. We also need an understanding of the lasting needs of society, and the importance of striking a balance with the ecosystem in designing our business and ensuring a light footprint with an impetus on regeneration and renewal. Purpose and motives need to be aligned with enterprise to shape sustainable outcomes. Finance needs to enable blending of the sun and water, the fertilisation by community of necessary goods and services, and laws and regulations which prevent expropriation and exploitation of both society and nature. This chapter will discuss the climate and chemistry needed for business to grow and flourish through purposeful finance.

Chapter 5 Inner Growth

Contemporary finance sees growth and prosperity as an incontrovertible goal, making it a sin to avoid growing and expanding. In reality, not all growth is desirable, and death and decay are normal and necessary to sustain the planet. Inter-generational equity is critical to an organic finance, and the focus on valuation encourages expropriation of future generations to shape greed and speculation in the present. Organic and holistic progress of people and communities is often undermined by economic calculations and short-sightedness. Entrepreneurship can lead to growth in giving and serving society and nature, something which also transforms the business leader to new levels of possibility and purpose. Materialistic growth also often leads to monopoly and market abuse, with inequality the unsustainable outcome. In this chapter, we will discuss the limits to growth, and the measures needed to monitor sustainable progress, enabling accountability to society and the environment. Trust and relationships nurtured with conscience and compassion can chart different patterns of growth beyond the material, whose possibilities finance diminishes and denies altogether.

Chapter 6 Forests of Hope

Forests are the life and lungs of a healthy planet, and we have actively destroyed them. To rebuild and nurture healthy forests, finance needs to cultivate a sense of humility and responsibility about its institutions and character. Interdependence needs to be encouraged not undermined by the systems of finance. This makes morality and ethics central to a new organic theory of finance. Normative idealist approaches are needed to shape responsible institutions and markets. Selflessness is normal for trees but absent in contemporary economics which encourage selfishness as critical to growth. How we rewire our science to shape growth and sustainability at a macro level will be a key focus of this concluding chapter. Finally, there is a succinct summary of the implications of this research on the study and teaching of finance for a sustainable future.

Notes

1 Research and investigation of over 30,000 finance articles in eminent journals demonstrates a significant narrowness of scope, parochial research methods, lack of inter-disciplinary knowledge, poor impact on the real world, and most seriously, a lack of ethical concern (Brooks et al., 2019; Brooks and Schopohl, 2018; Kay, 2015; 2011; Fleming, 2017a; 2017b).
2 Finance Nobel Laureate Shiller (2013) calls for a moral and ethical finance after the 2008 crash, but fails to mention either culture, tradition or belief community in the entire book. Religion as a source of conscience, a forum for ethical renewal and a major influence on conduct is just ignored. Such is the scientific apathy and denial.
3 As an example, the Jains have a whole science and philosophy of Ahimsa or non-violence, which can help demonstrate what a peaceful finance can look like. In fact, many practices in the global Jain diaspora show how this is done even today (Shah & Rankin, 2017).
4 Van Krieken (1999) and Williams (2012) give examples of the wisdom of indigenous cultures. Shah & Rankin (2017) detail the financial wisdom of the Jains, one of the oldest living cultures of the world.
5 Said (1996) demonstrates how even the idea of a black intellectual did not exist in Europe until the 1970s. The claim to knowledge superiority still runs very deep and has been reified by powerful institutions like Universities (Bhambra et al., 2018).
6 Todd (2016) even challenges the phrase 'ontology' as another word for 'colonialism'.
7 A biography, testimonials and publications can be viewed at www.atulkshah.co.uk – the life story of an empire 'subject' is relevant to the authority and authenticity of the wisdom, as this is where their living understanding of truth and knowledge is situated and reified.
8 In the last decade, a number of books have appeared which call for a systemic change in human culture, values and behaviour. Some examples of this are Alkon & Agyeman (2011); Ehrenfeld & Hoffman (2017); Lang et al. (2009); Meissner (2021); Shah (2022a).
9 Brooks (2018); Hurl & Werner (2024); Mazzucato & Collington (2024); Palan (2003); Shaxson (2012) provide examples of how professionals collude to support the elites and the wealthy at the expense of state revenues, which they expropriate deliberately and actively.
10 Shah (2024) is an auto-ethnography of my own experience of racism in the academy.

References

Abrudan, L.-C., Matei, M.-C., & Abrudan, M.-M. (2021). Towards Sustainable Finance: Conceptualizing Future Generations as Stakeholders. *Sustainability (Basel, Switzerland)*, 13(24), 13717.

Aggarwal, R., & Goodell, J. W. (2014). Culture, Institutions, and Financing Choices: How and Why Are They Related? *Research in International Business and Finance*, 31, 101–111.

Akala. (2019). *Natives: Race and Class in the Ruins of Empire*. Two Roads.

Alex, M., & Ichumbaki, E. B. (2024). 'Unless We Value the Intangible Heritage, the Tangible will never be Safe!' Linking the Tangible and Intangible Aspects of Heritage Sites in Africa. *Heritage & Society*, ahead-of-print, 1–20.

Alkon, A. H., & Agyeman, J. (2011). *Cultivating Food Justice: Race, Class, and Sustainability*. MIT Press.

Anderson, K. (2010). *The Political Economy of Agricultural Price Distortions*. Cambridge University Press.

Andrews, K. (2022). *The New Age of Empire: How Racism and Colonialism Still Rule the World*. Penguin.

Ardalan, K. (2023). *On the Methodology of Financial Economics: A Multi-Paradigmatic Look at Bias in the Mainstream*. Edward Elgar Publishing.

Armstrong, C. (2024). *Global Justice and the Biodiversity Crisis: Conservation in a World of Inequality*. Oxford University Press.

Armstrong, K. (2006). *The Great Transformation: The World in the time of Buddha, Socrates, Confucius and Jeremiah*. Atlantic Books.

Astrachan, J. H., Astrachan, C. B., Campopiano, G., & Baù, M. (2020). Values, Spirituality and Religion: Family Business and the Roots of Sustainable Ethical Behavior. *Journal of Business Ethics*, 163(4), 637–645.

Baars, G., & Spicer, A. (2017). *The Corporation: A Critical, Multi-Disciplinary Handbook*. Cambridge University Press.

Baddon, L., Hunter, L., Hyman, J., & Leopold, J. (2017). *People's Capitalism? A Critical Analysis of Profit-Sharing and Employee Share Ownership: 1*. Routledge.

Bakan, J. (2004). *The Corporation: The Pathological Pursuit of Profit and Power*. Free Press.

Bakan, J. (2020). *New Corporation: How 'Good' Corporations Are Bad for Democracy*. Vintage Books.

Banerjee, S. B. (2022). Decolonizing Management Theory: A Critical Perspective. *Journal of Management Studies*, 59(4), 1074–1087.

Barrera, A., & Amore, R. C. (eds) (2024). *The Oxford Handbook of Religion and Economic Ethics*. Oxford University Press.

Bastiat, F. (n.d.). *The Collected Works of Frédéric Bastiat*, Vol. 2. Ludwig von Mises Institute.

Bay, T., & McGoun, S. (2018). Critical Finance Studies. *Critical Perspectives on Accounting*, 52, 1–3.

Bay, T., & Schinckus, C. (2012). Critical Finance Studies: An Interdisciplinary Manifesto. *Journal of Interdisciplinary Economics*, 24(1), 1–6.

Bebbington, J., Österblom, H., Crona, B., Jouffray, J.-B., Larrinaga, C., Russell, S., & Scholtens, B. (2020). Accounting and Accountability in the Anthropocene. *Accounting Auditing & Accountability Journal*, 33(1), 152–177.

Beck, U. (1992). *Risk Society: Towards a New Modernity*. Sage.

Beliso-De Jesús, A. M., & Pierre, J. (2020). Special Section: Anthropology of White Supremacy. *American Anthropologist*, 122(1), 65–75.

Bell, E., Winchester, N., & Wray-Bliss, E. (2021). Enchantment in Business Ethics Research. *Journal of Business Ethics*, 174(2), 251–262.

Berry, W. (2004). *The Unsettling of America: Culture and Agriculture* (revised edition). Counterpoint.

Bhambra, G. K. (2023). *Rethinking Modernity: Postcolonialism and the Sociological Imagination*. Springer International Publishing.

Bhambra, G. K., Gebrial, D., & Nişancıoğlu, K. (eds) (2018). *Decolonising the University* (illustrated edition). Pluto Press.

Bharti, N. (2018). Evolution of Agriculture Finance in India: A Historical Perspective. *Agricultural Finance Review*, 78(3), 376–392.

Bhatnagar, N., Sharma, P., & Ramachandran, K. (2020). Spirituality and Corporate Philanthropy in Indian Family Firms: An Exploratory Study. *Journal of Business Ethics*, 163(4), 715–728.

Bischoff, K. (2021). A Study on the Perceived Strength of Sustainable Entrepreneurial Ecosystems on the Dimensions of Stakeholder Theory and Culture. *Small Business Economics*, 56(3), 1121–1140.

Blakeley, G. (2019). *Stolen: How to Save the World from Financialisation*.

Blakey, J. (2021). Accounting for Elephants: The (Post)Politics of Carbon Omissions. *Geoforum*, 121, 1–11.

Boatright, J. R. (2010). *Finance Ethics: Critical Issues in Theory and Practice*. Wiley.

Borch, C. (2020). Introduction: What is Critical Finance Studies? In C. Borch, R. Wosnitzer, R. Wosnitzer, & C. Borch (eds), *The Routledge Handbook of Critical Finance Studies* (pp. 1–25). Routledge.

Borch, C., & Wosnitzer, R. (2020). *The Routledge Handbook of Critical Finance Studies*. Taylor & Francis.

Boyle. (2010). *The Tyranny of Numbers: Why Counting Can't Make Us Happy*. Flamingo.

Brady, E. (2018). John Muir's Environmental Aesthetics: Interweaving the Aesthetic, Religious, and Scientific. *The Journal of Aesthetics and Art Criticism*, 76(4), 463–472.

British Business Bank (2020). *Alone, Together: Entrepreneurship and Diversity in the UK*. Oliver Wyman and British Business Bank.

Brooks, C., & Schopohl, L. (2018). Topics and Trends in Finance Research: What Is Published, Who Publishes It and What Gets Cited? *The British Accounting Review*, 50(6), 615–637.

Brooks, C., Fenton, E., Schopohl, L., & Walker, J. (2019). Why Does Research in Finance Have So Little Impact? *Critical Perspectives on Accounting*, 58, 24–52.

Brooks, R. (2014). *The Great Tax Robbery*.

Brooks, R. (2018). *Beancounters: The Triumph of Accountants and How They Broke Capitalism*. Atlantic Books.

Brunning, S., Yu-ping, L., O'Connell, E. R., & Williams, T. (2024). *Silk Roads*. British Museum Press.

Buller, A. (2022). *The Value of a Whale: On the Illusions of Green Capitalism*. Manchester University Press.

Bullough. (2018). *Moneyland: Why Thieves and Crooks Now Rule the World and How to Take It Back*. Profile Books.

Bullough, O. (2023). *Butler to the World: How Britain became the servant of tycoons, tax dodgers, kleptocrats and criminals*. Profile Books.

Burgis, T. (2024). *Cuckooland: Where the Rich Own the Truth*. William Collins.

Burrell, G., Hyman, M. R., Michaelson, C., Nelson, J. A., Taylor, S., & West, A. (2022). The Ethics and Politics of Academic Knowledge Production: Thoughts on the Future of Business Ethics. *Journal of Business Ethics*, 180(3), 917–940.

Çalışkan, A. S. (2022). *Homo Faber and Homo Economicus in the Scientific Revolution*. Routledge.

Campbell-Stephens, R. M. (2021). *Educational Leadership and the Global Majority: Decolonising Narratives*. Springer International Publishing.

Carnegie, G. D., Gomes, D., Parker, L. D., McBride, K., & Tsahuridu, E. (2024). How Accounting Can Shape a Better World: Framework, Analysis and Research Agenda. *Meditari Accountancy Research*, 32(5), 1529–1555.

Castree, N. (2021). Framing, Deframing and Reframing the Anthropocene: This Article Belongs to Ambio's 50th Anniversary Collection. Theme: Anthropocene. *Ambio*, 50(10), 1788–1792.

Chang, H.-J. (2011). *23 Things They Don't Tell You About Capitalism*. Penguin.

Chen, J. Z. (2009). Material Flow and Circular Economy. *Systems Research and Behavioral Science*, 26(2), 269–278.

Choat, S., Wolf, C., & O'Neill, S. (2024). Decolonising Economics and Politics Curricula in UK Universities. *Studies in Higher Education*, 49(9), 1504–1518.

Christensen, M., & Lamberton, G. (2022). Accounting for Animal Welfare: Addressing Epistemic Vices During Live Sheep Export Voyages. *Journal of Business Ethics*, 180(1), 35–56.

Christophers, B., Leyshon, A., & Mann, G. (2017). *Money and Finance After the Crisis: Critical Thinking for Uncertain Times*. Wiley Blackwell.

Clapp, J., & Fuchs, D. A. (2009). *Corporate Power in Global Agrifood Governance*. MIT Press.

Clark, G. L., & Wójcik, D. (2007). *The Geography of Finance: Corporate Governance in the Global Marketplace*. OUP.

Coggan, P. (2012). *Paper Promises: Money, Debt and the New World Order*. Penguin.

Cohen, D. (2014). *Homo Economicus: The (Lost) Prophet of Modern Times* (S. Emanuel, Trans.). Polity.

Constanza, R. (2013). *Building a Sustainable and Desirable Economy-In-Society-In-Nature*. Australian National University E Press.

Cook, D. (2011). *Adorno on Nature*. Acumen.

Cowen, T. (2002). *Creative Destruction*. Princeton University Press.

Crichlow, W. (2018). Western Colonization as Disease: Native Adoption Cultural Genocide. *Critical Social Work*, 3(1).

Cunningham, L. (2014). *Berkshire Beyond Buffett: The Enduring Value of Values* (illustrated edition). Columbia University Press.

Dalrymple, W. (2020). *The Anarchy: The Relentless Rise of the East India Company*. Bloomsbury Publishing.

Dalrymple, W. (2024). *The Golden Road: How Ancient India Transformed the World*. Bloomsbury Publishing.

Daly, H. E., & Cobb. (1994). *For The Common Good: Redirecting the Economy toward Community, the Environment, and a Sustainable Future* (updated, expanded edition). Beacon Press.

de Bruin, B. (2015). *Ethics and the Global Financial Crisis: Why Incompetence is Worse than Greed*. Cambridge University Press.

Deckard, S., Niblett, M., & Shapiro, S. (2024). *Tracking Capital: World-Systems, World-Ecology, World-Culture*. SUNY Press.

DePuy, W., Weger, J., Foster, K., Bonanno, A. M., Kumar, S., Lear, K., Basilio, R., & German, L. (2022). Environmental Governance: Broadening Ontological Spaces for a More Livable World. *Environment and Planning E: Nature and Space*, 5(2), 947–975.

de Santos, B. (2016). *Epistemologies of the South: Justice Against Epistemicide*. Routledge.

Deshpande, R. S., & Arora, S. (eds) (2010). *Agrarian Crisis and Farmer Suicides*. SAGE.

Dodd, N. (2014). *The Social Life of Money*. Princeton University Press.

Driver, C., & Thompson, G. (2018). *Corporate Governance in Contention*. Oxford University Press.

Dryzek, J. S., Norgaard, R. B., & Schlosberg, D. (2011). *Oxford Handbook of Climate Change and Society*. Oxford University Press.

Dundas, P. (2002). *The Jains*, 2nd edition. Routledge.

Dupont, Q., & Karpoff, J. M. (2020). The Trust Triangle: Laws, Reputation, and Culture in Empirical Finance Research. *Journal of Business Ethics*, 163(2), 217–238.

Durand, C. (2017). *Fictitious Capital: How Finance Is Appropriating Our Future* (D. Broder, Trans.). Verso Books.

Eckersley, R., 1958. (1992). *Environmentalism and Political Theory: Toward an Ecocentirc Approach*. UCL Press.

Egan, M. (2021). Diversity, Inclusion, and the Opportunities for Accounting Research. *Social and Environmental Accountability Journal*, 41(3), 201–207.

Ehrenfeld, J., & Hoffman, A. J. (2017). *Flourishing: A Frank Conversation About Sustainability*. Stanford Business Books.

Empson, L. (2017). *Leading Professionals: Power, Politics and Prima Donnas*. Oxford University Press.

Engelen, E., Ertürk, I., Froud, J., Johal, S., Leaver, A., Moran, M., & Williams, K. (2012). Misrule of Experts? The Financial Crisis as Elite Debacle. *Economy and Society*, 41(3), 360–382.

Engler, H. (2018). *Remaking Culture on Wall Street: A Behavioral Science Approach for Building Trust from the Bottom Up*. Springer International Publishing.

Fanon, F., Sartre, J.-P., Philcox, R., & Bhabha, H. K. (2004). *The Wretched of the Earth*. Grove Press.

Farley, J., & Luzzati, T. (2023). In memoriam: Herman Daly (1938–2022). *Ecological Economics*, 205.

Fenelon, J., & Alford, J. (2020). Envisioning Indigenous Models for Social and Ecological Change in the Anthropocene. *Journal of World-Systems Research*, 26(2), 372–399.

Ferguson, K., & Petro, P. (2016). *After Capitalism: Horizons of Finance, Culture, and Citizenship*. Rutgers University Press.

Finel-Honigman, I. (2010). *A Cultural History of Finance*. Routledge.

Fleming, P. (2014). *Resisting Work: The Corporatization of Life and Its Discontents*. Temple University Press.

Fleming, P. (2015). *The Mythology of Work: How Capitalism Persists Despite Itself*. Pluto Press.

Fleming, P. (2017a). Why Homo Economicus had to Die … Over and Over Again. In *The Death of Homo Economicus* (Vol. 1, p. 87). Pluto Press.

Fleming, P. (2017b). Wreckage Economics. In *The Death of Homo Economicus* (Vol. 1, p. 40). Pluto Press.

Fleming, P., & Spicer, A. (2007). *Contesting the Corporation: Struggle, Power and Resistance in Organizations*. Cambridge University Press.

Foroohar, R. (2016). *Makers and Takers: How Wall Street Destroyed Main Street*. Crown.

Frankopan, P. (2016). *The Silk Roads: A New History of the World*. Knopf Doubleday Publishing Group.

Frayne, J. F. (2017). *The Indian Hundi*. Lulu.com.

Freire, P. (2017). *Pedagogy of the Oppressed*, 13th edition. Penguin Classics.

Friedman, B. M. (2022). *Religion and the Rise of Capitalism*. Knopf Doubleday Publishing Group.

Furnham, A. (2014). *The New Psychology of Money*. Psychology Press.
Gendron, Yves, & Smith-Lacroix, J. (2013). *The Global Financial Crisis: Essay on the Possibility of Substantive Change in the Discipline of Finance*. Critical Perspectives on Accounting.
George, S. (2013). *Whose Crisis, Whose Future?*Polity.
Gerlach, P. (2017). The Games Economists Play: Why Economics Students Behave More Selfishly Than Other Students. *PloS One*, 12(9), e0183814.
Ghio, A., McGuigan, N., Stewart, O. J., Tharapos, M., & Wood, L. I. (2023). Diversity, Equity, and Social Justice in Accounting Education. *Issues in Accounting Education*, 38(1), 1–5.
Goodell, J. W., Kumar, S., Lahmar, O., & Pandey, N. (2023). A Bibliometric Analysis of Cultural Finance. *International Review of Financial Analysis*, 85, 102442.
Goodhart, C. (2010). How Should We Regulate the Financial Sector, The Future of Finance, LSE. www.futureoffinance.org.uk.
Gore, A. (2006). *Earth in the Balance: Ecology and the Human Spirit*. Rodale Books.
Graeber, D. (2014). *Debt: The First 5000 Years*, 2nd revised edition. Melville House Publishing.
Graeber, D. (2019). *Bullshit Jobs: The Rise of Pointless Work, and What We Can Do About It*. Penguin.
Graeber, D., & Wengrow, D. (2022). *The Dawn of Everything: A New History of Humanity*. Penguin.
Haidt, J. (2013). *The Righteous Mind: Why Good People are Divided by Politics and Religion*. Penguin.
Hamilton, L. (2016). Empire and Economics: Decolonising Colonialism and Its Legacies in Africa. *Theoria*, 63(147), 1–5.
Hampden-Turner, C., & Trompenaars, A. (1993). *The Seven Cultures of Capitalism: Value Systems for Creating Wealth in the United States, Japan, Germany, France, Britain, Sweden, and the Netherlands*. Currency Doubleday.
Hanson, S. (2015). The Case for Farm Finance. *Innovations: Technology, Governance, Globalization*, 10(1–2),139–146.
Harari, Y. (2015). *Sapiens: A Brief History of Humankind*. Vintage.
Harrison, R. (2015). Beyond 'Natural' and 'Cultural' Heritage: Toward an Ontological Politics of Heritage in the Age of Anthropocene. *Heritage & Society*, 8(1), 24–42.
Harvey, D., 1935. (1996). *Justice, Nature and the Geography of Difference*. Blackwell.
Hawken, P. (1994). *The Ecology of Commerce: A Declaration of Sustainability*. Phoenix.
Hawley, K. (2012). *Trust: A Very Short Introduction*. OUP.
Heffernan, M. (2011). *Wilful Blindness: Why We Ignore the Obvious at our Peril*. Walker.
Hertz, N. (2020). *The Lonely Century: A Call to Reconnect*. Hachette UK.
Hickel, J. (1982). *Less is More: How Degrowth Will Save the World*. William Heinemann.
Hilkens, A., Reid, J. I., Klerkx, L., & Gray, D. I. (2018). Money Talk: How Relations Between Farmers and Advisors Around Financial Management Are Shaped. *Journal of Rural Studies*, 63, 83–95.
Hines, R. D. (1988). Financial Accounting: In Communicating Reality, We Construct Reality. *Accounting, Organizations and Society*, 13(3), 251–261.
Ho, K. (2009). *Liquidated: An Ethnography of Wall Street* (illustrated edition). Duke University Press Books.
Hoang, K. K. (2022). *Spiderweb Capitalism: How Global Elites Exploit Frontier Markets*. Princeton University Press.

Hoppe, R. A. (2014). *Structure and Finances of U. S. Farms: Family Farm Report, 2014 Edition*. DIANE Publishing Company.

Hurl, C., & Werner, L. B. (2024). *The Consulting Trap: How Professional Service Firms Hook Governments and Undermine Democracy*. Fernwood Publishing Co Ltd.

Jaffe, S. (2021). *Work Won't Love You Back: How Devotion to Our Jobs Keeps Us Exploited, Exhausted and Alone*. C Hurst & Co Publishers Ltd.

Jäger, J., & Dziwok, E. (2024). *Understanding Green Finance: A Critical Assessment and Alternative Perspectives*. Edward Elgar Publishing.

James, O. (2007). *Affluenza: How to be Successful and Stay Sane*. Random House.

Jasanoff, M. (2011). *Liberty's Exiles: American Loyalists in the Revolutionary World*. Alfred A. Knopf Inc.

Jones, G., Escalante, C., & Rusiana, H. (2015). Reconciling Information Gaps in Organic Farm Borrowers' Dealings with Farm Lenders. *Agricultural Finance Review*, 75(4), 469–483.

Jordaan, M. J., & Eiselen, R. (2015). Organic Agriculture: The Trade-Off Between Financial and Non-Financial Benefits. *Journal of Economic and Financial Sciences*, 8(3), 875–889.

Kaiser, A. (2018). *The New Oxford Handbook of Economic Geography*. Oxford University Press.

Kay, J. (2011). *The Map Is Not the Territory: An Essay on the State of Economics*. Institute for New Economic Thinking.

Kay, J. (2015). *Other People's Money: Masters of the Universe or Servants of the People?* Profile Books.

Keasey, K., & Hudson, R. (2007). Finance Theory: A House Without Windows. *Critical Perspectives on Accounting*, 18(8), 932–951.

Kenadjian, P. S., & Dombret, A. (2016). *Getting the Culture and the Ethics Right: Towards a New Age of Responsibility in Banking and Finance* (Vol. 20). De Gruyter.

Keucheyan, R. (2017). *Nature is a Battlefield: Towards a Political Ecology*. John Wiley & Sons.

Kingston, L. (2015). The Destruction of Identity: Cultural Genocide and Indigenous Peoples. *Journal of Human Rights*, 14(1), 63–83.

Klein, N. (1970). *On Fire: The Burning Case for a Green New Deal*. Allen Lane.

Klocek, D. (2013). *Sacred Agriculture: The Alchemy of Biodynamics*. Lindisfarne Books.

Kuhn, T. S., & Hacking, I. (2012). *The Structure of Scientific Revolutions: 50th Anniversary Edition*, 4th edition. University of Chicago Press.

Kumar, S. (2024). *Soil, Soul, Society: A New Trinity for Our Time*. Parallax Press.

Kvangraven, I. H., & Kesar, S. (2023). Standing in the way of rigor? Economics' meeting with the decolonization agenda. *Review of International Political Economy*, 30(5), 1723–1748.

Lagoarde-Segot, T. (2015). Diversifying Finance Research: From Financialization to Sustainability. *International Review of Financial Analysis*, 39, 1–6.

Lagoarde-Segot, T. (2018). Sustainable Finance: A Critical Realist Perspective. *Research in International Business and Finance*.

Lagoarde-Segot, T. (2020). Financing the Sustainable Development Goals. *Sustainability (Basel, Switzerland)*, 12(7), 2775.

Laine, M., Unerman, J., & Tregidga, H. (2022). *Sustainability Accounting and Accountability*, 3rd edition. Routledge.

LaMothe, R. (2023). The Silence of Othered Species: The Anthropocene Age, Trauma, and the Ontological Rift. *Pastoral Psychology*, 72(3), 385–402.

Lang, T., Barling, D., & Caraher, M. (2009). *Food Policy: Integrating Health, Environment and Society*. Oxford University Press.
Langley, P., Anderson, B., Ash, J., & Gordon, R. (2019). Indebted Life and Money Culture: Payday Lending in the United Kingdom. *Economy and Society*, 48(1), 30–51.
Latour, B. (2014). *On Some of the Affects of Capitalism, Copenhagen*. Royal Academy.
Lazonick, W., & Shin, J.-S. (2019). *Predatory Value Extraction: How the Looting of the Business Corporation Became the US Norm and How Sustainable Prosperity Can Be Restored*. Oxford University Press.
LeVasseur, T., Parajuli, P., & Wirzba, N. (2016). *Religion and Sustainable Agriculture: World Spiritual Traditions and Food Ethics*. University Press of Kentucky.
Lewis, M. (1989). *Liar's Poker: Rising Through the Wreckage on Wall Street*. W. W. Norton.
Lewis, M. (2011a). *Boomerang: The Biggest Bust*. Penguin Books.
Lewis, M. (2011b). *The Money Culture*. Norton.
Lewis, M. (2014). *Flash Boys: Cracking the Money Code*. Penguin.
Lewis, M. (2010). *The Big Short: Inside the Doomsday Machine*. Allen Lane.
Lewis, S. L., & Maslin, M. A. (2015). Defining the Anthropocene. *Nature*, 519(7542), 171–180.
Llewellyn, D. T. (2005). Trust and Confidence in Financial Services: A Strategic Challenge. *Journal of Financial Regulation and Compliance*, 13(4), 333–346.
Luyendijk, J. (2015). *Swimming with Sharks: My Journey into the World of Bankers*. Guardian/Faber & Faber.
Lymbery, P. (2015). *Farmageddon: The True Cost of Cheap Meat*. Bloomsbury Paperbacks.
Macey, J. R. (2022). ESG Investing: Why Here? Why Now? *Berkeley Business Law Journal*, 19, 258.
MacKenzie, D. (2005). Opening the Black Boxes of Global Finance. *Review of International Political Economy*, 12(4), 555–576.
Mackenzie, D. (2006). *An Engine, Not a Camera: How Financial Models Shape Markets*. MIT Press.
MacKenzie, D. (2011). The Credit Crisis as a Problem in the Sociology of Knowledge. *American Journal of Sociology*, 116(6), 1778–1841.
Marquis, C. (2024). *The Profiteers: How Business Privatizes Profits and Socializes Costs*. Hachette UK.
Mazoyer, M., & Roudart, L. (2006). *A History of World Agriculture: From the Neolithic Age to the Current Crisis*. Earthscan.
Mazzucato, M., & Collington, R. (2024). *The Big Con: How the Consulting Industry Weakens our Businesses, Infantilizes our Governments and Warps our Economies*. Penguin.
Mbembe, A. (2019). *Necropolitics*. Duke University Press.
McGoun, E. G. (1997). Hyperreal Finance. *Critical Perspectives on Accounting*, 8(1), 97–122.
Meadows, D. H., Meadows, D. L., Randers, J., & Behrens, W. W. (1979). *The Limits to Growth: A Report for the Club of Rome's Project on the Predicament of Mankind* (new edition). Macmillan.
Meghji, A. (2021). *Decolonizing Sociology: An Introduction*. Polity.
Mehta, L., Oweis, T., Ringler, C., Schreiner, B., & Varghese, S. (2019). *Water for Food Security, Nutrition and Social Justice*. Routledge.
Meissner, M. (2021). *Intangible Cultural Heritage and Sustainable Development: The Valorisation of Heritage Practices*. Springer International Publishing.

Meyer, E. (2016). *The Culture Map: Decoding How People Think, Lead, and Get Things Done Across Cultures*. PublicAffairs.

Møller, V., Cocks, M., & Vetter, S. (2023). Nature-Connectedness and Well-Being Experienced During Best and Worst Times of Life: A Case for Safeguarding Biocultural Diversity. *Social Indicators Research*, 165(3), 1053–1089.

Monbiot, G. (2000). *The Corporate Takeover of Britain*. Macmillan.

Monbiot, G. (2017). *How Did We Get Into This Mess? Politics, Equality, Nature*. Verso.

Monbiot, G. (2023). *Regenesis: Feeding the World without Devouring the Planet*. Penguin.

Montgomerie, J. (2008). Bridging the Critical Divide: Global Finance, Financialisation and Contemporary Capitalism. *Contemporary Politics*, 14(3), 233–252.

Moore, J. W. (2016). *Anthropocene or Capitalocene? Nature, History, and the Crisis of Capitalism*. PM Press.

Muniesa, F. (2024). *Paranoid Finance*. Polity.

Muradoglu, G., & Harvey, N. (2012). Behavioural Finance: The Role of Psychological Factors in Financial Decisions. *Review of Behavioral Finance*, 4(2), 68–80.

Murau, S., & Pforr, T. (2020). What is Money in a Critical Macro-Finance Framework? *Finance and Society*, 6(1), 56–66.

Murphy, R. (2015). *The Joy of Tax*. Transworld Publishers.

Nair, M., & Njolomole, M. (2020). Microfinance, Entrepreneurship and Institutional Quality. *Journal of Entrepreneurship and Public Policy*, 9(1), 137–148.

Naude, P. (2019). Decolonising Knowledge: Can 'Ubuntu' Ethics Save Us from Coloniality? *Journal of Business Ethics*, 159(1), 23–37.

Naylor, L., & Thayer, N. (2022). Between Paranoia and Possibility: Diverse Economies and the Decolonial Imperative. *Transactions – Institute of British Geographers (1965)*, 47(3), 791–805.

Nesvetailova, A. (2012). Money and Finance in a Globalized Economy. In R. Palan (ed.), *Global Political Economy*, 2nd edition. Routledge.

Newell, P. (2013). *Globalization and the Environment: Capitalism, Ecology and Power*. John Wiley & Sons.

Newell, P., & Paterson, M., 1967. (2010). *Climate Capitalism: Global Warming and the Transformation of the Global Economy*. Cambridge University Press.

Ng, Y. (2019). KEYNOTE: Global Extinction and Animal Welfare: Two Priorities for Effective Altruism. *Global Policy*, 10(2), 258–266.

Nguyen, M.-H., Pham, T.-H., Ho, M.-T., Nguyen, H. T. T., & Vuong, Q.-H. (2020). On the Social and Conceptual Structure of the 50-Year Research Landscape in Entrepreneurial Finance. *SN Business & Economics*, 1(1), 2.

Niiniluoto, I. (2020). Social Aspects of Scientific Knowledge. *Synthese (Dordrecht)*, 197(1), 447–468.

Obach, B. K., & Tobin, K. (2014). Civic Agriculture and Community Engagement. *Agriculture and Human Values*, 31(2), 307–322.

Obeng-Odoom, F. (2020). *The Commons in an Age of Uncertainty: Decolonizing Nature, Economy, and Society*. University of Toronto Press.

Ortiz, H. (2017). A Political Anthropology of Finance: Profits, States, and Cultures in Cross-Border Investment in Shanghai. *HAU Journal of Ethnographic Theory*, 7(3), 325–345.

Ostendorf-Rodríguez, Y. (with González, R.). (2023). *Let's Become Fungal! Mycelium Teachings and the Arts: Based on Conversations with Indigenous Wisdom Keepers, Artists, Curators, Feminists and Mycologists*. Valiz.

Osterhammel, J., Geyer, D., & Petersson, N. P. (2021). *Globalization: A Short History*. Princeton University Press.
Ott, J. C. (2011). *When Wall Street Met Main Street: The Quest for an Investors' Democracy*. Harvard University Press.
Pabrai, M. (2007). *The Dhandho Investor: The Low-Risk Value Method to High Returns*. Wiley.
Paik, P. Y., & Wiesner-Hanks, M. (2013). *Debt: Ethics, the Environment, and the Economy: Vol. 6*. Indiana University Press.
Palan, R. (2003). *The Offshore World: Sovereign Markets, Virtual Places, and Nomad Millionaires*. Cornell University Press.
Parker, M. (2018). Why We Should Bulldoze the Business School. *The Guardian*.
Parlasca, M. C., Johnen, C., & Qaim, M. (2022). Use of Mobile Financial Services Among Farmers in Africa: Insights from Kenya. *Global Food Security*, 32, 100590.
Pattanaik, D. (2015). *Business Sutra: A Very Indian Approach to Management*. Aleph Book Company.
Pettifor, A. (2017). *The Production of Money: How to Break the Power of the Banks: How to Break the Power of Bankers* (illustrated edition). Verso.
Pettigrew, A., & Starkey, K. (2016). The Legitimacy and Impact of Business Schools – Key Issues and a Research Agenda. *Academy of Management Learning and Education*, 15(4), 649–664.
Pfeiffer, D. A. (2006). *Eating Fossil Fuels: Oil, Food, and the Coming Crisis in Agriculture*. New Society Publishers.
Pistor, K. (2019). *The Code of Capital: How the Law Creates Wealth and Inequality*. Princeton University Press.
Poyser, A., & Daugaard, D. (2023). Indigenous Sustainable Finance as a Research Field: A Systematic Literature Review on Indigenising ESG, Sustainability and Indigenous Community Practices. *Accounting and Finance (Parkville)*, 63(1), 47–76.
Prahlad, C. K. (2019). *The Fortune at The Bottom of The Pyramid*. Pearson Education.
Pretty, J. N. (2002). *Agri-Culture: Reconnecting People, Land and Nature*. Earthscan.
Prins, N. (2014). *All the Presidents' Bankers: The Hidden Alliances that Drive American Power*. Hachette UK.
Prins, N. (2018). *Collusion: How Central Bankers Rigged the World*. PublicAffairs.
Rajan, R. (2019). *The Third Pillar: How Markets and the State Leave the Community Behind*. Penguin Press.
Randazzo, E., & Richter, H. (2021). The Politics of the Anthropocene: Temporality, Ecology, and Indigeneity. *International Political Sociology*, 15(3), 293–312.
Rankin, A. (2010). *Many-Sided Wisdom: A New Politics of the Spirit*. Mantra Books.
Raworth, K. (2018). *Doughnut Economics: The Must-Read Book That Redefines Economics for a World in Crisis*. Random House Business.
Read, R. (2023). Touching the Earth: Buddhist (and Kierkegaardian) Reflections on and of the 'Negative' Emotions. *Religions (Basel, Switzerland)*, 14(12), 1451.
Reinhard, C., & Rogoff, K. (2011). *This Time is Different: Eight Centuries of Financial Folly*. Princeton University Press.
Renner, A., Daly, H., & Mayumi, K. (2021). The Dual Nature of Money: Why Monetary Systems Matter for Equitable Bioeconomy. *Environmental Economics and Policy Studies*, 23(4), 749–760.
Reurink, A. (2018). Financial Fraud: A Literature Review. *Journal of Economic Surveys*, 32(5), 1292–1325.
Reuter, C. H. J. (2011). A Survey of 'Culture and Finance'. *Finance*, 32(1), 75–152.

Rich, M. M. (2013). *The Hidden Evil: The Financial Elite's Covert War Against the Civilian Population*. Mark M. Rich.

Rifkin, J. (2001). *The Age of Access: The New Culture of Hypercapitalism, Where All of Life is a Paid-For Experience*. Jeremy P. Tarcher.

Robin, M.-M. (2012). *The World According to Monsanto*. The New Press.

Roettger, D. (2015). *Agricultural Finance for Smallholder Farmers: Rethinking Traditional Microfinance Risk and Cost Management Approaches*. Columbia University Press.

Sacks, J. (2003). *The Dignity of Difference: How to Avoid the Clash of Civilisations*. Continuum Books.

Sacks, J. (2010). *The Persistence of Faith: Religion, Morality and Society in a Secular Age (the BBC Reith Lectures)*. Continuum Compact Series.

Sahlins, M. (2013). On the Culture of Material Value and the Cosmography of Riches. *HAU Journal of Ethnographic Theory*, 3(2), 161–195.

Said, E. W. (1995). *Orientalism*. Penguin Books India.

Said, E. W. (1996). *Representations of the Intellectual: The 1933 Reith Lectures*. Vintage.

Said, E. W. (2014). *Culture and Imperialism*. Random House.

Sailesh Rao, E. (2020). *Animal Agriculture is Immoral*. Independently Published.

Samman, A., Boy, N., Coombs, N., Hager, S., Hayes, A., Rosamond, E., Wansleben, L., & Westermeier, C. (2022). After the Boom: Finance and Society Studies in the 2020s and Beyond. *Finance and Society*, 8(2), 93–109.

Sandel, M. J. (2013). *What Money Can't Buy: The Moral Limits of Markets*. Penguin.

Sanghera, S. (2021). *Empireland*. Penguin Books.

Schulz, J., Bahrami-Rad, D., Beauchamp, J., & Henrich, J. (2018). *The Origins of WEIRD Psychology*. https://ssrn.com/abstract=3201031

Sedgmore, L. (2024). *Presence Activism: A Profound Antidote to Climate Anxiety*. John Hunt Publishing.

Shah, A. (2015a). Systemic Regulatory Arbitrage – A Case Study of KPMG. www.academia.edu.

Shah, A. (2015b). The Chemistry of Audit Failure – A Case Study of KPMG. www.academia.edu.

Shah, A. (2018). *Reinventing Accounting and Finance Education – For a Caring, Inclusive and Sustainable Planet*. Routledge.

Shah, A. K. (2022a). *Inclusive and Sustainable Finance: Leadership, Ethics and Culture*. Routledge.

Shah, A. K. (2022b). Reform Lessons from Investigative Journalism. Review Essay of 'Beancounters' by Richard Brooks. *The British Accounting Review*, 54(3), 101069.

Shah, A. K. (2024). Racism in the Accounting Academy: An Auto-Ethnographic Case Study of British Higher Education. In H. Vollmer (ed.), *Handbook of Accounting in Society* (pp. 363–376). Edward Elgar.

Shah, A., & Rankin, A. (2017). *Jainism and Ethical Finance: A Timeless Business Model*. Routledge.

Shaxson, N. (2012). *Treasure Islands: Tax Havens and the Men Who Stole the World*. Vintage Books.

Shaxson, N. (2019). *The Finance Curse: How Global Finance is Making Us All Poorer*. Vintage.

Sheridan, J., & Longboat, D. (Roronhiakewen [He Clears the Sky]) (2006). The Haudenosaunee Imagination and the Ecology of the Sacred. *Space and Culture*, 9(4), 365–381.

Shiferaw, A., Hebo, M., & Senishaw, G. (2023). The Spiritual Ecology of Sacred Landscapes: Evidence from Sacred Forests of the Sebat Bête Gurage, Central—South Ethiopia. *Cogent Social Sciences*, 9(1).

Shiller, R. J. (2013). *Finance and the Good Society*. Princeton University Press. https://doi.org/10.1515/9781400846177.

Shiva, V. (2006). *Earth Democracy: Justice, Sustainability and Peace*. Zed.

Short, D. (2010). Cultural Genocide and Indigenous Peoples: A Sociological Approach. *The International Journal of Human Rights*, 14(6), 833–848.

Shrivastava, P., Ivanaj, S., & Persson, S. (2013). Transdisciplinary Study of Sustainable Enterprise. *Business Strategy and the Environment*, 22(4), 230–244.

Smith, A. (2023). *An Inquiry into the Nature and Causes of the Wealth of Nations*. Wiley-Blackwell.

Soukup, S. R. (2021). *The Dictatorship of Woke Capital: How Political Correctness Captured Big Business*. Encounter Books.

Starks, L. T. (2023). Presidential Address: Sustainable Finance and ESG Issues – Value versus Values. *The Journal of Finance (New York)*, 78(4), 1837–1872.

Stein, M. (2011). *A Culture of Mania – A Psychoanalytic View of the Incubation of the 2008 Credit Crisis*. Organisation.

Stiglitz, J. E. (2017). *Globalization and Its Discontents Revisited: Anti-Globalization in the Era of Trump*. Penguin.

Stiglitz, J. E. (2019). *People, Power and Profits: Progressive Capitalism for an Age of Discontent*. Allen Lane.

Stiglitz, J. E. (2024). *The Road to Freedom: Economics and the Good Society*. Allen Lane.

Stilwell, F. J. B. (2019). *The Political Economy of Inequality*. Polity.

Strevens, M. (2022). *The Knowledge Machine: How an Unreasonable Idea Created Modern Science*. Penguin.

Stuart, D. (2020). Radical Hope: Truth, Virtue, and Hope for What Is Left in Extinction Rebellion. *Journal of Agricultural & Environmental Ethics*, 33(3–6),487–504.

Sultana, F. (2023). Whose Growth in Whose Planetary Boundaries? Decolonising Planetary Justice in the Anthropocene. *Geo*, 10(2).

Taylor, B. (1997). Earthen Spirituality or Cultural Genocide? Radical Environmentalism's Appropriation of Native American Spirituality. *Religion (London.1971)*, 27(2), 183–215. https://doi.org/10.1006/reli.1996.0042.

Tett, G. (2010). *Fool's Gold – How unrestrained greed corrupted a dream, shattered global markets and unleashed a catastrophe*. Abacus, 356pp.

Tett, G. (2021). *Anthro-Vision: How Anthropology Can Explain Business and Life*. Random House Business.

Thomas, D. C., & Inkson, K. (2017). *Cultural Intelligence: Building People Skills for the 21st Century: Surviving and Thriving in the Global Village*, 3rd edition. Berrett-Koehler Publishers.

Thompson, H. (2017). *Oil and the Western Economic Crisis*. Palgrave Macmillan.

Todd, Z. (2016). An Indigenous Feminist's Take on the Ontological Turn: 'Ontology' Is Just Another Word For Colonialism. *Journal of Historical Sociology*, 29(1), 4–22.

Toledo, V. M. (2022). Agroecology and Spirituality: Reflections About an Unrecognized Link. *Agroecology and Sustainable Food Systems*, 46(4), 626–641.

Trompenaars, A., & Hampden-Turner, C. (2020). *Riding the Waves of Culture: Understanding Diversity in Global Business*, 4th edition. Nicholas Brealey Publishing.

Turner, A. (2015). *Between Debt and the Devil: Money, Credit, and Fixing Global Finance* (illustrated edition). Princeton University Press.

Turner, J., & D'Silva, J. (2006). *Animals, Ethics, and Trade: The Challenge of Animal Sentience*. Earthscan.

Tyrie, A. (2013). *Changing Banking for Good*. Committee Report HC175–111. UK: House of Commons Treasury.

Valentinov, V. (2021). Sustainability in Classical Institutional Economics: A Systems Theory View. *Sustainable Production and Consumption*, 28, 1500–1507.

Van Krieken, R. (1999). The Barbarism of Civilization: Cultural Genocide and the 'Stolen Generations'. *The British Journal of Sociology*, 50(2), 297–315.

Vanden Heuvel, K. (2009). *Meltdown: How Greed and Corruption Shattered Our Financial System and How We Can Recover*. Nation Books.

Veland, S., Gram-Hanssen, I., Maggs, D., & Lynch, A. H. (2022). Can the Sustainable Development Goals Harness the Means and the Manner of Transformation? *Sustainability Science*, 17(2), 637–651.

Verny, T. R. (2023). *The Embodied Mind: Understanding the Mysteries of Cellular Memory, Consciousness, and Our Bodies*. Pegasus Books.

Warren-Jones, A. (2017). Regulatory Theory: Commercially Sustainable Markets Rely Upon Satisfying the Public Interest in Obtaining Credible Goods. *Health Economics, Policy and Law*, 12(4), 471–493.

Wenger, E. (2000). *Communities of Practice: Learning, Meaning, And Identity*. Cambridge University Press.

West, B. (2003). *Professionalism and Accounting Rules*. Routledge.

Whitehead, A. N. (1979). *Process and Reality*. Free Press.

Whitley, R. (1986). The Transformation of Business Finance into Financial Economics: The Roles of Academic Expansion and Changes in U.S. Capital Markets. *Accounting, Organizations and Society*, 11(2), 171–192.

Whyte, D. (2020). *Ecocide: Kill the Corporation before it Kills Us*. Manchester University Press.

Whyte, D., & Wiegratz, J. (eds) (2016). *Neoliberalism and the Moral Economy of Fraud*. Routledge.

Wilber, K. (2002). *The Spectrum of Consciousness*. Motilal Banarsidass Publications.

Williams, J. (2012). The Impact of Climate Change on Indigenous People: The Implications for the Cultural, Spiritual, Economic and Legal Rights of Indigenous People. *The International Journal of Human Rights*, 16(4), 648–688.

Williams, J. W. (2014). Feeding Finance: A Critical Account of the Shifting Relationships Between Finance, Food and Farming. *Economy and Society*, 43(3), 401–431. https://doi.org/10.1080/03085147.2014.892797.

Yunus, M. (2003). *Banker to the Poor: Micro-Lending and the Battle Against World Poverty*. PublicAffairs.

Zhou, Y. (2015). Jain Irrigation Systems Limited: Creating Shared Value for Small Onion Growers. In Y. Zhou & S. C. Babu (eds), *Knowledge Driven Development* (pp. 163–179). Academic Press.

Zingales, L. (2015). Presidential Address: Does Finance Benefit Society? *The Journal of Finance*, 70(4), 1327–1363.

Zuboff, P. S. (2019). *The Age of Surveillance Capitalism: The Fight for a Human Future at the New Frontier of Power: Barack Obama's Books of 2019*. Profile Books.

2 Soil and Soul

The Earth is the ground on which society and life is built and sustained. Over millions of years, Gaia has learnt to create a balance between soil, water and air to nurture and sustain life. It is one of very few planets which have life. This growth was organic, not fuelled by finance or technology. The balance between species evolved over time, sometimes millions of years, through adaptation and assimilation. While life on earth was born some 3.8 billion years ago, it is only 70,000 years ago that humanity began its cognitive revolution to form cultures and communities. And money is only five thousand years old, and that too was in the form of local currency, with at times several coins and currencies prevailing in different kingdoms. International and mobile money are a much more recent phenomenon in human history, and ahistorical finance deletes this from memory or science altogether. It is critical that we put finance in this wider historical context and understand its role in creating the Anthropocene – the profound and irreversible attack on planet earth and its living systems.

This introductory chapter opens the wide canvas of finance, in terms of human history and diverse cultures, to expose how what we call the modern science and discipline is so profoundly dislocated from the ecosystem. Just as the interdependence of soil, air, water and soul has been universal throughout history, the rise of human violence and greed has come to overwhelm the planet. To claim that Net Zero technologies will solve all our problems and return life back to harmony, reversing climate change, is to profoundly misunderstand how our very thoughts, actions, institutions and cultures are a deep part of the problem. These will not be transformed by a technological fix called Net Zero. We need to go back to the ground of finance, and connect it with the soul, to begin to understand how it can be reformed for a harmonious ecosystem. That is the goal of this chapter – to lay the foundations of the new economic wisdom needed to make peace with Gaia.

For starters, it is important to understand that much later in the multi-billion-year life of the planet (only 300,000 years ago), the human species was born. For a long time, human life was local, populations were small, and there were no technologies for mass economics (like international bonds and money transfers) or mass food or agriculture. Some five thousand years ago, the human species decided to create money, to fund wars, collect taxes and ease certain trade and transactions (Graeber, 2014). For a long time, it was a very limited technology of life – it was rarely used, and that also in specific contexts and parts of the world.

Sadly, violence and war played a foundational role in the spread and reach of money, and it is still so today, also leading to ecological devastation and rising inequality. In Hindu science, it is believed that these foundational *nishasas* (bad energies) do not go away easily. As late as the sixteenth century, when the Spanish conquistadores invaded Mexico, they saw the locals mining and wearing gold and looted them as it was much prized in Europe and a source of wealth and fortune. Paradoxically, the natives did not see it as precious or valuable, and simply used it to wear for their jewellery, and had a different currency, based on cowrie shells, for their trade.

This dislocation of the economy from Gaia is critical to understand for us to be able to reform our science and knowledge in finance – humans are aesthetic beings, not robots or machines (Brady, 2018). The discipline has virtually eliminated all study of history or cultures, and instead imposed a new ideology which is neo-liberal and worships the market as the arbiter of all goods and services. In the process, the intimate knowledge and understanding of the nature and limits of money has been destroyed. The truth is that the world has a vast diversity of cultures, similar to the biodiversity of species on the planet, and these cultures have different attitudes and relationships with money, wealth and power. The advent of empire and globalisation has tried to conquer and subvert cultures, and unify economies and currencies, making it harder for different peoples to control their currencies and societies in line with their belief systems.

Money was not needed in the growth and evolution of the planet for millions of years but has today become critical to human society. We need to remember that we created it to serve us and not divide or conquer us. Money was never invented to overwhelm all aspects of our lives, including love, relationships, learning and development, happiness, our mental and physical health and well-being, organ purchases, child-care, institutionalisation of elderly people, and even purchase entertainment and holidays. It has eased many aspects of our lives, but along the way made us feel insecure, emotionally troubled and often lonely and isolated.

Nature-based Societies

Our human population on this planet has for a long time been limited and we have lived within our own local needs of food and shelter – there have been no states or borders as we know them today, and travel was constrained by the available means or the need to find new pastures, water or warmer climates. Born 85 years ago, my mother rarely left her village – many people in the world today still live highly local and rural lives. From the young age of six, she farmed the land, leaving early in the morning and coming home after dark. Her childhood was deeply immersed in nature, and that has helped her cope with the ups and downs of life by staying rooted in her soul, and simple in her values and aspirations.

Throughout history, fate and destiny were something to be accepted rather than challenged, and faith gave people that ability to live in balance with the ecosystem, and find joy in small things, like sharing a meal at lunch with co-workers (Harari, 2015). Danger and threats were all around, but so was family and community, and at many times in our history there was more non-violence than war. Money was used in limited ways if at all, and its access and possession was restricted, so was its storage and circulation. Transactions were mainly local and physical, and happened through sharing, trust and relationships. They often reinforced society instead of splintering it like we experience today.

Rivers were once very close to our homes, as they provided the fresh water necessary to sustain human life and agriculture. Societies were built close to the elements of nature rather than distant from it, using technology to transport, feed and nourish it as we do today in our large urban conurbations. Our lives were more grounded than they are today. Violence and aggression were limited to local populations, and often used more in self-defence than in attack. There were no technologies of mass killing, or murder and bombing from a distance. The killer had to fight with their own bare hands and see the victim with their own eyes. Today, finance can commit violence from large and growing distances and often stay invisible in the process. Take the example of factory farming or abattoirs, and how finance is key to their scale. The growing human inequality on the planet is another example of how not only can the rich stay invisible and unaccountable, but the media often actively celebrates their wealth and prowess in accumulation. The growth of money by humans is seen as the epitome of success.

Even if animals were eaten, the killing was not done on an industrial scale, and within limits and with respect to the sentience of all living beings (in the case of Native Americans and many Indian cultures for example). Factory farming of animals or even fruits and vegetables was not even a pipe dream in ancient times. Farmers had close contact with their soul, and bore the risks of climate and rain directly, putting their trust in the sun and the soil. They were forced to stay humble to the elements and suffered from the ups and downs of nature's harvests. Death was also common and natural, and led many to reflect on the deeper meaning and purpose of life. This gave birth to diverse indigenous religions and belief systems. Today, we have used wealth, medicine and technology to postpone and even deny the reality of death.

In short, for a large part of our human history, the population, culture and ethics were such as to force us to live within our means and not become too greedy or selfish. Technologies of war, globalisation and finance were simply not there, so damage could be limited. We also experienced joy, meaning and happiness without the need for money, and this gave us a deep sense of fulfilment and contentment. Without money, it is difficult to amass fortunes and amplify greed – the vice of greed was constrained by the absence of money. There were also social and cultural constraints to greed and accumulation. In many parts of the world, the rich saw it as their public duty to serve their community. Paradoxically, the modern-day alienation and lack of community has encouraged greed and accumulation as cushions of fear and loneliness. The extreme levels of wealth we see today have been facilitated by technologies like stock markets and globally transferable liquid currencies through virtual technology, which enable the private accumulation of power. If people experience love and sharing in their neighbourhoods and communities, they are unlikely to become greedy and selfish. The word *loot* is originally a Hindi word for stealing, but creeped into English as the British were seen as abject looters of India. Empire also stemmed from deep insecurity and a thirst for power.

Communities of Souls

In ancient times, there were risks of robbery or violence, and conflicts within families and neighbourhoods, but these tended to be local. Humans were organised in communities and collectives and did not know much about individualism, let alone greed and materialism. The risks of life were mitigated through belonging to local villages, and faiths and beliefs helped people to cope with death and disease. Yes, there were challenges in life, like attacks from wild animals, cold climates, shortages of food and shelter, wars and conflicts between local neighbours, but the scale was rarely such as to fundamentally disturb the balance of life. In contrast, money and insurance today give us the illusion that death is unlikely, but in olden times, death was a lived experience and not denied or ignored. It forced people to reflect on the deeper meaning of life and existence.

The discovery of agriculture led to more settled societies and communities, and an early attempt to tame the land for the sake of human needs. It reduced the anxiety over food and helped reduce the need for a nomadic and foraging life. Money was rarely used or transacted, and exchange and mutuality were the norms of social life. Trade was seen as not just an opportunity to profit, but also to learn and travel, and gain knowledge and wisdom too. The resulting surpluses were invested locally to help the poor and the needy, or to build schools or hospitals. Death and loss were everyday experiences due to poor healthcare, so resilience was cultivated through raw experience, faith and family. Technologies like brick housing and shelter, or fresh water on tap or schools, healthcare and hospitals were rare and not accessible to all. There were class elites and hierarchies, which created inequalities of wealth and power.

The inability to fly or to travel quickly led to more grounded and rooted cultures and customs. Simple products like shoes, which we take for granted today, were not available widely even three hundred years ago, and people had to walk barefoot, enabling them to feel the ground. In Hindu weddings, there is a custom where the bride's parents wash the feet of the groom. This act would normally be seen as bemeaning and shameful but was done with joy and pride. This is a symbolic gesture of respect, a ritual which was often done to welcome new visitors to their homes and help keep them tidy.

The feet are the contact point between the human spirit and planet earth, and this groundedness can keep souls earthbound and rooted. Feet enable movement but do not disable connection. Jain monks and nuns, one of the oldest living cultures of the world today, are not allowed to travel by car, air or sea, and have to live nomadically without carrying any money. Their feet develop a very thick skin over time, to cope with the harshness of the terrain – they adapt. Their life and survival today as monks and nuns show that such a life is possible and human growth, high thinking and spirituality are not restrained by a lack of money. Over time, Jains have learnt to transcend the fear of death, and thereby understand the limits of materialism and possession.

Modern transport in cars, trains and airplanes displaces us from this earthen groundedness, and technology gives the impression of immediacy and transparency. However, this also removes people from context and subsumes that we do not need to understand people's histories, traditions or backgrounds. It cheats us into thinking that we know people and understand them, when in truth we have spent little time enquiring about their personal histories, beliefs or upbringing. We also assume that we do not need to understand people in order to fix the deal or complete the transaction – a polite greeting is sufficient. Subconsciously, we try to make people the same, when in reality relations are more complex and depend on power, politics and inter-cultural intelligence. Social groupings and belonging among people are also deemed irrelevant, except when supplemented by chains of influence and expropriation, when networks and class become very important. The equations of finance eliminate all these subtleties actively and deliberately.

Wisdom as Wholesome, Responsible and Accountable Knowledge

Knowledge benefits from groundedness and wholeness if we are to lift ourselves from anthropocentric thinking. It has to find a way of embracing Gaia, and the interdependence of all life (LaMothe, 2023). The soil and soul of finance are trust and relationships, conducted within a strong moral and ecological compass. They make the ground on which money can be created and circulated, and the breakdown of trust and relationships will lead to the breakdown of money and society. We are already in this scenario, where planetary expropriation is rising, species extinctions and animal cruelty are growing exponentially, and human wars and inequality are increasingly being normalised.

Our public health and mental well-being are diminishing in spite of the advancements of science and knowledge. Markets, seen to be the panacea for all greed and excess, have ended up breeding monopolies and oligopolies instead of the competition and consumer choices that were promised. Companies like Amazon have used the stock market to expand and grow, and then subverted competition by abusing their size and power, extracting wealth from both customers and suppliers, even when the corporation does not make anything. Platform companies have now come to dominate the producers and remove the competition, seizing the global power in retailing and distribution. Google, Microsoft and Meta do this with information for highly lucrative private profits.

Money and finance have become technologies which usurp our trust and relationships, and while promising a comfortable life, end up taking away our comforts and displacing our social networks, making us feel disconnected and isolated. To find out whether or not we can trust someone, we are forced to use technologies like TrustPilot, instead of asking a neighbour for a recommendation. The communities of old were the real 'banks' of trust and relationships, but today they have become extinct or ignored by modernity. Mutuality makes exchange normal, and payment an insult. Sharing reinforces caring, and removes isolation, setting an example for future generations of the resilience of communities. The meetings of people necessary to establish an opportunity to befriend and trust have now gone on-line and virtual, making them incomplete and partial. Soil has become separated from soul, and the ground of living communities is now routinely trampled upon by cold, calculating finance such that children growing up in broken families or with few or no relatives, have no idea what trust and relationships feel like.

Care and Compassion

For food to grow, we need to plant the seeds, sow the land and nourish it with water, and pray for the sun and rain to do the magic. Food is vital to life on earth, and wild foods are hard to find and digest. Before the advent of agriculture, humans would have needed to develop this intimate understanding of which wild fruits, leaves and grasses could be edible and out of necessity would have had to be nomadic to seek better pastures. Animals would have been a source of food, but tools for killing, roasting and preserving meat would be needed to ensure that it can be made edible by humans as we cannot eat raw meat. Like so many animals today, it is possible that all our time was spent in seeking food, and there was no such thing as jobs, factories or even economies whose life is governed by interest rates, inflation and exchange rates.

There was time to build relationships and communities, and a direct experience of mutuality as a form of self-defence against violence, and a resource for collecting and sharing food, which gave us life and security. Communities were also the source of knowledge and learning, and the individual was never separate from the collective. In fact the etymology of the word individual comes from the Latin *in-divisio* that which is indivisible and cannot stand on its own. Even our language has been usurped to serve the need for western societies to justify their universalist worldviews. Just as empire was an attempt to civilise cultures, neo-liberalism used science and the enlightenment to continue that crusade and diminish *primitive* cultures and behaviours.

Today, money has seeped so deep into our lives that it has separated us from both soil and soul. For many, it has given them the illusion of power and control, and helped distance their lives from growing food and building an intimacy with the land. Our inner spirit or soul has become diminished by our materialistic lifestyles and, for many, simply putting food on the table to feed the family has become exhausting, with little time for prayer or reflection. The economy has produced and grown inequality, and specialisation has meant that farmers produce the food, which we can purchase in supermarkets to feed our families. The food supply chain, and its super-marketing, has also ensured a growing distance from soil, such that children often believe that food is grown in super-markets, and has no connection with the land. The factory production and packaging of meat has also meant that none of us have to see or hear the pain and cries of the animals that are on our plate – we have distanced our food from the souls of animals.

Yet with all this specialisation, and the relative ease of modernity, neither our soil nor our soul is happy and fulfilled. We have a global crisis in physical and mental health, and, for the affluent, instead of bringing security, money has led to more and more restlessness and insecurity. In the textbooks of finance, there is no mention of either soil or soul – such is the depth and breadth of abstraction. Even culture, ethics and morality have disappeared from sight, as the science is so desperate to be objective that it has no need for such subjective beliefs and diversity. Just as humanity has distanced itself from the land, finance has detached itself from virtue and morality.

Displacement

When we look deeply at farming, even the farmer has become displaced and distanced from the land or the spirit, when using combine harvesters, manufactured chemicals and mechanisation to fertilise the soil and maximise produce. We call this progress and modernisation, but is it really? The soil quality is directly attacked by these methods, and the factory farming of animals mean huge carbon emissions and an attack on their sentience for the sake of human food. It is power over soil and animals which we use to exploit and extract, and use finance to mass produce or mass kill, without any shame about the health and environmental externalities and side effects. The technologies of food production are such that they cannot be obtained without significant financial investment. Their scale and the capital investment required concentrates ownership, even corporatise it, removing the need for food and farming communities and traditions which preserve and conserve land and animals. In this sense, finance removes the need for a farmer to be grounded with his soil, and for the pain of animals to be felt and experienced. A cognitive dissonance from soil, soul and suffering is the result. This is not sustainable.

Finance has a tendency to impose its own cold logic wherever it is used. Concepts like economies of scale, efficient production, or the use of chemicals and pesticides, have become normalised, routinised and justified as scientific methods of food production in spite of the evidence of pollution, public health failures, soil and environmental degradation. Now that these side effects have come to the fore, finance has come up with 'solutions' like ESG, filters which are supposed to encourage businesses to invest ethically, without abandoning the logics of efficiency or scale. It raises a simple but profound question – how can a tool and technology whose basis is the attack of soil and soul be reformed to become a protector of the environment, without reforming the systems of knowledge which have led to the crisis in the first place?

It is, therefore, not an exaggeration to say that money today manufactures food and super-markets it, reducing the need for human farmers or any sense of connection with soil and sentience. It is paradoxical that an economic technology humanity has shaped is today overwhelming soil and soul, plundering the very fabric of nature. The food industry is one example of this transformation, but such analysis can also be extended to other critical needs of human life and well-being like education, housing, health and social care, and work, careers and employment. More and more, money and finance control and limit our choices, and we are forced to become slaves to the engines of commerce, losing our ability to question or challenge the systems and processes which dominate and overwhelm our souls. Finance actively and overwhelmingly disconnects us from fundamentals like trust, relationships, culture, well-being and community, forcing us to become selfish, distrusting and isolated automatons, detached from our inner spirit. We have become externalities to the systems of globalisation and financialisation, groundless and soul-less.

The Multinational Corporation: A Combine Harvester of Global Destruction

The public corporation is a legal fiction and human construct, similar to money (Bakan, 2004, calls it a psychopath). It has amassed huge power over the last hundred years, with access to global capital markets and technologies of production and distribution which allows them to be everywhere at the same time (Stiglitz, 2017). Platform companies like Google, Meta, Amazon have their tentacles into every household in the world, silently collecting commissions and revenues on the back of other people's data and preferences. Even worse, they are now shaping human behaviour and culture, subverting it to highly commercial and selfish corporate motives – Zuboff (2020) calls this 'behavioural surplus'. In terms of the economy, the corporation has become a key driver all over the world, and provider of useful goods and services. Even professional firms like accountants, lawyers and management consultants have become multinational corporations, with significant size and influence. Contrary to the free market liberalism of economists, these organisations have become monopolies and oligopolies, as opposed to the perfect competition that was promised to us, which would have led to the best priced products for the ultimate consumer. Even worse, they have often undermined state regulatory processes, minimised tax payments, captured politicians and governments, effectively preventing any sense of accountability (Bakan, 2020).

In terms of soil and soul, these multinational corporations have neither soul nor grounding, and are everywhere and nowhere at the same time (Stiglitz, 2019). They have managed to become *uprooted* from the 'ground' of the society that created them, in a similar way to money. While soil plays a critical role in holding and nourishing the roots of plants and trees, helping them to absorb water and nutrients, the corporation nourishes itself from 'man-made' finance, which it then uses to uproot from duty, accountability and responsibility. From an ethical perspective, we can see that the corporation is an extension of the fiction of money – a kind of fiction *squared* – which has made finance even more difficult to control and regulate. The poisonous side effects of this, in terms of social and environmental upheaval, are now dumped onto our ecosystem, without any remorse or guilt on the part of these giant vampire squid corporations. Given their diffuse and anonymous ownership, we cannot point any fingers at any specific human beings for these heinous crimes. The US and UK congressional and parliamentary hearings against these giants after the 2008 financial crash and other scams exposed how powerless even governments are to make them accountable (Bakan, 2020).

In terms of revenues and profit extraction, they are global, and in terms of tax payments or loyalty to local citizens and societies, they are fickle and irresponsible (Brooks, 2014). They actively use state infrastructures like roads, utilities, education, laws and crime prevention to protect their assets and provide their products, but don't want to pay the appropriate taxes and use their power to undermine state controls. The globalisation of world trade has helped them to expand their power and interests, but at the same time they have used these to play states against one another to maximise their subsidies, and even influenced the rules of free trade to benefit their short-term and parochial interests. Given our huge public health, economic inequality and environmental challenges, their transformations in terms of social and environmental responsibility are simply cosmetic and deeply selfish.

Planet earth has given birth to the multinational corporation, and the genie is out of the bottle – it has become a power unto itself. When we come back to the basics of nature, soil and soul, this soullessness is a deep problem which we need to accept, and remedy through constraining the legal structures and powers of these giant economies. Their rootlessness is a deep problem for the planet, and the lack of democratic control a major catastrophe, as accountability is removed and extraction is magnified. The fact that a plant or tree is fixated in one place makes it highly grounded and accountable, and also limits its power for growth and expansion. An animal or tree's absence from an economic model of money, profits and marketing teaches us important lessons about the limits of corporate enterprise, and the criticality of containing its power and reach. This corporate 'impersonal person' is a deep contradiction, and society has to find ways to limit its rampant and irresponsible growth.

The multinational corporation has become a giant killing and poisoning machine, owning large factory farms which slaughter the 400 billion animals a year we consume on this planet. Similarly, the oil industry taps energy buried underground for tens of thousands of years, and poisons the planet, polluting our air and water, and irreversibly destroying our ecosystem. The waste that the oil refining process creates is recycled into plastics and chemicals, which help spread the poison far and wide. The smoke that comes from petrol engines pollutes the air we breathe, without which no soul can survive on this planet. Just 20 multinationals produce 71% of all fossil fuel emissions on the planet. None of this can be done without access to big finance and capital, and laws which allow them to pollute freely.

Democratic Failure

Shareholders who are the ultimate owners of corporations, are significantly divided and inactive in using their influence to transform the conduct and behaviour of the organisations which they control (Lazonick & Shin, 2019). Their priorities too have become financial – they simply want to tap into the profits and gains in share prices, without asking any serious questions about how they are made, and what damage has been done to the 'externalities' of society and the environment. In many cases, personal 'soulful' shareholders are at the lowest denominator of the food chain of money, having invested indirectly through fund managers such as pension providers, or insurance companies or mutual funds, where they have little say in how their money is gambled or invested. Financial markets have become giant speculating platforms for the rich to trade, exploit and extract, without much effort or sweat – increasing their personal fortunes whilst workers see their real incomes decline, the insecurity of their jobs grow, and their health and well-being damaged as a result of corporate irresponsibility.

Intermediaries like banks, fund managers and other financial institutions have also come to dominate soil and soul, even though they are managing other people's money, and ought to be grounded and act in the best interests of their clients (legal fiduciary duty). They have become huge clusters and concentrations of power, such that even when they fail or are mismanaged, governments bail them out – they have simply become too big to fail. The moral hazard they create, by taking all the winnings and dumping all the losses to society lead to serious fissures and cracks which are unsustainable.

Although there are laws which regulate financial institutions, the reality is that the complexity of the financial system and collusion among central bankers has distanced the effectiveness and enforcement of these laws (Prins, 2018). Employers and pension funds delegate their financial management to intermediaries, without much power to enforce their moral or environmental concerns. Fund managers like Blackrock or State Street have become so big globally through managing other people's money, that despite being middlemen, they are now able to control large global corporations in the interests of the managers and employees of Blackrock. This is also unsustainable.

If corporations draw upon financial capital to feed their growth and expansion, financial institutions are warehouses of money which not only collect it, but also create it through the multiplier effect. As a result, they are able to host large surpluses of 'financial energy' and use their credit-creating capacity to multiply this man-made resource. If they are ethical and responsible, they would use this power in a guarded manner, ensuring that money is lent to organisations which serve to invigorate society and protect the environment. Instead, they become large concentrations of hubris and arrogance, channelling finance to industries and enterprises which lack the values needed to protect soil and soul. The sense of responsibility and accountability that ought to come with being a bank of other people's money disappears and becomes overwhelmed by greed, selfishness and excessive risk-taking. There is profound dislocation from culture, community and responsibility inside these organisations, which is unsustainable.

Context in Finance Nourishes the Soul

The living context of finance matters. Its science and production machinery have been aggressively and arrogantly created by humans, and that even not very long ago in our history, in one thousandth of the time we have been on planet earth. Our acceleration of planetary destruction has resulted directly from our markets and institutions of finance. Nature and the living ecosystem provide us with deep wisdom and science to rewire our knowledge, if we allow ourselves to learn from it and apply it to our contemporary challenges. As human educators and scientists, we need to open our hearts and minds, to tap into wider knowledge systems and translate them to our challenges today.

We need to rediscover a finance language of groundedness and community, of limiting the need for and use of money and capital, and help society in distinguishing between public goods and private needs. The public space of finance needs to be reclaimed, and its obsession with markets as the arbiter of all economic activity, dismantled. If specialisation separates us from our relationships and communities, we need to rethink its need, and understand its limitations. It is culture and context which really give confidence and value to money, and we urgently need to find a way of rewiring finance to grassroots mutuality and coexistence. Trust has been removed from the study of finance, and even the fiction that is money has been converted into a fact, beyond any question or doubt. We need to admit to ourselves, and to society, that such scientific fraud is unsustainable. The technocracy that has been built around it has tried to cushion itself from critique, by building jargon and language which alienates and closes the knowledge at the same time. The disciplinary walls of finance need to be demolished, and its scientific power to overwhelm other subjects and understandings need to be questioned and challenged.

Earth and soil are very deep – several kilometres lie between the surface and the core of our planet. In the same way, cultures and traditions often have significant depth and heritage, but modernity sees only the surface, and rushes to its judgement and analysis. Racism is just one example of this, but appearances and buildings matter too – a high tower financial institution or accounting firm looks down on society, and commands status and prestige in doing so. These institutions have come to overpower the roots and ground on which they were constructed and are now all too dominant in their reach and impact.

Anthropologists and sociologists have developed a context scale and culture map (Meyer, 2016, Chapter 1), where nations with long histories and traditions are put at the higher end, in contrast with countries like North America, which are young and founded by immigrants. High-context countries like India or Japan have a deeper tradition of mutuality and relationships, whereas individualism is more common in low-context nations. Even the UK has been put in a lower-context scale, whereas France is more towards the higher-context end. Such analyses prove that to understand the varying 'soils' of finance, we need to engage with cultural and social histories and norms. To detract from this would be to misunderstand and misrepresent the varieties of meanings of money between nations and cultures. In finance science, low-context countries have imposed their individualism, materialism and distrust on the rest of the world.

Through its ignorance of culture and the human social fabric altogether, finance science denies the existence of this depth, and the nuances of cultural wisdom. This heritage is what has hitherto glued our societies and institutions together, and made them responsible and accountable. It has also prevented money from becoming very powerful and controlling, by keeping a number of important customs and relationships completely outside the financial system. Not only is trust nurtured in these contexts, it is nourished, valued and protected. Paradoxically, North America had a deep high context history among the Native Americans, but this was destroyed by the conquistadores and European greed-merchants (Jasanoff, 2011).

Earthly Morality and Living (not Philosophical) Ethics

Morality needs to be recentred in finance to help create a grounding and connection between soil and soul. It can no longer be peripheral or ignored altogether. There is a universal ethic of fairness, equity and justice, which we now know to be not simply an exclusive domain of humans to each other. Our science ought to embrace our duties and responsibilities to all living beings, even where they do not have the power or language to respond directly to our behaviours or technologies. Ethics and morality are neither purely intellectual nor fixed in time, and evolve with experience and are influenced by our friendships and work environments too.

Creation is not there simply for our use and expropriation, but something to be protected and preserved, *for its own sake*. This requires a major transformation in our textbooks and pedagogies, but there are significant positives also when we recraft finance in this way. Furthermore, our obsession with rationality and science has also resulted in humanity becoming more argumentative and judgemental, making dialogue and conversation more difficult (Haidt, 2013). The significant secularism and technocratic pyramids of finance mean that moral conversations become impossible, and pluralism and contextual differences are banished altogether.

Fragments of culture, belief, trust and community still prevail all over the world, to different degrees in spite of the growth of money and its influence. Soil and soul are still alive and well and help nourish whole families and societies in many villages and towns. Even today, farming in many parts of the world is small and local, organic and natural, with farmers working and living within their means, and learning from the generosity of nature to care and share. They are contented and enjoy the fresh air and nourishment that comes from living in rural areas and belonging to the land, rather than owning or possessing it. Communities also flourish and survive in spite of the growth in individualism, as a reaction to its coldness and loneliness. All over the world, people still give to charity, without any expectation of return, often donating much more than money – their skills and time. Many find in charity a way of coming to terms with materialism, keeping it in check and helping children to see life beyond earning and accumulating.

Given that soul is innate to every living being, its flame is always flickering deep within us, and can be experienced if we stop denying it. Yoga and meditation are ways of lighting the spirit and awakening it. In deep meditation, we can discover the limitations of money, and the baggage that comes with its accumulation. Through reflection, we open a personal dialogue between body and soul, and help nurture a deeper sense of purpose and meaning to give us a springboard of hope and kindness. As we go inwards, we begin to see how material life and consumption is limiting in its potential to create lasting meaning and fulfilment. We begin to appreciate the importance of this relationship between soil and soul, how both are essential to life, and both need to be protected and nourished to find peace and tranquillity. We also discover the pain of this separation and cognitive dissonance, when our science denies the very existence of an inner spirit. It has long separated not only body and soul, but also the natural world from our health and well-being.

While it may appear daunting to find a language and terminology in finance which connects both soil and soul, the truth is that in our cultures and traditions, we have long meditated on the role of money in everyday life. Dodd (2014) offers a good summary of this. Faith traditions are a classic example of this, but so are smaller cultures and communities which developed their own local customs and beliefs. These cultures were dismissed as backward or pagan when in reality, they often worshipped the soil, sun and water, and did not make money and materialism central to their belief narratives. Even the ownership of land, which we now take for granted, was seen as unfair and unjust – soil was seen as not something to be 'owned' but property which belongs to planet Earth and is a public good rather than a private asset. We forget that for a long time in human history, money was an alien concept, and life continued without money, with exchange bringing people closer together in trust and bondage.

The experience of camaraderie and brotherhood transformed many cultures and belief systems and ensured that wealth and its accumulation were not seen as the overwhelming purpose of life. People experienced the joy of giving and sharing, and the limitations of owning and possessing, and professions like teaching or the priesthood were seen as high status, worthy and desirable. Having a sense of purpose and meaning in life was highly valued. The confusion created by money and wealth in the provision of certain goods and services, like education or healthcare, often attracted people who sought the joy of public service and lived contented lives. Such people in turn became role models for younger children and adults, who too aspired for honourable vocations.

Shared Learning and Identity

We are social beings, and learn from our elders, family, neighbourhoods and friends all the time – we forget that classrooms are a modern invention. Animals have always been our teachers (pet-owners know this) and the soil has nourished and given life to us, with trees becoming our umbrellas of hope and possibility. Nature was our classroom, and it is in the wilderness that we learnt to find and grow food to nourish our bodies, and in groups that we found shelter, comfort, well-being and security. Individualism has been a creation of modernity which has been significantly amplified by a western culture of greed and materialism, and an active distancing from faith, belief and conscience. Empire has led to a global stampede against culture, heritage and community, and modern methods of education have emphasised the classroom and competitive, impersonal examination rather than wisdom, tradition and communities of learning.

Education research shows that shared and experiential learning is very powerful and grounded within the context of the real world. In fields like medicine, clinical experience is critical to graduation and embedded into the university curriculum. Not so in finance, where it is abstracted from the real world and there is no apology for this. On the contrary, students learn to construct this abstract world as the real world, and apply this training when they eventually work in finance. This is seriously damaging, and needs to be changed if we wish to create a better sustainable world. What follows are examples of concepts and methods which can be applied to make finance soulful and grounded. Family and community are the first place to start.

Families and communities need not always be local, insular and parochial. There are examples of villages and localities in history, but, even then, to call them decadent or backwards is to misrepresent the comfort and security they often provided local people. Today we have a global crisis of isolation and loneliness, resulting in depression and mental illness, often afflicting people from all ages and backgrounds, especially in large urban conurbations. Paradoxically, large cities are making us even lonelier, and people who live in them are cold, calculating and selfish, often not even knowing the names of their next-door neighbours. For some, sharing and belonging is risky and painful, and they would rather live their life without needing to trust or rely on anyone. Our ground of family, friendships and relationships, has often become a desert without any soul, and we reach for drugs and alcohol to cope with the displacement this creates.

In denying or ignoring the importance of trust, contemporary finance has grown distrust in society, encouraging people to be more selfish, individualistic and materialistic. In calling finance a science, it has given authority and credibility to a worldview which denies the beauty and richness of interdependence. In removing culture from its equations, finance has diminished the importance of different traditions and belief systems all over the world, and their abilities to check the expansion of money and contain its coldness and exploitation. Culture and belief are the soil in which people are born, the ground where respect and relationships are sown, and host to a network of communities and societies, sharing and trading with one another. Souls are born out of culture, and in their growth and progression, nourish society in ways far deeper than money can ever reach.

When we lose our connection with our past, or narrow our lens to specific histories of power and violence, we lose sight of the diversity of histories that have come to shape life on earth. In particular, rich micro-stories of local villages and communities diminish in importance, and wars, struggles and conquest come to dominate our memories. Peace is not a popular story, but a worthy one. Music, poetry and literature have sprung from man's desire for understanding and meaning, and are often expressions of a quest to connect body and soul, and find ways of connecting to traditions and heritages that we have inherited for free. Narrative has power to etch into memory and travel far and wide, often transcending the barriers of communication like printing and reading, with many cultures of the world having very sophisticated oral traditions.

High Context Cultures: History and Tradition

In developing a science of sustainable finance, the past provides us with nuggets of wisdom which we would be foolish to ignore. The absence of powerful technologies like smartphones, cars or piped water, banks and financial markets led to different innovations, and a bigger focus on character, sharing and community. The *hundi* or written paper bond between a borrower and a lender (Frayne, 2017), relied on trust and honour to regulate money, and it worked – in fact, it helped grow and develop one of the richest states in the world in the eighteenth century, the state of Bengal. World trade was financed from here, and there was a deep understanding of the relationship between credit, trust and social capital, and the importance of keeping money grounded in self-discipline and honour (Dalrymple, 2020). In such a context, trade and the economy flourished because of the communities of enterprise, and the lack of short-term greed or selfishness. Finance created opportunity, but did not destroy contentment. Risk was experienced directly rather than ignored or cushioned by insurance or hedging products. Unfortunately, when the British looters arrived in India, their low-context minds could not fathom the long-term damage to the deep culture that they were expropriating.

When the soil of life sustains a variety of cultures, beliefs and practices, it is wrong to dismiss this diversity simply because it does not fit our theories or equations. Just as the United Nations recently prepared a Declaration on Biodiversity, we need to ensure that finance engages with and protects the wide variety of cultures and communities on the planet. Micro-finance was developed to help small and marginal communities who were struggling to survive and empower them to manage their own money and play an active role in economic life by providing necessary products and services. What is critical to the success of micro-finance initiatives is the local knowledge, language and needs, and the patient education and training given to help these people manage their finances, connecting effort and reward without impoverishing or enslaving them. Where these schemes were properly administered, they led to the growth in self-belief and empowerment, showing how small amounts of money can make large differences to the life experiences of whole communities.

Even within one family, there can be big differences in how people deal with money or cope with it. Some may spend whatever they earn, and others may be more prudent. Some choose to work hard, and others can be happy go lucky, not worrying too much about career or ambition. There are differences as a result of gender, age and influences that people experience when they go to school and college. Money independence at an early age can make one person responsible, and another profligate. These experiences can shape future attitudes to money in diverse ways. The death of a parent at an early age, and the resulting poverty, can drive someone to be highly motivated to make money and live a comfortable life. Teachers and role models can also influence what someone becomes, and how important money is to their career choice.

Inter-dependence

Soil allows plants to grow and trees to flourish. Their roots bind the soil, and the soil entwines the roots, giving them a firm grip and connection to the ecosystem. Unlike humans, plants and trees are unable to move or to roam. Yet they find ways to grow and flourish in spite of this restraint. They have developed an ability to combine sun, rain and soil to draw energy and convert it into food for other living beings. Their logic and goal in life seems to be to provide and give generously to others, without charging any fees. The sun is the main source of energy for the plants, and even that comes totally for free, and is abundant all year round.

If we contrast these acts of sharing and giving with the modern-day logic of money and finance, we immediately encounter many contradictions. For example, how can a plant or tree work hard all day and night in growing the fruits or vegetables, and give them away totally for free? It is also surprising that these actions are repeated every season. Where is the logic – are they stupid not to charge a fee for this vital life-giving service to animals and humans? We could also ask why it is that they do not move around and travel to the best locations and markets where they can fetch the highest prices for their produce. Furthermore, plants could raise finance so that they can multiply and spread all over the world, and earn even more profits by increasing supply and production, and globalizing their capacity to grow and nourish life on earth. Instead of plants serving farmers, shoots and trees could instead hire farmers to work for them in spreading the seeds and ploughing the land, ensuring that as producers of food, they hold the ultimate ownership rights. Given the stakeholders of soil, water and sun, the plants could operate ethically and give a share of their profits to each of them for their vital services in fuelling and maintaining the food production machine.

We will soon see that this logic is becoming absurd and unrealistic. It is so important for society that nature maintains its core values of symbiosis and cooperates selflessly to nourish us. Costs, revenues, finance and profits seem completely alien in this context and such calculations would disrupt the rhythms and values of nature. However, we humans seem to have developed a way of imposing our power and greed on the ecosystem, such that we have forgotten the hard work done by the plants in cooperation with soil, sun and water to give us food without which we could not even sustain life. We seem to have overpowered nature, and learnt how to exploit and expropriate it, without its permission or authority. Our abilities to monetise food, and grow it through finance, has meant that we have become even more distanced from the pristine principles of nature. Like the character of money, we have become cold and calculating, especially when we move into large scale agriculture, and create global food business multinationals.

Plants Connect Soil to Soul

A plant comes in between soul and soil. It is the link which nourishes society selflessly. Whilst it is a living being, it also becomes a giver, without poisoning the air or water, or charging for its fruit. It has no interest in marketing nor in raising finance to expand and grow. Money can never be a source of its food or nutrition as it is completely fictitious and has no energy or natural value of its own. There are no middlemen when it comes to food production – the plant works with sun, soil and water and intermediates their energies to prepare quality fruit and vegetables. It has no intention of building its own power base, or exploiting its stakeholders to profit and accumulate wealth. It grows organically, within natural limits, and can die every season after the work is done and food is provided. Plants do not fear death or worry about it, nor do they strive for comfort or security. They will bear the hot sun, the cold weather or the rainstorm with equal stoicism, and in the case of trees, even provide shade for others on a hot or wet day, without charging for the service.

All the research shows that the soil of the earth has been severely depleted by human action, and its rich bank of minerals is disappearing at an exponential rate. Large-scale agribusiness is one of the biggest culprits, pumping the soil with chemical fertilisers for the sake of increased productivity and profits. These corporations, ruin it instead of allowing the soil to grow food with its own natural minerals at an organic rate, rather than with externally induced growth hormones. The intimate understanding of the nature of food, and its relationship with humans and the ecosystem has become lost or undermined by combine harvesters who mechanically plunder the soil day and night, exhausting its capacity to grow food over the long term. We need to rekindle the ancient knowledge systems of agriculture, and understand the deep links between soil and soul, where farmers provided for their local communities, and experienced the risks of the seasons directly, finding solace in their faith.

At a time when unemployment worldwide is growing, these organic methods of farming could rekindle jobs and communities, helping improve health, wellbeing and mutuality through kindness, patience, and local technologies. Farmer suicides have grown exponentially even in the West, as instead of working within their own resources and means, they are forced to borrow to finance costly seeds, chemicals and machinery, and when the weather changes and they are unable to repay, they are not forgiven but instead bankrupted by society. The juggernaut of finance increases distance between soil and soul, and its cold calculating machinery kills both soil and humans, breaking the mental health of farmers and forcing them to abandon all hope or faith. Even at the point of contact with planet earth, where farmers are contented simply to earn a small profit and keep a roof over their head, our systems are instead creating restlessness, debt slavery and destroying villages and communities in rural areas. We are denying the opportunities for farmers to truly have a spiritual experience by immersing themselves in the rhythms and bounty of nature.

Animals Are People too

That animals have soul and spirit can be certified by any pet owner – they are living beings who often have no understanding of ego, selfishness or even greed, words and deeds which are simply not in their vocabulary. That they cannot speak our language, and we have overwhelming power over them, has allowed humanity to callously grow and kill them at an exponential rate. A factory farm is a very cold mechanical pain machine, where the freedom of animals is removed from birth, and we have even invented words to help us to deny their personality and character – a pig is pork, a cow is beef, and dead animals are meat, without ever having possessed a soul. The industry of finance wants to fatten animals as quickly as possible, to gain the greatest return on investment in the shortest possible time. The food the animals eat is highly processed, chemicals are injected to influence their meat productivity, and the effluent they produce is pumped into our soil and rivers, without care or concern for the public health and environmental consequences. The entire process of animal killing is made invisible to the public eye, and it is never called a holocaust or mass murder. What is even worse is that even after the animals are killed, and meat is produced after significant use of water and energy, humans still waste a significant amount of food – just as the animal's life was wasted, so was its death. This is soul destroying and unsustainable, and once again finance is a major hidden culprit in this industry of animal and environmental exploitation.

Finance urgently needs to talk about animals, and not silence their reality or existence. They are a core fabric of our living planet and have no say in its development or destruction. Animals are both souls and soil, as they often live underground or as insects and micro-organisms who actively enrich the soil. When we breed animals purely for human consumption and exploitation, we directly attack the fundamental interdependence of all living beings in an irreversible way, through our sheer power, violence and species-related arrogance and hubris. The culture and consciousness of animals is undermined and undervalued. A society built on such attitudes to other species will end up destroying itself unless we reverse this monstrous violence. Lending and investment in animal factories and slaughterhouses should be curbed and monitored, and instead investment made in organic meat production where animals are raised in natural conditions with freedom to graze the land and live healthy lives.

Land: Ownership or Trusteeship

Who owns the soil? It is the land, and it has been cultivated over generations, and if anyone has rights of ownership, it is the farmers who live on it and cultivate it. Private land ownership really confuses our relationship with history and community. In some cultures, the people feel that they are owned by the land, and there is a deep intimate connection and responsibility which ought not be broken. When humans own land for the sake of private profit and with the rootedness and loyalty required for responsible ownership, society should allow them to own it and exercise stewardship, rooted in local customs, community and traditions. For inter-generational sustainability, the economy should permit future generations to own and farm it, and stay connected and rooted to their locality. New knowledge and technology could help reform farming practices, but it is critical that ownership remains local and responsible.

Not all land is devoted to farming. We need land for housing, and also for commerce, trading, warehousing and manufacturing. For personal housing, land can be owned, but not for purposes of speculation or property gains – it ought to be for family living. Alternatively, if land is rented, then it can be at rates which are not greedy and recognise the need for local communities to housing and shelter. We have public housing, social housing and shared ownership, which are variants of this theme. Ideally, people should be restricted from owning more than one property, and taxes and incentives can encourage wider participation and democratic housing such that the land is not a source of private profit or speculative gambling.

In corporate finance, the private ownership of land is taken as a given – there is little reflexivity about the nature of land and its connection with people, heritage, traditions and community. Even speculative ownership of land is described as either an investment, or a risk asset, for which owners should be compensated for the risk, when there is rarely any significant downside to property values over the medium to long term. The state provides a legal framework which protects private ownership rights, and firms who own land are entitled to fully profit from it. Even the tax treatment of property gains is favourable for landowners as capital gains taxes are usually lower than income taxes.

When corporations own land and property, the personal connection is further removed because shareholders who are the ultimate owners are removed from the decision-making process related to the land, and proxies and agents make these decisions on their behalf. We need to find legal codes where such ownership is given a soul and conscience, duties and responsibilities, and not allowed to be speculative, distant and reckless.

Contemporary finance science *removes* the soul from property ownership. While soil is host to millions of microorganisms, property has become objectified and made immortal by finance theory. Its soul is seen as irrelevant and unnecessary. The unstated assumption is that land is an object which can be traded freely, without any need for personality or soulfulness. It also forgets history and community, and allows distant and impersonal ownership, through corporate structures. Tax is treated as a cost to be minimised, rather than a distribution, giving the government its due stake in the profits of the enterprise given its free provision of public infrastructure. Tax minimisation is a direct attack on the legal system provided by the state which protects private ownership, a framework which costs a lot of money to operate, enforce and adjudicate.

For a sustainable planet, we need to reflect deeply on the subject of property ownership. At the very least, we need to morally agree that ownership comes with duties and responsibilities, and should not be purely speculative or soulless. Ideally, we need to find frameworks of protecting land for home ownership and housing, because these are necessities of life, and for those who cannot afford to own, there should be subsidised housing so they can choose to live in the communities they prefer and closer to their families and workplaces. The uprooting of land ownership from historic communities should be prevented as far as possible. Soulfulness, even if it's not measurable, is valuable and worthy of protection and nourishment.

Landlords can profit from ownership over generations without significant cost or effort – the income from tenants keeps accruing, creating inequality and hereditary gains for a few, and precarious lives for the many who live or work on the land. We need to find a way of constraining this accumulation to ensure inter-generational equity and reduce the inequalities created by excessive wealth gained without much effort. Otherwise, there will be different classes of people who will constantly be in debt, always sweating while others gain without much toil. We will break the interdependence between soil and soul when we allow concentrated property ownership, and inter-generational transfers of those rights.

Lessons for Finance Theory

There are profound lessons here for our theories of organic finance. We should try to keep finance local and grounded, and keep it respectful of its stakeholders, which may not always be human beings, nor have a direct voice or power to enforce. We are not owners of the soil – the soil is the owner of the plant and produce, one could argue, or it just is soil without any desire for ownership. At the very least, we can learn to respect the humility, modesty and generosity of sun, rain and soil, and remind us constantly that money is simply a means and not an end in itself. It lubricates life and production but should not be allowed to ignore its natural stakeholders whose selflessness and generosity is boundless. The deeper we allow finance to rule life on earth, the more dislocated we will become from the rhythms and harmony of an inter-dependent ecosystem.

The mobility and liquidity of money also has the power to uproot and disrupt society. We have plenty of experience and evidence on this from our research on globalisation and financialisation. Concentrated banks of capital and money allow us to multiply production exponentially, rather than to grow it according to the pace and rhythms of nature. Furthermore, we have lost control over the direction of this seed capital – trillions go to the fossil fuel industry, or to financing armaments or industrialised and chemicalised agriculture, which attacks the soil, disrupting its capacity to grow organically. The more universal money becomes, the greater its ability to globalise its power. It also concentrates significant influence among Banks and Financial Institutions which control the supply and movement of money, exacerbating hubris and inequality. The soil can never accumulate such power over others – it stays where it is and grows what it can.

Seen from a perspective of soil and soul, this seems very dangerous. It appears to be another means of 'colonizing' the planet and its ecosystem, suppressing the rich biodiversity and balance that Gaia has developed over millions of years. While plants and trees cannot move, seeds are exported and transplanted all over the world, without regard to their origin and climatic conditions. Mass agriculture can help in providing cheap food but it can also displace humans from the land, destroying local communities of contentment who had built a relationship of respect, awe and humility. The values that they had learnt from the land now become displaced, marginalised or suppressed, leading to a decline in our trust and relationship capital so vital to living sustainably.

Agricultural finance is not in the syllabus of corporate finance education anywhere in the world – neither in MBA programmes or in Master's in Finance programmes. The universalist science of corporate finance has been developed such that it applies to all firms independent of industry or national or cultural context, even when we have plenty of evidence which proves that industries and cultures are different, and their differences have real influences on how business is done, and how success is defined and sustained. In this sense, science and education have themselves become uprooted from the ground, and given the global footprint of business schools and business education, including professional training, the impact on knowledge and education is very significant. Subconsciously, it conveys the impression that big is good and small is bad. Rootedness, localism and wider natural stakeholders are unnecessary and a nuisance.

Yet context matters deeply in finance as in life. Culture and communities are contexts too as we have already seen. Finance sees context as an irritation to do away with, rather than a reality to embrace and embed into its science. In removing context, we are left with education and training which is fundamentalist, highly dogmatic, and deeply impersonal and cold. To practice and work in finance, we are forced to become cold and calculating ourselves, displacing us from our inner nature, identity and inherently social character. We are both decultured and acculturated at the same time, and it is no surprise that people who work in finance often suffer from deep mental health issues, because they have to live bi-polar lives. Centres of finance often predominate in large urban cities like London or New York, where traditional norms of community get severed and individualism thrives. Huge financial power and influence is concentrated in these cities, making decisions which influence the whole world.

To 'factualise' money, removing context becomes convenient, even if it is an abstraction which traps society into a fallacy of misplaced concreteness. We can see parallels here with farming, where produce and markets are given more importance than growing and soil maintenance. For the meat industry, animals are simply products for consumption, rather than living beings whose killing has real cultural and environmental consequences. Separation and commodification harm us in the long term, even when it may seem temporarily convenient or profitable. We need to rediscover ways of weaving our lives back into the fabric of the land and communities, and understand the significant limitations of a materialist society when it comes to sustainability. This knowledge needs to be woven into our finance education methods and programmes.

It is impossible to ignore the evidence that finance is a key part of the problem of the environmental catastrophe. Its theoretical and institutional universalism and standardisation is simply wrong – there is no other way of putting it. Worse than wrong, it is deeply violent and damaging to the ecosystem. Given that money was created from culture, trust and relationships and requires public confidence to sustain its value and reliability, we need to bring back the study of its fundamentals. This dislocation of money and its ramifications for both humanity and the planet need to be understood and acknowledged, if we are to make a start at reforming our knowledge.

Chapter Summary

When we examine finance from the ground up, new perspectives and insights emerge. In this chapter we looked at the basics of money, its promise built on human trust and relationships, and how through its spread and globalisation, it has ended up depleting both society and planet. Trust has become displaced and disrupted by money such that we no longer even know what relationships mean, and what it means to be generous and selfless. Culture has become displaced and usurped by big money and technology such that we have become unwitting servants and consumers to the giant corporate machine. Context varies between countries and its importance on the diversity of attitudes to finance should not be ignored. In modernity, our data and choices are not owned by us, and instead corporatised and subverted often sub-consciously without our knowledge or permission. We analysed the new institutions of finance, the multinational corporation and financial warehouses, to show how these organisations have become clusters of power with little responsibility and accountability.

The private 'ownership' of land has not spread human democracy but instead encouraged accumulation and inequality, enhancing displacement and the breakdown of communities. Even our cultural and traditional understandings of land, as something far *beyond* human ownership and control, has been completely ignored by finance science which has instead turned it into a speculative tool to be possessed and used to possess others. In the rush to shape an 'objective' science, finance has uprooted itself from culture and community, eliminated diversity, and suppressed any engagement with morality, in spite of the fact that the whole discipline collapses if we remove human trust and confidence in money. We looked at the nature of soil and soul, their selflessness in nourishing society and rootedness in the ground, to understand what happens when financial energy is uprooted and loses human control.

In particular, we can directly see how the fiction of money, created to ease social and cultural life, has become globalised, subverted and out of human control. No longer is it a servant of society, but instead a master – a genie which has long left the lamp, and is now dominating the lives of billions of people, even when it has no meaning or intrinsic value of its own. Corporations and financial institutions have collated and usurped money to amass huge power and influence with little responsibility and accountability. In fact, they have multiplied the fiction and coldness of money, and distanced themselves from the pain and injury caused to the environment and society. Even democratic governments are powerless to hold corporations to account – such is the remote control they have created.

Even though soil and soul have no voice, they possess a secret intelligence, and values of immortality and sustainability from which we can learn a lot. They help us to ground our thinking about money, to discern its truths and fictions, and begin to understand how culture, our human core of being and connectivity, gets undermined and subverted. When there are debates about corporate social responsibility, or environmental accountability, we cannot resolve the dilemmas and contradictions without going to the very roots and grounding of finance, and its relationship with multinational corporations. Our specialisation and partiality has actually disabled us from real critique of the discipline, as we have lost all the words, traditions, practices and languages which have for long connected soul with soil, and encouraged humans to be responsible stewards of the ecosystem. In the next chapter, we focus on seeds, the key catalysts of growth and nourishment, fertilised by nature. We examine the financial ingredients and environment needed to nourish and multiply seeds – with trust, relationships and belief critical to organic growth.

References

Bakan, J. (2004). *The Corporation: The Pathological Pursuit of Profit and Power*. New York: Free Press.

Bakan, J. (2020). *New Corporation: How Good Corporations Are Bad for Democracy*. Vintage Books.

Brady, E. (2018). John Muir's Environmental Aesthetics: Interweaving the Aesthetic, Religious, and Scientific. *The Journal of Aesthetics and Art Criticism* 76(4), 463–472.

Brooks, R. (2014). *The Great Tax Robbery*. One World.

Dalrymple, W. (2020). *The Anarchy: The Relentless Rise of the East India Company*. London, Oxford, New York, New Delhi, Sydney: Bloomsbury Publishing.

Dodd, N. (2014). *The Social Life of Money*. Princeton University Press.

Frayne, J. F. (2013). *The Indian Hundi*. Lulu.com.

Graeber, D. (2014). *Debt: The First 5000 Years*, 2nd revised edition. Melville House Publishing.

Haidt, J. (2017). *The Righteous Mind: Why Good People Are Divided by Politics and Religion*. London: Penguin.

Harari, Y. (2015). *Sapiens – A Brief History of Humankind*. Vintage.

Jasanoff, M. (2011). *Liberty's Exiles: American Loyalists in the Revolutionary World*. New York: Alfred A. Knopf Inc.

LaMothe, R. (2023). The Silence of Othered Species: The Anthropocene Age, Trauma, and the Ontological Rift. *Pastoral Psychology* 72(3), 385–402.

Lazonick, W., & Shin, J.-S. (2019). *Predatory Value Extraction: How the Looting of the Business Corporation Became the US Norm and How Sustainable Prosperity Can Be Restored*. Oxford University Press.

Meyer, E. (2016). *The Culture Map: Decoding How People Think, Lead, and Get Things Done Across Cultures*. New York: PublicAffairs.

Prins, N. (2018). *Collusion: How Central Bankers Rigged the World*. New York: PublicAffairs.

Stiglitz, J. E. (2017). *Globalization and Its Discontents Revisited: Anti-Globalization in the Era of Trump*. London: Penguin.

Stiglitz, J. E. (2019). *People, Power and Profits: Progressive Capitalism for an Age of Discontent*. Allen Lane.

Zuboff, P. S. (2019). *The Age of Surveillance Capitalism: The Fight for a Human Future at the New Frontier of Power: Barack Obama's Books of 2019*. Profile Books.

3   Seed

Soil needs seed and soul to help humanity feed and nourish itself (Berry, 2004; Klocek, 2013; Pretty, 2002). Just one teaspoon of soil contains more microorganisms than the total human population on planet earth. Without soil and seed, settled life as we know it today would not be possible. Through our rush to specialise, we have separated soul from both soil and seed, as we saw in the last chapter. Books in finance today say very little or nothing about food even when it is vital to life. Farmers are now specialists in cultivating the land, when only a couple of hundred years ago, farming was common in communities all over the world, and there was a deep and intimate connection with the land. Farming was a shared collective activity, with finance and money playing only a small role in agriculture (Mazoyer & Roudart, 2006). Through modernity's increasing industrialisation and specialisation, society has *grown* its distance and remoteness from the land, and increasingly taken food for granted, and turned small organic farmers into slaves to the corporate system of food production and concentrated agribusiness (Gore, 2006).

Finance has forgotten the criticality of seed to sustainability. Seeds are souls in infancy, with a capacity to nourish and give life to others. They need the highest respect, and their growth and survival depend on a range of factors from soil quality, to water availability, sunshine and organic fertilisers to provide the chemistry for growth and multiplication. They require democracy, justice and community, to survive and flourish – farmers need to be treated fairly and not exploited, let alone turned into the slaves of market forces (Shiva, 2006). Their cultivation requires knowledge, tools and equipment, and an intimate understanding of the local conditions and climate, including crop rotation to keep the soil healthy. In the last chapter we saw how even the seed of wisdom critical to sustainable finance learning and education has been completely subverted by finance. Satish Kumar (2024) explains that soil, soul and society are a trinity for our time, and, for finance to be sustainable, it needs to be a component and servant to this trinity.

Agribusiness Attacks both Soil and Soul

Agribusiness operates on an industrial scale, aiming for economies of scale, high productivity, profit maximisation and efficiency through chemical fertilisers,

DOI: 10.4324/9781003534532-3

expensive technologies and combine harvesters (Clapp & Fuchs, 2009). It places a huge focus on animal farming, which is the most inefficient means to serve a large human population (Turner & D'Silva, 2006). To get a calorie of energy from grain is a thousand times more efficient from vegetables than from meat. The environmental cost of meat production is catastrophic and unsustainable, if animals are farmed on an industrial scale. Their soul and sentience are denied and plundered violently.

Agribusiness attacks small farmers and local communities, destroying their intimacy with the land, and as a result, displacing rural society and transforming human culture towards urban insecure 'jobs' (Lymbery, 2015). This is not dissimilar to how big business has destroyed many small businesses all over the world and removed the local store and supplier of goods and services altogether. Finance calculations do not value community and social capital. The fertiliser chemicals and factory manufacturing processes poison our soil and water systems, not to mention the farmers themselves. Animal waste exacerbates our climate crisis, and destroys our rivers and land through large scale poisoning (Monbiot, 2017; Robin, 2012).

The conditions for animals in these concentration camps are such that they are stripped of life from birth, and fattened beyond their natural capacity to increase profits, and then killed mercilessly in cold blood, very far from the bankers who finance it all – the height of immorality (Sailesh Rao, 2020). The cognitive dissonance surrounding the supply chain of finance needs to be removed urgently – at the very least financiers should be made aware of their decision and impact chains (Boatright, 2010). Genetic engineering by global companies like Monsanto help concentrate financial muscle and pass on risks to farmers and society through cold calculated greed, poisoning our air and water systems in profoundly irreversible ways (Robin, 2012). Their industry ethos and focus are profit and wealth rather than soil and soul.

Industrialised agriculture has genetically engineered seeds to maximise productivity and efficiency, concentrating financial power even more, and turning soil, seed and farmer into slaves of a food production machine (Pfeiffer, 2006). It has successfully disconnected and dislocated society from the land, and broken our rootedness and social cohesion, whose side effects and externalities, finance science has not even begun to measure. All forms of power have significant difficulty in reconciling and acknowledging their excesses and hubris. Finance science, through its denial of history, politics and the social construction of money, has deliberately and pro-actively alienated itself from earthly accountability. Çalışkan (2022) goes further to show that the combination of the scientific revolution and the industrial revolution had to *artificially create* a new species called *Homo Economicus* to justify its colossal violence and brutality – it was a fabrication, *Homo Faber*.

Just as agriculture has distanced itself from the farmer, finance science has detached itself from the criticality and importance of trust and community. It is simply unwilling to take the blame for its own role in removing and displacing trust, and destroying human social capital and communities. Given that the experts benefit from the fruits of their own power, and have created this vast abstract edifice of financial economics, they have now become incapacitated from reforming its very soil and seed (McGoun, 1997). Lots of challenges have come from the margins, but the core has so far managed to keep itself impenetrable.

For seeds to flourish is not simply a matter of biology. Or chemistry. Nor will technology simply reproduce life without side effects. Seeds need human caring and agency not just for planting, but for growth and harvesting (Monbiot, 2017). Given the biodiversity of our planet, and the varieties of climate conditions, soils, temperatures and local technologies, to universalise farming and treat it like a production machine is violent, destructive and ultimately, an unsustainable science. It is materialist economics overpowering the soil and soul, subverting the logic of nature. Suicides of farmers are not just financial bankruptcies, but social and emotional ones too, where we have failed to nurture the local knowledge and support the cultural intimacy with the land so critical to healthy food production (Deshpande & Arora, 2010). If finance removes itself from the human and ecological cost of industrialised food production, it will end up uprooting our economies from any sliver of sustainable hope.

Horticulture is the science of soil but has the key word 'culture' which means it requires balance and human sensitivity and nurturing to preserve and protect it (Berry, 2004). This beautiful living host to millions of micro-organisms invisible to the naked eye, powerfully moulds it to give life and host peaceful coexistence and mutuality of a wide range of species. Its health and well-being have a significant impact on the whole of society and our ecosystem – something which economics has undervalued and ignored for generations. It is our duty to correct this flawed logic, and transform the models and equations, such that the health and well-being of all living beings is taken into account in investment decision-making.

Perils of Standardised Wholesale Finance

Wholesale finance may be easy to lend, but is often also very easy to lose, as borrowers are not souls but other corporations and institutions, who have learnt not to take personal responsibility or have a conscience (Turner, 2015). Given that each seed is unique and comes with its own potential, we need to recover the intimacy and localisation of finance, and find ways to control the greedy moneylenders or loan sharks. In the past, the names of the lenders were known to the borrowers, and there was personal accountability on both sides, whereas today, there is no personal lender, and that makes it very difficult for farmers to share any temporary problems they may encounter. Distance between borrower and lender also reduces trust and relationships, weakening the bondages of society so critical to our health and well-being.

The opportunity that seeds carry is the hope of a better, more equal and prosperous future not just for the farmer, but the whole local community. Prosperity here is not in terms of money or wealth, but in terms of social and cultural upliftment, better health and well-being, and the protection of tradition and heritage which has sustained the test of time. It also means the availability of grounded and holistic learning and education, with new science and technology to help improve local yields and output, without damaging the soil or soul. Farmers who experience the deeper connections with the land, also come to understand the nature and limits of money. It is critical that their produce is valued and not monopolised by large and powerful customers who dictate the terms and prices by controlling the market.

Growth, progress and success are therefore defined in terms which are above and beyond finance, and not limited by it. The development of wisdom and understanding is often highly prized by local communities, and so too is the cooperation and harmony. Nature teaches them the science of interdependence in the classroom that is the farm, such that they learn a deep awe of, and humility towards, its power and respect its catalytic abilities to shape opportunities and success. Seasons are also teachers of life, growth and death, and when farmers live and work with the seasons, they increase their respect for the rhythms and harmony within nature. Finance science, in its ambition for perennial growth of income and wealth, has tried to deny seasons and even the constraints of time, and instead pursued money for its own sake. The rhythms of nature can feel like a nuisance to finance. It is no exaggeration to say that locality, biodiversity, seasonality and climate are a nuisance for perennial finance, whose goal is the abolition of all constraints, including soil, weather and fertility.

Through grounding ourselves in the nature of seeds, and their relationship with the land, bio-culture, human agency and enterprise, we come to understand the variety of ingredients which need to come together for a sustainable finance. Trust and relationships are key to the cultivation of hope, patience and opportunity, and so are discipline and wisdom. Just as the soil binds the roots of a plant to give it firmness and stability, finance comes from community and shared success, and ought to nourish this interdependence. It should not seek to outgrow or outcompete the community that has given money its trustworthiness and value. The criticality of balance, seasonality and patience cannot be overemphasised in the journey of financial growth.

Interdependence

The seed and ground that is needed to nurture sustainable finance is a combination of human culture, entrepreneurial spirit, communities of trust and social capital, and a profound understanding of the interdependence of all life (DePuy et al., 2022). It is not simply about loans, financial management, risk mitigation or market efficiency. Knowledge of the business and industry makes a significant difference as to whether or not the enterprise will survive and grow. Some of that knowledge may be obtained in a business school or university, but the breadth of understanding about the product, its usefulness, market potential, quality and sustainability, also requires experience, field training, coaching, and mentoring. Traditions and communities were also host to this wisdom and passed it down the generations. Localised experiential knowledge should be valued and not dismissed (Williams, 2012).

Finance is *not* a seed but, if we understand its capacities and potential, can help nourish the soul of food and therefore society. For example, there is a long, slow and patient time gap between planting the seeds and benefiting from the harvest. In that time, the seeds need to be watered, the soil needs to be weeded and the sun needs to do its work to give the growth energy to the plants. How will a farmer feed his or her family in that time? What happens if the conditions change and the climate fails to nourish due to changes in seasonality? There is both investment and risk, which finance can help manage to ensure that the farming family can harvest the fruits and vegetables and take them to market to collect the revenues. Modernity has sadly corrupted this relationship in profound ways (Williams, 2014). We need to find ways of creating an empathetic finance which understands subsistence farmers and does not exploit their ignorance or illiteracy when it comes to money matters. For an inclusive society, enhanced by local and organic supplies of healthy food, we need them as much as they need us.

Micro-finance: Seeding Small Entrepreneurs

Nobel laureate Mohammed Yunus understood the criticality of finance and credit for the severely poor and marginalised women in Bangladesh society (Yunus, 2003). He could also understand their culture and resilience, and trustworthiness. Initially, he started to give them small loans, sometimes from his own pocket. Alongside the loans, he gave them advice about how to look after the money, how to record it, and ensure that it is repaid when maturity comes. In this way, he slowly started a revolution and managed to attain near 100% repayment – a loan performance truly rare anywhere in the world. This practice is known as micro-finance – where money is lent directly to individuals in small amounts, rather than through banks or intermediaries, which is the norm. When poor people are abandoned by finance, they seek credit from loan sharks who rip them off the little they have.

Yunus planted seeds of credit strategically and sensitively, understanding local culture, needs and empowering the marginalised borrowers. He could not see the pain of their suffering, and as an economist, wanted to live by what he taught his students, and cared for his community. It started initially as an experiment but soon grew and later became a global phenomenon. Unfortunately, the patient, localised and organic manner in which he operated was not a formula all lending institutions understood, and they could not achieve the same success rates (Nair & Njolomole, 2020). Yunus understood the soil of finance, his community, and cultivated trust and provided more than money – the knowledge to account for the borrowings and repay them in time. In the process, he ended up growing even more trust.

Hundreds of millions of subsistence farmers in the world are illiterate. Even the basics of finance require literacy, and the industry and its products are often so complicated that they need even more literacy for people to simply use them and apply them to support their farming. Even if rural finance were available from the state, there are barriers such as forms to fill, and the Banks may be far from the farms. As we saw earlier in Chapter 1, financialisation has meant that the finance industry thrives from illiteracy and exploits it, instead of changing its culture and services to serve society. Industrialised chemical-based farming makes farmers even more vulnerable, as they lack the knowledge to apply the chemicals safely without harming themselves. The additional fact that farmers' culture and values are those of nature, contented and generous, rather than calculating and materialistic, we have a deeper problem with the logics of finance. This is happening at a time when we want land to build peace with nature, through an organic farming industry which is rural, inclusive and protective of nature.

Finance becomes the 'inter-temporal energy', which helps nourish society. However, for it to work, small farms and communities need to be valued and supported (Hanson, 2015). Credit needs to be fairly priced, place trust in the farmer and understand and support the risks her family are taking and be patient. Modern mobile technology helps finance reach far and wide, deep into rural areas. If the crop fails for any reason, finance should not be cold and cruel, but compassionate and tolerant, allowing the next harvest to help repay the loan. There is evidence which shows that farmers are not always comfortable to learn about finance or give importance to its sound management (Hilkens et al., 2018). Their intimacy with the land can make it difficult to manage something that is inorganic like money. This needs to change, and can also apply to small entrepreneurs in other lines of business. However, this weakness in financial literacy should not be exploited by lenders as we need good soil management to sustain our future.

The banker needs to understand the science of agriculture, and also through the local community networks, keep in touch with the farmers and stay informed about the horticultural conditions. Over time, they could build contacts with experts who know the soil and the local climate, and share this wisdom with all the farmers they have lent money to. When Jain Irrigation started providing drip irrigation equipment to farmers in India, they helped with both the finance and the training to ensure farmers were able to use the equipment properly (Zhou, 2015).

Farm banks could become more than simple lenders who maintain a distance, coldly calculating the returns on their loans, and quickly bankrupting farmers when they experience crop failure or seasonal fluctuations. Instead, if bankers understood the larger sense of purpose behind agriculture, and respected local conditions and wisdoms, they could become the real catalysts of seed and growth, helping to fertilise both soil and society at the same time. This requires banking to have a strong local presence, and understanding of the industry, and the needs of the local community – for many farmers, timely access to finance is a significant problem (Bharti, 2018). It also means that bankers should not just specialise in finance, but have a wider breadth of knowledge, and see themselves as ethical local developers and horticulturalists. Micro-communities require diverse approaches to finance rather than a standardised, hierarchical model which is top down and institution-centred rather than farm-sensitive.

Their role as wholesalers and distributors of money can be performed responsibly and efficiently if they see the big picture as brokers of the skills needed to transform seed to fruit and are willing to learn and teach (Jones, Escalante & Rusiana, 2015). Some of this science may come from heritage and tradition, and some from new technology and experimentation. Such banking rekindles a strong sense of purpose and meaning which can catalyse hope and friendship, far beyond the lending transaction. Financiers should humbly provide the energy to help seed turn to harvest and ensure a fair return for both farmers and the local community. The risk of lending needs to be shared, and the joy of harvest can also be celebrated by both banker and farmer, as a fruitful partnership – the harvest celebration can enhance meaning and purpose for the banker who facilitated it. This happiness will nourish the soul of the lender as much as the borrower and perform a very important service to both society and the ecosystem.

Trust

Soil provides an invaluable support and nourishment mechanism for plants and trees (Klocek, 2013). It gives home to roots, which become the firm base and foundation and help the trees stand tall and upright, against all forces of wind and rain. The soil is the means through which water and nutrients are fed to the plant and gives life to the spirit. It is the very core of grounding for the life which is going to nourish all of humanity. Paradoxically, the roots also help bind the soil and keep it firm on the ground, ensuring that the rich topsoil does not get blown away by the wind. The interdependence of life is experienced in the very surface of planet earth. It is practiced silently, without any fanfare.

In a similar way, trust is the glue which enables the seed of finance to grow and replenish itself – its practice requires culture and behavioural change (Engler, 2018). It is the ground and root of social life, and the core from which community is built and society is established. What happens under the soil cannot be seen to the naked eye, yet every farmer knows that the health of the soil is vital to the success of his harvest. Just as the soil quality cannot be taken for granted, so is the criticality of trust to finance and its very root in society. We know that every currency note is merely a promise by the central bank – it has no value of its own. It is society which gives it trust and therefore value. Modernity has destroyed trust in society, and the increasing reach and spread of money and finance, combined with a growing transactional culture have caused this devastation (Sandel, 2013). Paradoxically, the society which has the most extreme problems is also the intellectual guru of the world, such is American power and influence today.

Trust stems from rootedness and community (Daly & Cobb, 1994). Faith and belief are very important keys in the building and nourishment of trust. Trust is a belief that the neighbour, friend or relative will honour their commitment which may or may not have anything to do with finance. It requires good character, conscience, reliability and self-discipline – there ought to be a strong personal desire to be worthy of trust. Children have no choice but to place complete trust on their parents – for their food, rest and play. Here trust is not even a bargain or a reciprocal act – it is complete. At home, trust cannot be guaranteed – parents may have their own struggles in life, and at times even when they want to care, circumstances prevent them from doing so. Basic access to finance to earn a fair wage and look after young children is also problematic for many families all over the world today, and growing inequality is increasing the strains (Stilwell, 2019). In retail financial services, trust is critical to long-term customer satisfaction and repeat business, so it is in the strategic interest of the provider to self-regulate their behaviour such that trust is replenished rather than undermined (Llewellyn, 2005).

Like love, trust cannot be measured, and it is a mistake to ignore its criticality simply because of this (Hawley, 2012). Furthermore, trust has to be experienced to be valued. For so many people in life, especially in cities and in many parts of the western world, which has been built on war and empire, trust is a highly suspicious and precarious quality. Distrust is their religion. Urbanisation promotes selfishness and individualism – life is very competitive and often removed from nature. As a result, many people today have little personal experience or appreciation of its criticality. Scholars have developed a trust triangle which shows that the quality of trust in any society depends on culture, regulatory environment and reputational capital – all three are critical to cultivating the soil of trust (Dupont & Karpoff, 2020).

Laws and institutions have been created to engender trust and provide people with a safety net against crime, fraud and deceit. However, access to justice has become more and more costly and laws have also become codified such that they lose their core spirit – the legal system creates and spreads inequality, by emphasising the protection of private capital and private property and elite interests (Pistor, 2019). In communities, there may not be strict codes and written rules, but norms which have been established for generations, and are sustained by parents, beliefs and neighbourhoods. Children are brought up in a sea of trust, and personally experience its vitality through a rich social life and upbringing. They do not need to be constantly suspicious and insecure and find it easy to give trust and honour their commitments to others.

Trust is the basic foundation needed for seeds of community to establish themselves and grow (Rajan, 2019). It is both the soil and the soul of society. The success and sustainability of finance significantly depends on this bank of trust, and its failure can also arise from the breakdown of trust. The establishment and protection of trust need not require lawyers and courts to enforce it, especially at a community level. That is why all over the world, there are local rules and adjudication mechanisms to monitor and regulate trust, and to provide quality culturally sensitive justice. Viewed with a liberal western lens, these may seem unjust and unfair, but they have a significant strength in the locality and intimacy of justice. Furthermore, the economies of trust are significant and material – short-term lending, selfless expert advice, sharing of contacts and networks, mentoring junior entrepreneurs or farmers – happens instinctively in such communities. There is a significant generosity of spirit which the West has failed to understand and respect, and often cannot see it even when it is happening in front of their very eyes.

Soul Distance and Denial

When there is detachment from soul and soil, the ground of finance, the distance and abstraction from truth, grows over time. The tools and techniques built to cultivate this abstraction become ever more sophisticated and obtuse. After a while, they become the only language known to the expert, and finance experts and markets, *grow* new products to profit from trading and speculation (Mackenzie, 2006). In this way, society not only suffers from the pain of inequality, but from the hubris of its science. Humanity is now rendered incapable of unravelling truth and wisdom which we have long buried very deeply – environmentalists long for a rediscovery of truth and wholeness (Stuart, 2020). While regulators and politicians lament the breakdown of culture in banking and finance (Goodhart, 2010; Kenadjian & Dombret, 2016; Tyrie, 2013), they are unable to see that the markets and institutions they have boldly promoted, have themselves become agents of cultural destruction. All reforms are bound to fail unless we understand the source of this cancer.

Seeds, the very hope of life, embody this hubris when we unapologetically manufacture, patent, standardise and industrialise them. Nature generates seeds for free and has done for thousands of years, but we have now patented them and use them to make money. We have forgotten the importance and value of birth, and the deep care and nurturing required for the preservation of life (Kumar, 2024). Through the growth of distance from, and mechanisation of the very ground which has shaped life on earth, we have removed ourselves from a caring and compassionate finance. It is urgent that we go back to the very roots of soil, soul and seed if we wish to build and nurture a sustainable science of finance. At a basic level, this could start from taking finance students to a local farm to learn about the business, and the connections between soil, seed, money and growth. For some sceptics, this may seem odd and irrelevant, and the trip can be used to open their eyes about the diverse natures of finance.

Industrialised and corporatised agriculture colonises and subjugates the seed to the structures of mass production (Shiva, 2006). This reduces biodiversity to standardisation and uniformity, making the seeds globalisable rather than locally adapted to suit the soil and climate conditions (Armstrong, 2024). Nature and its vast ocean of differences become subjugated, biologically and genetically modified to suit the structures and motives of agri-business. The real-world diversity of culture is removed from agriculture and replaced by a*greed*culture, disrespecting soil, soul and seed. The potential of seeds to bloom and adapt is curbed, and over time, the standardisation can actually reduce resistance to a variety of threats that can arise from different soil and climate conditions. So far, we have tried to restrain human cloning, even though we rarely understand human diversity, let alone respect it. As seeds have no voice, they are deemed to be stupid and deserving of our control and subjugation. The attitudes that led to the Anthropocene still prevail.

Shortages of water and failures of rain can mean death for seeds. Through finance, we can prevent these by sophisticated systems of irrigation and continue growing and harvesting food, irrespective of the weather. However, in doing so, we remove society from experiencing the challenges and opportunities of nature, and try to grow seeds in conditions which are totally under human control. Something is gained and something is lost at the same time. For finance to sustain itself, society needs to experience its limits, and learn to cope and adapt to it, just as farmers all over the world adjusted before industrialisation. During those times, there were hardly any chemical fertilisers, so farmers had to rotate the crops, grow them in small scale and develop an intimate understanding of the soil and climate conditions.

Farmers' personal and soil health and well-being were enriched by organic methods of farming and not decimated by the use or cost of chemical fertilisers (Jordaan & Eiselen, 2015). It takes a long time for chemicalised soil to become organic again – all that investment is saved when farms stay organic. During times of drought and famine, Farmers learnt about the mastery of nature, and developed beliefs and traditions to thank it for the harvests, and pray for the rain. Today, we have forgotten to pray or to thank nature, and, when it is beyond our control, we come up with concepts like Net Zero, to try and tame it to preserve human life, without any changes in culture or behaviour. Prayer and festivals can be an important form of farm risk management, giving hope and resilience in times of challenge. Most cultures of the world have prayers and festivals for farmers which are part of their tradition and handed down over generations.

A combine harvester has no need for 'experiencing' nature. It is designed to attack it, overpower it, and reap its bounty as fast as possible. It has no soul or feeling, but is efficient and productive. Humility, respect and awe are not in its engineering – even the soil is taken entirely for granted and plundered without any emotion or feeling. Seeds, the hope and potential of life, are the servants of the combine harvester, designed to suit its hunger for a large, standardised and predictable harvest. Society has allowed its ability to shape powerful technologies to overwhelm the rhythms and genius of nature, often without understanding or respecting its wisdom. Chemical fertilisers used to expand production are the by-products of the extractive and environmentally poisonous oil industry. They end up poisoning our soil too, making our food unhealthy and destroying the soul of the earth in which seeds are planted. The number of jobs removed by such giant machines are ignored by economics, and so is the break-up of farming communities.

Hope, Potential and Opportunity

Seeds from nature, developed locally and adapted to the soil and the climate, are the hope that feeds local communities and enables them to live fulfilled, contented, and cooperative lives. They come from nature, and are planted back into nature, continuing the organic relationships between the past and the present. The soul of the local population is entwined with the seeds, and their growth is carefully nurtured, and weeds removed by stealth and natural crop rotations. The knowledge required for successful harvests is also local, and openly shared without any need for copyright or control – it belongs to everyone and respects the forefathers for their collective wisdom and experience.

While the quality of the soil and its critical importance in grounding the plants and nourishing them may not be easily visible to the naked eye, farmers have learnt over generations how to tame it and get the best from it. This is localised wisdom, which should not be seen as irrelevant, backward or even unscientific. Tradition plays a role in shaping habits, and these can be reformed through respectful and creative approaches to education. The language and customs of the land ought to be respected by finance and not ignored simply because it cannot understand them or globalise the practices. It is said in finance that what gets measured is valued and protected – we need to find ways to measure the knowledge and cultural capital that comes from organic farming. Furthermore, the social and trust capital built in village communities where people are close to the land and grounded, can also be measured. However, there are also dangers in making the intangible, tangible and reduced simply to money, income or value (Williams, 2014).

The potential latent in seeds can be unleashed by a combination of wisdom, discipline, patience and conscience. Farmers need patience and discipline to allow the sun and soil to do their work in nurturing and growing the seeds. This process cannot be rushed to suit the needs for loan repayments for example. Loans would be needed to finance the farmer and her family from the time of seed-planting to the time of harvest (Hanson, 2015). However, these loans should not be priced to rip off the vulnerable farmer, or disrespect their valuable skills in taming the land and feeding the local community. If the rains are delayed, or do not come in time, calling the loan in means that the lender has no share in the risk that comes from the seasons, nor any patience in recovering their money. To preserve and conserve both the farm and the farming family, lenders could extend the loan and roll it forwards to the next harvest, empathising with the seasonal uncertainty, and respecting the honesty and integrity of the farmer to provide a valuable service to society, as without food people cannot live, even if the loans were repaid on time. Agricultural finance needs to be land, seasons and community-sensitive, and learn about faith and patience.

Discipline in tilling the land, removing the weeds, and planting, watering and harvesting on time are critical to the success of the farmer and the repayment of the loan. This discipline comes from culture, character and inter-generational reputations and conditioning. Local lenders would be able to assess the characters of the farmers, and be able to evaluate their promises often in a far better way than distant technocrats. Bankers today look at all loans in the same way, and recall their payments without respect to the context and local circumstances. They also hate small loans as they cost a lot to police and control, and prefer making big loans which they can lose in a wholesale manner. Like the combine harvester, Banking today has created systems and processes to overwhelm the borrowers, overpower them, and coldly exploit and expropriate them from their high and distant comfortable seats (Murau & Pforr, 2020). Bankers cushion themselves from experiencing the pain and injury caused by their decision-making and then society wonders why agriculture fails to feed fresh, healthy produce which is locally grown and nurtured.

Seed Multiplication and Replication

Nature can multiply seeds, and spread them with the help of wind or insects. They will grow anew provided there is good soil and water nearby, and will do even better if they are managed and protected by human beings. Alternatively, farmers can store last year's seeds and replant them to grow in the next season, and generate more produce. However today, giant corporations have copyrighted the ownership of seeds, such that they can only be replanted when purchased and paid for. The organic nature of seed multiplication has been blocked, prevented or severely curtailed my multinational agribusinesses, who also ensure that the diversity of seed varieties is minimised (Robin, 2012). Their actions help monopolise and control the growth and spread of seedlings, which are the very source of natural life and nourishment for humans on planet earth. Furthermore, systems of protection and trade wars can also mean that agricultural incentives are distorted by state actions (Anderson, 2010).

If finance is a seed which helps firms and organisations grow and expand, then its monopolisation and standardisation, within various parts of one country and across industries also becomes a serious problem – we live in an era of deep financialisation (Blakeley, 2019). It can mean that applicants for loans or capital have to follow standard rules and processes and may have to travel a fair distance from the source of business or enterprise to get the vital support they need to grow. In this process, both seed manufacturers and lenders can and have become more powerful than the farmers or entrepreneurs. The banks can dictate the terms of the finance, and coldly pull the plug whenever they feel like.

Instead of becoming a catalyst for growth, finance can become a costly burden as there is no loyalty or empathy for the borrower, nor an understanding of the business or farming practice. Numbers and metrics replace the nuances of relationship, trust and judgement critical to good decision-making and long-term sustainability (Boyle, 2010). Power and wealth become more and more concentrated in financial institutions, when the actual seeds and efforts are made by others who often have no choice but to submit themselves to the whims and demands of the lenders. Farming is a labour-intensive activity, and provides vital health to society with fresh produce.

The judgement of soil, soul and seed that is required to sustain farming and ensure its continued success becomes secondary to the lending process. Instead, the financial security provided by the borrower, and the minimisation of risk for the lender become the priorities. The nuanced understanding of purposeful enterprise, and skilled farming that is required for seeds to grow and flourish now becomes undervalued and subject to highly routinised and transactional evaluation mechanisms – to widen finance availability and access, different methods need to be adopted (Roettger, 2015). If we are not careful, this conservatism can lead to financial systems which become very risk averse, short-termist and purposeless, reckless in their understanding of the needs of the economy and society. The skill in allocating finance towards economic growth and sustainable development becomes less and less relevant.

The wider goals of economic management, which are to help allocate scarce resources to necessary products and services become undermined and corrupted. The related responsibility and accountability that comes with this, is abrogated by big financial institutions and capital providers – micro-finance is *not* wholesale finance, but retail finance, with significant grassroots potential. If governments do not provide state-backed finance, and delegate such provision wholly to the private sector, the economic mismanagement is exacerbated (Bharti, 2018). Public priorities and needs are rarely valued by private finance. Furthermore, if the private sector financial institutions are themselves servants of large and anonymous capital markets, the chains of interdependence and ethical financial management are broken down even more, and what results is a cold, technocratic and irresponsible allocation of finance.

Education and Training

Research in education demonstrates that people learn and grow from social interactions and practical experiences (Wenger, 2000). Classrooms or business schools can actually remove learners from society, abstracting knowledge in a way which can be seriously damaging. Instead of nurturing a sense of purpose and meaning through learning, classrooms and individualist structures of examining, subconsciously diminish social conscience and a sensitivity of the impact of one's actions on wider society and nature. Our methods of education and training are transforming expert finance 'seeds' into selfish individuals, even when they are social and caring beings. This is profoundly damaging and counterproductive. The context of family, neighbourhood, belief, culture and relationships influences learners profoundly, and this shapes their future character and ethics. Ignoring this through factory-based methods of *seed-planting*, we industrialise expert behaviour and should then not be surprised when they behave so greedily and selfishly.

Such training would require inter-disciplinary skills, including character and cultural evaluation, specific training related to the product such as agricultural knowledge if the lending is to the farming industry, and an ability to obtain expert help when needed to support the borrower and evaluate risk (Hanson, 2015). Bankers often are in a powerful position to pool different skill sets and advisors to support a borrower who is in trouble, as another business or customer may have solved the same problem elsewhere. Here they become responsible relationship brokers, keeping the bigger picture in mind of supporting wider economic growth and development with a long-term, multi-stakeholder mindset.

Lenders should see their loan as a stake and not just a transaction, and it is possible that this will give them a lasting sense of meaning and purpose in their job, as opposed to a role which is cold, calculating and ruthless. Loans can be monitored by visits of bankers to the farms, rather than data on a spreadsheet. Locally adaptable techniques can be used to develop a field force, and even chiefs of villages or elders can be helpful in obtaining valuable information early, in the interests of both the borrower and the lender. Training Bank representatives for rural areas can also help create rural jobs and ensure the necessary support is received locally and in time before it's too late for the farmer.

Just as seeds require the right soil, climate, water and sun, so does sustainable finance. It is a joint venture, and the risks can be reduced where there is good understanding, trust and relationships between the lender and the borrower, and a system of local and fair justice if problems arise. Methods and systems need to be locally sensitive and adaptable, and patience, understanding and communications can allay challenges before they mushroom out of control, providing early warnings and remedies. The shorter distance between the lender and the borrower means better quality and more effective information and remedial mechanisms than would otherwise be the case. At times a combination of private and public finance can help make the investment sustainable, as opposed to pure private finance.

Faith and Belief

Trust is the *horticulture* critical to seed funding (Engler, 2018). It is an expression of faith in the borrower, and an injection of hope, which the debtor ought to respect and be grateful for. When the farm manager sees his or her job as one of wealth extraction from the soil, there is a deep disrespect to the variety of natural resources which help create income and prosperity. If instead the finance is seen in terms of a respectful and nurturing relationship, where neither party wants to damage the fabric of the society from which seeds turn into fruits, we have a binding contract of shared prosperity – and there is evidence which shows this enhances development and civic participation (Obach & Tobin, 2014). Trust can be an expression of deep humility, an understanding that we are but passers-by on this planet, committing ourselves to a light but joyful footprint. Here the journey is as important as the destination, and there is a desire not to let the other side down.

When one is immersed in the service to nature, faith (religious or otherwise) becomes the glue which holds people together and reinvigorates it to higher levels of personal growth and fulfilment (LeVasseur, Parajuli & Wirzba, 2016). The depth of understanding of one's duty on this planet, and the importance of aligning with the rhythms and seasons of nature to ensure quality food production, keep both the financier and the farmer, grounded. Their knowledge of growth and prosperity shifts as a result of this intimate relationship, and interdependence continues to be a living experience not muddied by money or finance. Culturally and spiritually, finance is put in its place and not allowed to overwhelm community, nature or society. To equate faith with fundamentalism and dogmatism is common in modernity, but not always true or applicable universally, to all cultures and belief systems. Furthermore, we have seen how finance today is in many ways a faith disguised as science – it can be equally dogmatic and fundamentalist, with ruinous consequences for modernity. We need to acknowledge that given the finality of death, all humans need to believe in something to give them hope and motivation in life.

Faith is often a force that creates, nourishes and enriches community, and has been economically important throughout human history (Barrera & Amore, 2024). For many small farmers all over the world, faith is a natural occupation and risk manager, often stemming from their love of the soil and sun. It is both the seed and the flower of trust. It is at the same time emotional and rational, and respects the magic of creation through prayer, meditation and singing (LeVasseur, Parajuli & Wirzba, 2016). Faith is the spirit which teaches and transforms human interdependence at the same time – it can take friendships to levels which either party could not even have anticipated. Faith has many layers of wisdom and understanding, communicated through art, literature, poetry or science. Relationships and human encounters provide an opportunity to invigorate faith and hope, which is very different from a purely cold and transactional approach to finance, where the inequality of power for the small farmer is exacerbated by the spirit underpinning the loan.

Faith can enhance and multiply trust – even where banks lose money from microfinance as a result of their trust in farmers or communities, the size of the loss is much more limited compared to commercial business lending, which is often done on a macro scale. Like the seed's latent power to grow, spread and nourish, faith carries within it an infinite energy for transformation. If we can successfully allow finance to stay grounded and humble, society can grow in ways beyond the reach of human orchestration and forecasting. As a group, we need to elevate our consciousness and analysis of money such that we value the things it cannot accomplish, and actively inhibit it from disrupting our relationships and communities. The frontiers of finance ought to be bordered and policed consciously, otherwise it will end up disrupting our moral, collective and ecological fabric.

Local Pooling of Seed Funding

For small businesses, communities and social capital can also provide very valuable and timely seed funding and trusted commercial advice, locally and periodically (Daly & Cobb, 1994). Lending is combined with mentoring, with a good awareness of the local market and conditions, and an early warning system for any risks or opportunities. Not just the borrowers, but lenders too have 'skin in the game' as they have risked their own money to help the farmer or the new business enterprise. Often new entrepreneurs are supported by the extended family, who want their relatives to be independent and self-sufficient. Even the shortage of labour during harvest times is supported by the extended family and village, so a shared sense of community is nurtured and invigorated through lived experience. Trusted knowledge of the local markets and opportunities is vital to a successful start-up, and the training and commercial skills become as invaluable as the money borrowed. Even in a highly developed country like the USA, a majority of farms are family-owned, although in terms of output, it is the industrialised farms which dominate (Hoppe, 2014).

Equipment and technology needed to support the business can be borrowed from friends and neighbours in the early days. I have heard many stories of start-ups where the owners slept at night on the shop floor to save on housing costs. Free labour from families can significantly help reduce the wage overheads, when these can simply be unaffordable. It can also be provided very flexibly throughout the day, ensuring that there is no need for overtime pay for hotels, restaurants or businesses which require late opening hours. This is a significant early financial investment which is undervalued or ignored in modern finance theory which has forgotten the value of family and social capital. Often debt and borrowings are encouraged to maximise returns for equity owners, instead of sharing and skimping, ignoring the risks of bankruptcy and loss of a whole family support system.

When finance and resources are borrowed from the local community, the obligation to repay is not purely legal, but also a key part of belonging and honour. There is a self-regulation of conduct which can encase the entrepreneurial seeds into pods of security and accountability which ought to be respected and valued. While these obligations may not be contractual, they can often be deeper and more effective. They serve to strengthen community ties and bonding, enhancing the social capital.

Finance in its universalist and rational calculative mode, has over time not only ignored such factors, but served to diminish their true value and effectiveness in sustainable enterprise. The very existence of local wisdom, entrepreneurial skills, knowledge-sharing, credit and labour-capital is sub-consciously denied (Prahlad, 2019), serving to harm the training of business students and graduates who come from such communities and social networks. This education can turn bankers into cold, calculating and suspicious nerds, rather than entrepreneurs who are able to acknowledge and value trust, nurture it, and also appreciate its long-term value for commercial success. Their own cultural wisdom and inheritance is often irreparably damaged by such education and training. There is also a growing arrogance from financiers towards borrowers, who are the front-line of enterprise and help give valuable returns to lenders from very little effort or sacrifice. A much wider range of skills and resilience are required from entrepreneurs than from financiers.

Biodiversity of Seeds

Just as humans are not standard, neither are seeds. The difference in varieties makes for challenge, competition, adaptation and learning. Different models of performing similar tasks, or different attitudes and cultures needed to build successful enterprises compete in the world for innovation, growth and scale.

They become laboratories where some seeds fail to germinate, and very few survive more than a year. Unfortunately, with large and powerful technologies today, it is easier to overpower and overwhelm the soil, such that biodiversity is eliminated and monopoly and significant market penetration become the norms. Fintech is a combination of finance and technology which can have significant adverse consequences for micro-businesses, and with globalisation, it can reduce the biodiversity of business enterprises on a global scale, with seriously harmful consequences. This is not to underscore some of the benefits, like M-Pesa in Kenya, which has enabled farmers and vegetable sellers to transact effectively through the ease of financial transactions and money transfer – although research shows that the technology is not used for finance (Parlasca, Johnen & Qaim, 2022).

When the diversity of seeds (or human cultures) is removed from nature, over time we lose their varieties of resilience to different soils and climate conditions, such that when there are big crop failures, we have little in the way of remedy. Similarly, disease and epidemics can flourish in mono-cultures, such that what may seem as productive and efficient in some years suddenly becomes a very costly shortage and global problem in other years. In the case of finance, we have experienced this over decades with booms and crashes, with the 2008 global financial crash being the largest and most damaging to the whole planet and our social and environmental ecosystem. It led to vast inequality, unemployment and a bailout of the fraudulent institutions, increasing their size and influence rather than allowing them to go bankrupt.

The greater the size and power of an enterprise, the more resistant it becomes to change and transformation, preferring instead to make monopoly returns and extract revenues from a guaranteed customer base. The innovation needed to change with the times and diversify according to the needs of different customers is reduced and sameness is preferred as it is easier to control and monitor. Global banks are an example of this greed and power, where often they are keen to minimise the interest given to savers and maximise the interest charged to borrowers, rather than operate fairly and justly in line with market interest-rate movements. Credit-card companies charge very large interest rates and fees to retail customers, in spite of their relative ability to repay, and often do not want them to repay their loans on time, as they can extract compound returns and high fees over a long period of time.

Mono-culture and globalisation lead to a counter-culture where multinationals subvert and diminish variety and competition, trampling on the lives of millions of people all over the world, making them slaves to anonymous and distant markets and institutions. In such circumstances, it is easier to proclaim 'the end of history' and forget that this can have significant costs and potentially irreversible side-effects for our ecosystem in the long term. The coldness of finance becomes routinised and its power to turn humans into precarious slaves increases, making humans all over the world more and more vulnerable. Another result of such behaviour is the unequal concentration of financial muscle and power, whereby even regulatory and political systems can be subverted by such cold calculating and irresponsible mega-corporations. The gaps and differences in regulatory systems between different countries, including tax obligations by multi-national corporations, can be actively exploited by these giants to enhance their extraction machines.

Grounded Seed Finance

It is critical that finance stays as close to earth as possible, to ensure its control, accountability and manageable scale. We know that the only place that seeds can grow is in soil and on earth. This limits the potential multiplication and growth like the entropy of nature. In contrast, financial compounding implies that growth can be infinite and limitless and there is no decay and entropy so far as money is concerned. This myth is dangerous and often leads to abuse of financial power. Nature has the potential to remind lenders to stay humble and respectful, and to help nurture fledglings, rather than pull the rug at any little sign of danger or challenges.

Soil has skin in the game. It owns the plants as much as the plants own it. There is reciprocity and symbiosis. Grounded finance, where roots, shoots and seeds are seen as potential for hope and discovery, catalysts for feeding and nourishing current and future generations is worth encouraging. It celebrates and reinvigorates local systems of shared social capital, transparency, trust and honour, and creates a symbiosis between nature and human resourcefulness. The harvest festival is an example of the gratitude that farmers express to nature for its bounty and generosity, and in finance, we too can have festivals which celebrate fair returns on investment and good systems of accountability. Such human gatherings can help inspire satiation and contentment rather than greed, expropriation and irresponsibility.

When 'seeds' *respect* the ground from which finance originates, they learn to understand and accept the interdependence of life, and nourish the wisdom that grows from this knowledge. Their expression of satisfaction comes not only from the fruits and vegetables produced, but also from a sense of meaning and purpose about the motives and outcomes of their fledgling enterprise. A very small and one-man business – a fruit-seller in India – recently told me, 'I am providing health nourishment for my customers, and use the returns to educate my three children, helping them to contribute to the wider economy'. The smile on his face when he said this, and the confidence with which he spoke for me epitomises the grounded strength that finance can give both to society and the borrower.

Like 'trust', the phrase 'respect' has disappeared from technocratic finance science. It is seen as irrelevant or subjective and unnecessary to the pure world of abstraction and materialism constructed by this science. However, from the perspective of nature, it is critical to building a sustainable ecosystem where there is recognition of the sources of nourishment. There is an understanding that in life, there is give and take, and while this need not be reciprocal, the symbiosis is real and a fact of existence and survival. Seeds are a very important product of nature and in time, they become a vital resource for other living beings. Seen from this perspective, the distancing of what is ultimately a very humanistic science, economics or finance, from human emotions, relationships and experiences is fundamentally damaging to birth, growth and death. It should therefore not come as a surprise to society that this ignorance ought to be rectified as it is a misrepresentation of truth.

Wisdom is deeper and much more ethical, holistic and cultured than knowledge. Finance lacks wisdom and denies its importance even when it is trying to be sustainable. Correcting this ignorance is not simply a matter of changing the equations or of adding new terminology or incorporating the 'externalities' shaped by finance. It demands a paradigm shift in the discipline, and a deeper collective effort by scholars to learn from the insights of other subjects like sociology, political science, history, anthropology, environmental science, biology and psychology. To begin this dialogue, there needs to be an open and public admission of the vast damage to the planet the ignorance and greed have created in the world today.

The seed that is finance knowledge ought to be genuine, responsible and accountable. It impacts our understanding, our professions and knowledge production mechanisms, and the future course of all living beings on planet earth. Its presumptions of universality and ignorance of ecosystem biodiversity and human cultural and social differences is deeply problematic. Patches to the science, like ESG, become a big part of the problems of knowledge and incapacitate humanity from cultivating truly sustainable policies and mechanisms (Macey, 2022). They end up endorsing and reifying damaging structures and practices, displacing genuine critique and challenge.

Simple Living, High Thinking

Leadership is a subject completely avoided in finance, and the theory gives the impression that it is irrelevant – all that is needed are projects with positive net present value and cash flows, and excellent financial analysis and knowledge (Shah, 2022). Once the science is implemented, the organisation has no choice but to grow and flourish is the unstated immortal dream. The reality is so very different – many high value organisations turn to dust overnight, and the incompetence of leadership and management can damage valuable institutions. Even though in the study of business, leadership is a highly important subject, in finance, it is simply ignored and dismissed as irrelevant. The truth is that the nuances and complexities of leadership end up confusing the equations and calculations of finance.

For seeds to flourish, they need to have some clarity of goals and direction. If the goal is purely materialistic and financial, it is simply unsustainable in the context of our wider ecosystem (Hilkens et al., 2018). It will displace and misallocate resources both in time and space, and can easily end up concentrating power and reducing accountability. The state which guarantees the value and credibility of money can find itself captured and undermined by this concentration of corporate power. In nature, seeds are voiceless yet productive, selfless and generous, without any materialistic ambition whatsoever.

Humanity ought to learn such qualities from seeds. Birth, growth and death need to be understood and embraced, and today we have vast reservoirs of knowledge and wisdom on these themes that we can draw upon. There is no excuse for our human ignorance, let alone denial of the relevance of these profound cultural characteristics and values for one of the most intelligent and powerful species on the planet. The fact that our habits and ethics are influenced and shaped by upbringing, beliefs and education makes it very harder to shake them off, especially when we are in influential positions, and are recruited, incentivised and promoted for our greed and selfishness. The fact that finance science has avoided these profound cultural dialogues and reflections is also evidence of its polarity and fundamentalism.

As social scientists, it becomes our public duty to challenge these false disciplinary segregations at their very core, otherwise we are all doomed to extinction, and deserve to be. We need to publicly recognise the damage our science has so far wrought, apologise for it, and go back to the very basics of life on earth to nurture and nourish a better and much more responsible and accountable framework of finance knowledge. What I have seen so far from many concerned scientists is a jump towards alternatives, without going through the apologia, or the humility required to do so.

Learning and Adaptation

Seeds are not selective about what they learn or where and how they get their knowledge. They simply adapt to their environment and learn and grow with it. There are no formal classes of induction or training, nor mechanisms for their certification and acceptance. They do not want to 'free' themselves or liberate themselves from nature and in this sense have no individual identity, but only a collective one. This makes us question our institutions of knowledge production, their brands and authoritative influence, and ways in which they are regulated, policed and captured by powerful interests. In the pretence of liberalism and freedom, we are being fed a very particular, narrow and mono-cultural diet in the name of science. If seeds were planted in this environment, they are likely to rebel or die out, such would be their 'natural' alienation. Their sense of community and esteem would be undermined by the soil and ground in which they find themselves. The push towards individualism and selfishness would make them rot and decay very quickly as it would feel very unnatural. As a result, we have a resulting global epidemic of loneliness today (Hertz, 2020).

This forces us to reflect on our systems of knowledge production, pedagogy and dissemination, and the ways in which they are in sync with the natural environment, or instead alienating and 'foreign'. So detached have our finance education systems come from the wider ground and communities in which they are produced and disseminated, we have come to create our own alien worlds and cultures which fit into our ideologies and theories. We have celebrated and glorified our separation from culture and diversity and seen this as central to our 'objectivity'. As Frederic Bastiat (n.d.) has said:

> When plunder becomes a way of life for a group of men in a society, over time they create for themselves a legal system that authorises it and a moral code that glorifies it.

Our knowledge systems have become deeply problematic and adversarial towards nature, biodiversity and community. They are planting seeds which are dangerous, and command significant influence in society. Significant institutions like multinational corporations, financial institutions and markets, regulators and the professions of accounting, finance and business, draw from this certified pool of 'talent'. Laws and regulations are often designed to promote 'free' markets and materialism, utilitarianism and individualism, denying the possibilities of other worldviews and belief systems. People who do not conform to this way of thinking are classified as backward and ignorant, and there is active brainwashing at universities to force students to subscribe to this science and achieve good grades. Even where 'seeds' come from different cultures they are co-opted and subverted in the name of branded quality education.

Denial of Social Needs and Relationships

In truth, finance is an extension of the deculturation of human life, and a direct cause of it too. Where seeds require culture to grow and flourish, the same is true of human infants, who are completely dependent on their parents in the early years of their critical development. They need love and care, regular nourishment and a comfortable and safe environment in which they can explore, play and experience risk. They are fully dependent on their parents and/or grandparents for this support. The reality is that good upbringing depends on the beliefs and values of the elders, the parents' own emotional stability and dedication to guardianship. It also needs an economic base which gives them resilience through which they can spend time with their children and also afford to take them on outings and adventures. This stability can become more tenuous with job insecurity, costly housing and in liberal individualist cultures where the parental responsibilities are contested rather than seen as a duty without choice. Extended family cultures can be a huge source of support and help in the early years of parenting, but these resources are not available in all traditions or even to families who come from those traditions.

Relationships among adults have become more and more precarious over time, making the 'seeds' of finance, future professionals and adults, very vulnerable. This can result in society having very tense and unhealthy attitudes to money, where poor people end up lacking in confidence, and either wanting too much, or not knowing how to live with and manage money. Middle classes are likely to have more prudence and care with money, and the upper classes would be obsessive about its accumulation and preservation, birthing generations of privileged 'seeds' who have lost any experience of the raw edges of life (James, 2007). Loneliness has become an epidemic in the West (Hertz, 2020), precisely at the time when greed and materialism have increased. However, it is not a topic or phrase even in the back index of finance textbooks – such is the denial to face reality.

The worst damage of deculturation comes from the education curricula, which choose not to engage at all with personal behaviours and attitudes to money. There is a recent wave of fashion around improving financial literacy, but this again is made objective and impersonal, and the focus is on maths and numeracy skills, ignoring the deep cultural training required to understand and manage money (Furnham, 2014). Paradoxically, even in specialist finance education there is very little literacy training – if anything the education is one of abstraction and complexity. Students are not even taught how to manage their own budgets or finances – so impersonal is the training. Furthermore, there is active and deliberate abuse and expropriation of the human *seeds* and their parents by financial institutions, and experts who work for them. This is done through poor returns on savings, high credit card interest rates, low access to affordable finance for the vulnerable, active promotion of debt and buy now-pay later schemes, and exploitation by fund and pension managers of hard-earned savings. It makes a mockery of all financial literacy training.

Trade, Travel and Adventure

Birds and bees carry seeds to new grounds and horizons. Sometimes, seeds are deliberately spread through wind and storms, taking them away from their 'comfort' zones, and not all seeds survive in new climates or soils. Risk is real, and neither managed nor avoided. It simply becomes a part of life, of birth and death. It can also happen that seeds mutate and adapt to the new lands, finding new ways of growing and nourishing. Humans have learnt to carry seeds with their travels or for the sake of their own needs, experimenting with them and assimilating them to different climates and environments. Finance has also travelled far and wide, often invisibly and by separating itself from the human/culture nexus, using cold calculating instantaneous technologies, institutions and money transfer systems to disguise its social construction (Coggan, 2012). When leaders and executives fly in and out of countries without spending any time locally to see and experience the effects of their powerful decisions, we increase the distance between finance and the real world.

Currencies like the dollar now dominate world trade and commerce. Institutions like Banks have branches and operations all over the world and play a critical role in the finance of trade, imports and exports. For global businesses, they are an invaluable ally in the facilitation of payments and the collection of sales revenues. Fluctuations in exchange rates can be very problematic for import/export businesses, but banks can help them manage this risk. We need to find a way of regulating international money flows such that the diversity of economies is protected and not exploited. Certainly, the growth of international banking and finance should not be celebrated as an uncritical good and boost to globalisation, as the side-effects and externalities of financial mobility need to be taken into account.

Human travel opens opportunities for inter-cultural respect, understanding and growth in knowledge and wisdom. The history of the Silk Road is pregnant with such stories of exchange and belief, where trade was about much more than profits or wealth creation (Frankopan, 2016). Trade brought diverse peoples into dialogue. It is a miracle how long-distance trust and relationships were built at that time, without technologies like the telephone or the internet. There is evidence that religion and belief played a central role in the cultivation of trade and mutuality (Brunning et al., 2024), and even rare manuscripts were gifted or exchanged, with merchants travelling with their holy books.

If anything, this reinforced respect and trust, even where cultures and beliefs differed – trade brought them tolerance, and a win-win attitude to life as opposed to a win-lose transactionality and mindset. Recent human experience has demonstrated that the growth and influence of finance has meant that such respect is deemed unnecessary and even counterproductive. Instead, short-termist and greedy attitudes prevail, and instead of mutuality, uneven power is sought to dominate and enforce trade (Vanden Heuvel, 2009). This spreads short-termist mindsets which directly transform local cultures in very unsustainable ways – the behaviours of multinational corporations directly undermine the seeds of culture which have been planted in many nations over hundreds and thousands of years.

Seeds come from biodiversity and help our ecosystem to enrich it. They are a product of biodiversity and when they are grown by a variety of human cultures in various parts of the world, they spread their fruits and nourish different peoples over large distances. Over time they develop a relationship with local populations, who come to understand the soil and weather conditions needed for their growth and development, and respect these in the ways they are farmed and cultivated. They help cultivate an intimacy which is far beyond textbook knowledge or efficient farming methods, and seeds keep this wisdom local and grounded, having been filtered and passed through generations of experience.

Universalist scientific knowledge about seeds, which is often produced and disseminated through education factories, needs to be adapted to local customs, traditions and knowledge too. Farming is a human and land symbiotic relationship, and this cannot easily be stripped away by globalisation, urbanisation and industrialisation. Ground, soul and seed come together to feed society. Standardised seeds have now become corporatised by multinationals like Monsanto, who have patented them and copyrighted them to ensure maximum profits and royalties. Such behaviour directly attacks both species and human diversity on the planet and should not be endorsed by big finance. It is highly damaging when corporate finance theories and textbooks ignore the criticality of relationships between food systems, human cultures and public and environmental health. They assume that money and the free market will solve all the misallocations of resources, without the supporting evidence, with the result that our ecosystem is damaged irreversibly.

Chapter Summary

Seeds carry the potential for life, nutrition and growth. They need a combination of factors to support this journey, including good soil and climate, careful and mindful agriculture, and nurturing which is sensitive to their needs in terms of rain, sun and fertilisers. The logic of finance is not synchronous with the logic of nature – and yet finance needs to protect nature, not destroy or exploit it. Seeds and humans interact with one another in the methods of farming and the choice and timing of planting in rhythm with the seasons. Finance and credit are needed to support the family of the farmer in times in between seed and harvest, and the risks that are entailed in the critical industry of farming. Too little finance can lead to hunger and deprivation, and too much finance can lead to mass production and alienation from the land, with a concentration of power in fewer and fewer hands. For small organic farmers, the industry of finance needs to find way of encouraging and supporting them, and making finance accessible, as they are providing a priceless service for the protection of our soil and environment.

Globalisation and industrialisation have tried to standardise food production and alienate the need for human culture and diversity in the care needed to harmonise earth, seed and soul. The result in many parts of the world has been the financial slavery of farmers, leading to bankruptcy, suicides and alienation from the land, with new generations preferring to have urban jobs than to take the risk of toiling with little reward. Tenant farmers can be forced to think in a short-term way to obtain the necessary revenue, and this may be unhealthy for soil and society – their rents need to allow for sustainability. While trust and faith are central to finance, they can also be undermined by the transactional systems which have come to replace them. The result is that humans have come to lose traditional knowledge systems and inter-generational relationships and whole farming communities critical to sustainable development have been wiped out.

Even the biodiversity of seeds, and their varied species and methods of farming have become supressed by the economic production engine, whose goals are higher and higher financial efficiency, without due consideration to the impact upon local cultures, rural lifestyles and communities of farming wisdom. Markets and incentives have not been able to value localism, nor shape new support and financing structures which encourage organic farming processes and systems. Financial growth has come to overwhelm the growth in local health, well-being and nutrition, increasing inequality and rural displacement. Even soil quality has suffered as a result of mass agriculture and chemical fertilisation such that the very land becomes unproductive over time, so exhausted it has become from the demands of high economic efficiency.

Finance has the power to seed new enterprises and businesses, and often does so with good outcomes. However, this power should not be used purely in terms of financial return and performance – it needs to take into account of a wide range of impact and performance measures before the decision to lend or invest is made. These criteria should include impact on our soil, water and energy systems and on cultures and communities too. A large number of small family-owned farms can be significantly beneficial to the planet, if supported by science, education and accessible finance, as they can help revive rural jobs and communities.

Finance education and training need to be reformed and made more accessible to ordinary people, including farmers. Traditions and wisdom which may be different from universal ideas of progress and happiness should be respected and engaged with rather than dismissed or ignored as being backward and regressive. Just because the value of cultures or relationships cannot be measured does not mean that they ought to be ignored or suppressed in the investment decision-making – the methods of evaluation need to be altered to take such intangibles into account. Businesses with the potential to amass significant power and influence in a short time through technology should also be carefully evaluated for their longer-term repercussions before being financed. Inter-generational fairness and equity ought to be a key consideration when finance is given.

Finance needs to extend its science to understand seed production, fertilisation and harvesting, ensuring that the human relationships and capital are not ignored or undermined. Local commitments to protecting the land for future generations come from rootedness, tradition and beliefs, and are critical to preserving our food ecosystems and supplies. The importance of this should be incorporated into the calculations of finance, and valued rather than suppressed. Rituals like planting and harvest festivals help humans to reinforce their communities and maintain rural rootedness. Even song and dance are critical to help farmers cope with routine work and nourish their spirits to help them invigorate their larger purpose of feeding the nation. The mechanisation of human labour can lead to idle minds and cold hearts and is not always a positive development for society. The dignity of work ought to be valued and protected. When financial systems and cultures forget to sing and dance, or to introspect on their purpose and meaning, we have serious problems in sustaining our human futures on planet earth. In the next chapter, we examine how our knowledge and education systems can be rewired to produce this harmony, celebrating the good practices that have long been hiding in plain sight.

References

Anderson, K. (2010). *The Political Economy of Agricultural Price Distortions*. Cambridge University Press.

Armstrong, C. (2024). *Global Justice and the Biodiversity Crisis: Conservation in a World of Inequality*. Oxford University Press.

Barrera, A., & Amore, R. C. (eds) (2024). *The Oxford Handbook of Religion and Economic Ethics*. Oxford, New York: OUP.

Bastiat, F. (n.d.). *The Collected Works of Frédéric Bastiat*, Vol. 2. Ludwig von Mises Institute.

Berry, W. (2004). *The Unsettling of America: Culture and Agriculture*, revised edition. San Francisco: Counterpoint.

Bharti, N. (2018, 1 January). Evolution of Agriculture Finance in India: A Historical Perspective. *Agricultural Finance Review* 78(3), 376–392.

Blakeley, G. (2019). *Stolen – How to Save the World from Financialisation*. Repeater.

Boatright, J. R. (2010). *Finance Ethics: Critical Issues in Theory and Practice*. Hoboken, NJ: Wiley.

Boyle, D. (2010). *The Tyranny of Numbers: Why Counting Can't Make Us Happy*. Flamingo.

Brunning, S., Yu-ping, L., O'Connell, E. R., & Williams, T. (2024). *Silk Roads*. London: British Museum Press.

Çalışkan, A. S. (2022). *Homo Faber and Homo Economicus in the Scientific Revolution*. Routledge.

Clapp, J., and Fuchs, D. A. (2009). *Corporate Power in Global Agrifood Governance*, Vol. 1. London, Cambridge, MA: MIT Press.

Coggan, P. (2012). *Paper Promises – Money, Debt and the New World Order*. Penguin.

Daly, H. E., & Cobb, J. (1994). *For The Common Good: Redirecting the Economy toward Community, the Environment, and a Sustainable Future*, updated, expanded edition. Boston, MA: Beacon Press.

DePuy, W., Weger, J., Foster, K., Bonanno, A. M., Kumar, S., Lear, K., Basilio, R., & German, L. (2022, 1 June). Environmental Governance: Broadening Ontological Spaces for a More Liveable World. *Environment and Planning E: Nature and Space* 5(2), 947–975.

Deshpande, R. S., & Arora, S. (eds) (2010). *Agrarian Crisis and Farmer Suicides*. Delhi, London: SAGE.

Dupont, Q., & Karpoff, J. M. (2020, 1 May). The Trust Triangle: Laws, Reputation, and Culture in Empirical Finance Research. *Journal of Business Ethics* 163(2), 217–238.

Engler, H. (2018). *Remaking Culture on Wall Street: A Behavioral Science Approach for Building Trust from the Bottom Up*. Cham: Springer International Publishing.

Frankopan, P. (2016). *The Silk Roads: A New History of the World*. Knopf Doubleday Publishing Group.

Furnham, A. (2014). *The New Psychology of Money*. Hove: Psychology Press.

Goodhart, C. (2010). How Should We Regulate the Financial Sector, The Future of Finance, LSE. www.futureoffinance.org.uk

Gore, A. (2006). *Earth in the Balance: Ecology and the Human Spirit*. New York: Rodale Books.

Hanson, S. (2015, January). The Case for Farm Finance. *Innovations: Technology, Governance, Globalization* 10(1–2), 139–146.

Hawley, K. (2012). *Trust: A Very Short Introduction*. Oxford: OUP.

Hertz, N. (2020). *The Lonely Century: A Call to Reconnect*. Hachette UK.

Hilkens, A., Reid, J. I., Klerkx, L., & Gray, D. I. (2018, 1 October). Money Talk: How Relations between Farmers and Advisors around Financial Management Are Shaped. *Journal of Rural Studies* 63, 83–95.

Hoppe, R. A. (2014). *Structure and Finances of U. S. Farms: Family Farm Report, 2014 Edition*. DIANE Publishing Company.

James, O. (2007). *Affluenza: How to Be Successful and Stay Sane*. Random House.

Jones, G., Escalante, C., & Rusiana, H. (2015, 1 January). Reconciling Information Gaps in Organic Farm Borrowers' Dealings with Farm Lenders. *Agricultural Finance Review* 75(4), 469–483.

Jordaan, M. J., & Eiselen, R. (2015, October). Organic Agriculture: The Trade-off between Financial and Non-Financial Benefits. *Journal of Economic and Financial Sciences* 8(3), 875–889.

Kenadjian, P. S., & Dombret, A. (2016). *Getting the Culture and the Ethics Right: Towards a New Age of Responsibility in Banking and Finance*, Vol. 20. Berlin, Boston: De Gruyter.

Klocek, D. (2013). *Sacred Agriculture: The Alchemy of Biodynamics*. Great Barrington, MA: Lindisfarne Books.

Kumar, S. (2024). *Soil, Soul, Society: A New Trinity for Our Time*. Parallax Press.

LeVasseur, T., Parajuli, P., & Wirzba, N. (2016). *Religion and Sustainable Agriculture: World Spiritual Traditions and Food Ethics*. University Press of Kentucky.

Llewellyn, D. T. (2005, 1 January). Trust and Confidence in Financial Services: A Strategic Challenge. *Journal of Financial Regulation and Compliance* 13(4), 333–346.

Lymbery, P. (2015). *Farmageddon: The True Cost of Cheap Meat*. London: Bloomsbury Paperbacks.

Macey, J. R. (2022). ESG Investing: Why Here? Why Now? *Berkeley Business Law Journal* 19, 258.

Mackenzie, D. (2006). *An Engine, Not a Camera: How Financial Models Shape Markets*. MIT Press.

Mazoyer, M., & Roudart, L. (2006). *A History of World Agriculture: From the Neolithic Age to the Current Crisis*. London: Earthscan.

McGoun, E. (1997). Hyperreal Finance. *Critical Perspectives on Accounting* 18, 97–122.

Monbiot, G. (2017). *How Did We Get Into This Mess? Politics, Equality, Nature*, reprint edition. London: Verso.

Monbiot, G. (2023). *Regenesis: Feeding the World without Devouring the Planet*. London: Penguin.

Murau, S., & Pforr, T. (2020). What Is Money in a Critical Macro-Finance Framework? *Finance and Society* 6(1), 56–66.

Nair, M., & Njolomole, M. (2020, 1 January). Microfinance, Entrepreneurship and Institutional Quality. *Journal of Entrepreneurship and Public Policy* 9(1), 137–148.

Obach, B. K., & Tobin, K. (2014, 1 June). Civic Agriculture and Community Engagement. *Agriculture and Human Values* 31(2), 307–322.

Parlasca, M. C., Johnen, C., & Qaim, M. (2022, 1 March). Use of Mobile Financial Services among Farmers in Africa: Insights from Kenya. *Global Food Security* 32, 100590.

Pfeiffer, D. A. (2006). *Eating Fossil Fuels: Oil, Food, and the Coming Crisis in Agriculture*. Gabriola Island, BC: New Society Publishers.

Pistor, K. (2019). *The Code of Capital: How the Law Creates Wealth and Inequality*. Princeton, NJ: Princeton University Press.

Prahlad, C. K. (2019). *The Fortune at The Bottom of The Pyramid*. Pearson Education.

Pretty, J. N. (2002). *Agri-Culture: Reconnecting People, Land and Nature*. London: Earthscan.

Rajan, R. (2019). *The Third Pillar: How Markets and the State Leave the Community Behind*. New York: Penguin Press.

Robin, M.-M. (2012). *The World According to Monsanto*. New York: The New Press.

Roettger, D. (2015). *Agricultural Finance for Smallholder Farmers: Rethinking Traditional Microfinance Risk and Cost Management Approaches*. Columbia University Press.

Sailesh, R. (ed.) (2020). *Animal Agriculture Is Immoral*. Independently published.

Sandel, M. J. (2013). *What Money Can't Buy: The Moral Limits of Markets*. London, New York, New York, Ontario: Penguin.

Shah, A. K. (2022). *Inclusive and Sustainable Finance: Leadership, Ethics and Culture*. London: Routledge. doi:10.4324/9781003164746

Shiva, V. (2006). *Earth Democracy: Justice, Sustainability and Peace*. London: Zed.

Stilwell, F. J. B. (2019). *The Political Economy of Inequality*. Cambridge: Polity.

Stuart, D. (2020). Radical Hope: Truth, Virtue, and Hope for What Is Left in Extinction Rebellion. *Journal of Agricultural & Environmental Ethics* 33(3–6), 487–504.

Turner, A. (2015). *Between Debt and the Devil: Money, Credit, and Fixing Global Finance*, illustrated edition. Princeton: Princeton University Press.

Turner, J., & D'Silva, J. (2006). *Animals, Ethics, and Trade: The Challenge of Animal Sentience*. London: Earthscan.

Tyrie, A. (2013). *Changing Banking for Good*. Committee Report HC175–111. UK: House of Commons Treasury.

Vanden Heuvel, K. (2009). *Meltdown: How Greed and Corruption Shattered Our Financial System and How We Can Recover*. New York: Nation Books.

Wenger, E. (2000). *Communities of Practice: Learning, Meaning, And Identity*. Cambridge: Cambridge University Press.

Williams, J. W. (2014). Feeding Finance: A Critical Account of the Shifting Relationships between Finance, Food and Farming. *Economy and Society* 43(3), 401–431. https://doi.org/10.1080/03085147.2014.892797.

Williams, J. (2012). The Impact of Climate Change on Indigenous People – the Implications for the Cultural, Spiritual, Economic and Legal Rights of Indigenous People. *The International Journal of Human Rights* 16(4), 648–688.

Yunus, M. (2003). *Banker to the Poor: Micro-Lending and the Battle Against World Poverty*. New York: PublicAffairs.

Zhou, Y. (2015). Jain Irrigation Systems Limited: Creating Shared Value for Small Onion Growers. In Y. Zhou & S. Chandra (eds), *Knowledge Driven Development* (pp. 163–179). San Diego: Academic Press.

4 Eco-System of Finance Beliefs

Rivers all over the world have been a critical source of fresh water without which life on earth for many living beings, including humans, would be impossible. A river flows from the mountains to the valleys, often travelling hundreds of miles to nourish mother earth, without charging a fee, nor drinking a drop for itself. In most indigenous cultures of the world, rivers were seen as sacred and worshipped and thanked for this elixir of life that gave life to others so selflessly. This simple fact about rivers and their generosity is totally absent from finance science, and fresh water has long been taken for granted, and therefore, ignored altogether.

The same is true of oxygen and air quality, without which humans would perish. Air is our lifeblood, and we need to breathe several times a minute simply to stay alive, and all this comes for free. The science of yoga places a significant emphasis on the quality, methods and depth of breathing, and its relationship with health and well-being. Contemporary medicine in contrast, has no science of breathing that is taught in medical school, so it too takes oxygen for granted, until patients struggle to breathe. Water and air are our life force, which are priceless and free, yet we have forgotten to acknowledge and respect their generosity, let alone value it. Through our pollution and waste, we routinely damage these sacred resources, and finance is critical in the expansion of factories, pollution and consumption, where waste products are grown in millions of tons every day without penalty. Human health and well-being are directly entwined with nature, and communities and social cohesion flourishes when nature is respected and protected (Pretty, 2002).

Modernity has emphasised economic growth and consumption at any cost and failed to value environmental and public health. Individualism and WEIRD psychologies have meant that western euro-centric cultures have become selfish and impersonal (Schulz et al., 2018), damaging hopes for a collective conscience, critical to a sustainable planet. Climate and weather too have been taken for granted, used, polluted and damaged beyond repair, and now that we are dying, we start turning green. We are obsessed about protecting ourselves at any cost, avoiding a deeper reflexivity about our morality and responsibilities to the planet and ecosystem. If our actions and science are a cause of harm and pollution, we will be unable to recover unless we face up to our scientific violence, and transform the very frames of our thinking.

DOI: 10.4324/9781003534532-4

As Big Pharma has taken over the definition of well-being, its industrialised and materialistic logic means that illness is more profitable than wellness. What we have done to soil is also what we are doing to human health – shaping an ecosystem of disease and death, of other living beings and humans too. The parallels with our financial knowledge ecosystem are similar – we are suffocating society and the planet knowingly and deliberately. Nobel Economics laureate Joseph Stiglitz (2019) demolishes the obsession with market fundamentalism, and argues for a more balanced economy approach which looks at the diversity of forces from charities, cooperatives, public bodies and small businesses to create a balanced economy. He is especially critical of micro-economics and its weird assumptions, which have had a big influence on corporate financial economic science today. Some argue that the industry of finance has actually become paranoid and obsessed about itself, losing connection with reality altogether, entirely self-referential, whilst at the same time commanding significant power and influence (Muniesa, 2024).

In this chapter, we focus on the ecosystem of finance knowledge and beliefs, to understand the structures and theories which impact the institutions and organisational cultures and behaviours in finance. We examine the fences constructed by the knowledge, the boundaries which are made impenetrable by outsiders, and the denial of the very politics and ideological nature of so-called 'objective finance'. The emerging science of systems thinking looks beyond silos and examines the webs of inter-actions and inter-dependencies which shape our outputs and outcomes (Chen, 2009; Deckard, Niblett & Shapiro, 2024; Renner, Daly & Mayumi, 2021; Toledo, 2022; Valentinov, 2021). When humans engineer systems, they can and often do develop a power unto themselves, whereby it is very difficult to unwind such forces. However, to shape sustainability, it is important for us to understand such systemic forces and how they impact upon the real world, often in unpredictable and damaging ways, even when they are designed by humans.

Stein (2011) psychoanalyses the 2008 Global Finance crisis and shows that there was an underlying culture of mania and psychopathy which became endemic. Group psychology, combined with power and distance from society for financial traders, has a significant impact on the global economy even today, especially when power is concentrated in a few very large and globally influential institutions (Turner, 2015). Technology helps concentrate this power. There are a number of critiques about capitalism given its spate of failures, and significant questions are being asked about whether or not such a system structurally breeds moral corruption (Ferguson & Petro, 2016; Rifkin, 2001; Stiglitz, 2019; Whyte & Wiegratz, 2016; Zuboff, 2019).

As we saw in Chapter 1, there are calls for a diversification of finance research along a variety of themes from ontology to epistemology, diverse research methods, and concern and empathy for the real world and the consequences of finance for society and nature (Brooks et al., 2019; Lagoarde-Segot, 2015). All the evidence points to the significant politicisation of accounting and finance knowledge, and the resulting deep resistance to critique. We have no choice but to expose the politics and the damage done by this pedagogy, in order to transform it. Micro-normative approaches are encouraged, where researchers explicitly take a moral position and try to solve the problems of society from different perspectives like critical realism or interpretive and radical humanist paradigms. Nature and animals have been divorced and 'othered' from the discipline, and even behavioural finance is now a separate subject, rather than the research integrated to transform the mainstream. In fact, its findings expose the irrationality of financial models and assumptions, but this is sidelined and segregated.

In this chapter, we show how this knowledge ecosystem can change if we allow diverse perspectives and cultures to share their own stories and experiences of finance, and point to the urgency of more research which exposes the differences in knowledge and relationships with money. A super-imposed universalist theory of finance is harmful to the large variety of diverse cultures and societies in the world. Qualitative and interpretive research is able to penetrate these nuances, but hitherto has been marginalised and removed from the core science. The incentives for this type of research have also been diminished by elite journals. It needs to be revived and encouraged, including descriptive and analytical research which helps us build case studies of real-world diversity in finance.

Specialisation as Border-creation and Boundary Policing

Knowledge specialisation has become so sophisticated that ethics is a separate subject for philosophy departments, and ecology is for the environmental sciences. The simple idea that ethics is not something that can be implemented by learning in a course or professional exam, but needs to be nourished and reminded for adults to maintain an ethical conscience is somehow presumed immaterial in Business education. Objectivity impersonalises and removes reflexivity at a time when we sorely need it. Environmental and organisational influences on ethical behaviour need to be discussed regularly by professionals as part of their continuing certification – this is where communities of identity and belonging can transform moral behaviour. Furthermore, if other subjects like finance, marketing or even leadership are encouraging unethicality through their silos and framing – this is also not debated. Silos can be convenient tools for removing critique and challenge (Burrell et al., 2022; Choat, Wolf & O'Neill, 2024), and complexity can easily disguise the assumptions and build convenient fences of expertise.

Business has been incentivised on every means of making financial profits and maximising them by minimising costs, responsibilities and environmental protection – there is geography of power which has significant influence on the real world (Clark & Wójcik, 2007). Business schools and professional bodies in accounting and finance multiply and expand the spread of this dis-ease on a global scale – their textbooks and frameworks are identical. Within the discipline of business, finance specialises on credit and cash, irrespective of how it is borrowed, whether or not it is accessible to all, or to what purpose it is utilised. As to the culture and politics by which credit is created and supplied, finance is consciously dismissive, seeing money as an endless resource for any projects which generate positive cash flows and dis-counted net present values.

Knowledge devoid of honesty and integrity, and irresponsible to mother earth and its creation, cannot be sustainable and is itself highly political (Keucheyan, 2017; Monbiot, 2017). As we saw in Chapters 1 and 2, soil, soul and seed matter in the creation of enterprise and they work in a symbiotic relationship. Interdependence is critical to the growth of any plant, and there are no separate rights or responsibilities of different elements – nature simply fuses them to give us nutrition and nourishment. The broad catchphrase of environment, which has become topical today, even in such cold calculating disciplines as finance needs to be unravelled for its true essence. It needs to be defined on its own terms, not through the lens of a science which has ignored its importance and value for decades.

Money is a social, cultural and political construct, and something that is plural rather than singular (Dodd, 2014). Unfortunately, the modern 'environment' of finance knowledge is primarily composed of human agency, corporate and financial institutions, economic production, markets and financial systems, though it needs to change (Renner, Daly & Mayumi, 2021). It is presented as transactional, value-free, neutral and detached from animals and nature, whose role is to serve humanity. After the 2008 crash, there was one important leadership call by the President of the American Finance Association, Luigi Zingales, where he questioned the divorce of the science from taking responsibility for the significant rise in frauds and asked whether finance benefits society (Zingales, 2015). Sadly, this did not result in significant changes in the research methods and theories (Brooks & Schopohl, 2018).

Education is not about primary human needs like air or water quality and supply, but about the context in which finance is nurtured and nourished, and how it remains responsible and accountable to the society from which it originates. The values and morality shaped in this environment are critical to the success or failure of finance. We need to instil ways to ground finance and relate it to the protection of society and nature. The methods by which money systems understand and embrace life, and respect its critical elements, foundations and resources are crucial to human sustainability (Murau & Pforr, 2020; Sandel, 2013). Products, services and markets need to be designed such as to maintain this deep sense of responsibility and accountability – otherwise, life on earth for humans will disappear altogether.

Additionally, finance research should remove its segregation from pedagogy and methods of training future professionals in finance. Investigative journalists outside the academy have done pioneering work in growing the knowledge base in finance, yet their work is constantly ignored and marginalised (Shah, 2022) they are journalists not scientists! However, if scientists do not analyse scandals and financial frauds, then journalists' forensic, public interest motivated work is critical to our understanding. One of the significant emerging public issues in finance is that of literacy – everyday financial products are so complex that ordinary people often get confused and cheated by them! Guess what, even financial literacy is not taught in a finance class – it jumps straight into the complexity without demystifying the basics! This is a lost opportunity in engaging and empowering students to think of everyday finance by personalizing it.

There is virtually no reflexivity among elite scholars about the methods and principles of finance education. While researchers have not measured the extent of the de-culturation among students and professionals, the fact that financial crises are so common is evidence of recklessness among leaders and institutions. It is possible that ethical students and professionals get weeded out by the system very early on, at a significant cost to society. We need much more research on the kinds of people who leave the profession or choose not to join because of discomfort with its values and morality. The damage caused by this elitist system of separation between science and pedagogy is significant given the increasing importance of finance knowledge in society. The simple fact that finance is a product of human imagination means that its implementation depends on what and how the science is taught. In hindsight it appears as if this separation has now become so deep that to rehumanise finance is to crash the entire pyramid of knowledge it has constructed. This can be scary for the elites who control the editorial boards, provided they even understand the need to personalise finance.

We need to shape an inclusive system of research and teaching where the two reinforce one another, and plurality is allowed and encouraged in different parts of the world (Shah, 2018). In the field of medicine, it is routine to provide clinical training as part of the curriculum, but in finance the two are separated completely. The theory is already distant from reality, and if pedagogy is segregated, even the opportunity to question the assumptions and models from a generation whose very future depends on human sustainability is reduced. Teachers have no choice but to 'preach' from Anglo-American textbooks, and, in many countries, only foreign PhDs and research journals are recognised in elite institutions, spreading the malaise even more deeply and profoundly. This can also result in self-selection, where the technocratic students major in finance, and the rounded and ethical students leave the discipline altogether, as it is incapable of addressing their questions or concerns. Taking students instead on business and finance field trips can open their eyes to the wider roles of finance in nature and society and give them memorable experiences.

Unsustainable De-culturation *Caused* by Finance

We have seen the criticality of culture, community and conscience in building and sustaining a moral culture around earth, animals, nature, money and finance. This is the most basic fabric of any economy. The diversity and plurality of cultures enriches this ecosystem of relationships, creating opportunities to learn from each other, and win-win trading enterprises which help build bridges of respect and tolerance (Hampden-Turner & Trompenaars, 1993). Allowing human diversity to engage in the variety of meanings and contexts of finance, we can create a healthy debate which challenges monotheism and universalism in the science. Such dialogues would also expose the variety of contexts and perspectives in which business and finance actually operate (Trompenaars & Hampden-Turner, 2020). Research on culture in finance is siloed, relatively thin and disparate (Goodell et al., 2023; Reuter, 2011), and there are even calls for a new field of 'cultural finance' increasing the silos! Even family and community are missing from the textbooks, let alone the concept of society. At best, the research method reduces culture to a subject for quantitative analysis – that is the only tool finance academics have. In finance textbooks, culture has yet to enter the syllabus.

This makes finance a highly partial, insensitive and quantitative science, and one which obfuscates truth and sustainability, and is the cause of so much pain and economic anguish in modernity. It also suppresses the variety of customs and relationships people have with money and its importance in social and public life (Sandel, 2013). Even institutions which are designed not to make money but to spend it, like state schools or public hospitals, are seen as wasteful and a betrayal of market logic and efficiency. Private good, public bad is the finance motto, spread globally through its textbooks and large business education footprints. Many students of such courses would graduate without having any understanding or respect for public organisations and their criticality to economic well-being. There is a strong negative social externality resulting from a highly commercial and globalised finance curriculum.

Debt slavery is another example in history where people who owed money often became slaves for life (George, 2013; Langley et al., 2019; Paik & Wiesner-Hanks, 2013) – examples include indentured labourers, the treatment of slaves as property, and the trading and financing of slaves as a profitable business. Slavery destroys culture and removes identity and self-belief altogether – it is deeply dehumanizing. Today, we still have debt slavery all over the world – people who cannot pay their mortgages are made homeless overnight, there are payday loan sharks who demand extortionate interest, child labour in many developing countries, extremely poor treatment of workers in many factories all over the world, extortionate credit card interest rates and charges – these are all everyday finance issues which are not on the curriculum. However, if the human stories are discussed in class, students would be sensitised to the politics of finance much earlier on, and empowered to behave differently when they graduate into employment.

There is a subliminal deculturation in finance science and education which is causing irreversible damage to our knowledge ecosystem in an increasingly globalised world (Montgomerie, 2008). It is removing our understanding of mutuality, family and community, and displacing our mental and physical health from the world of money and financial well-being. Walls, silos and barriers are created for different parts of social sciences to interact and engage with our understanding of economics, making them very difficult to break, and at the same time preventing a holistic understanding of finance. Even when behavioural finance shows how human psychology is critical to financial decision making, and is rarely rational (Muradoglu & Harvey, 2012), the world of corporate finance assumes that markets and corporate investment and lending have to be rational. There is some evidence that culture impacts financial decision-making (Aggarwal & Goodell, 2014), although much more research of this vein is needed.

The unwillingness to separate small business finance from the science of corporate finance expands the damage caused by this ignorance. I attended a keynote from a world-famous finance professor where corporate finance models were used to theorise small business finance – he had no clue that he was spreading the poison from top to bottom! When I called out the sham, he had no defence. What was most disturbing was how he had little understanding of the real world of business, and did not even think he needed to know, so steeped he was in his equations! Subliminally, finance education encourages future managers and leaders to be cold, transactional and materialistic, ignoring any cultural or psychological nuances. Fixed meanings are assigned to its models, when in reality, the meanings and interpretations vary significantly even between finance professionals (Ortiz, 2017).

Against such a background, it becomes very difficult to talk about corporate culture or psychology in finance, or about the behaviours of teams of accountants or financial controllers inside a corporation. Elite networks and 'communities' of finance trading and dealmaking are eliminated from debate and discussion. Even the nuances of power and status within finance managers and leaders, and how they impact business decision-making are not discussed in the training, with people having to cope with them on their own when they enter the big bad world. However, all these factors matter in how financial decisions are made and executed. The real-world influences on corporate finance are rarely rational or predictable, and more about who knows whom, and who can blame others for their financial hubris and get away with it.

The biggest problem comes from the fact that shareholders have delegated the responsibility of financial resource allocation of giant corporations to boards and management, on materialist and extractive principles, leading to 'ecocide' (Whyte, 2020). Furthermore, there is a vast and growing literature on financial fraud, which finds that conflicts of interest, complexity, technology and ignorance contribute to its growth (Reurink, 2018). Decisions relating to millions and even billions of dollars are made by agents rather than principals, and the evidence is littered with waste, scandal, fraud and even destruction of large and historical corporations by the actions of a few people. Yet the free and efficient competitive market narrative prevails. Furthermore, the academy thrives in growing the complexity of finance (Engelen et al., 2012; Mackenzie, 2006; MacKenzie, 2011) and denying its own conflicts of interest.

Ignorance and Suppression of Human Diversity

The diversity of human society, seasons, climates and resources on planet earth mean that there can *never* be one universal theory of the financial system. Instead, we need to redesign our knowledge and understanding to embrace a variety of customs, traditions and practices of money (Egan, 2021; Ghio et al., 2023), embracing pluralism in place of universalism. In his review of 5,000 years of human history, Graeber (2014) amasses a wide range of true stories and cultural practices relating to exchange, debt, beliefs, taxes, accounting records, famines, wars, loan sharks and money. None of this breadth and diversity is in contemporary research and teaching in corporate finance and accounting. In hindsight, it appears as if history and diversity have been stamped and bulldozed by these modern sciences and professions. Cultural ignorance and insensitivity can be very costly to business leaders and policy-makers, as the outcomes of practices and initiatives may become counter-productive and damaging even (Meyer, 2016).

We need to help create knowledge incentives, structures and institutions which embrace and protect this plurality, rather than suppress or decimate it. Only then will we achieve truly sustainable economic development. There is no one size which fits all. As an example, small local family-owned businesses provide a large ecosystem of work and rural development, where skills of enterprise are learnt from childhood, and so is quality service and contentment. They are agile and adaptable to local needs, and understand the local customs and languages, and can also be open to new knowledge and understanding about the importance of environmental protection.

A financial system which recognises the criticality of small business, and supports their survival and resilience, can have significant value in sustainable rural development. Even our understanding of finance can be enriched by documenting these small business practices and the ways in which they help build trust in society. Instead, subliminally, modern students of business learn that the science comes from big business and their strategies and practices, and if anything, this theory should percolate downwards to small business. *The Dhandho Investor* is a rare example of a cultural finance book based on examples of Indian business success in North America, showing how family unity, prudent risk management, focus on cash flows and financial control, and hard work helped the Patels dominate the Motel industry, starting from zero capital (Pabrai, 2007). It was not written by a finance academic. It also shows cultural adaptability to different countries and contexts.

At the opposite end, universalist institutions and markets aim to standardise production and work, removing their responsibility and accountability to local cultures, communities and environments. They can easily mechanise processes with the help of technology, such that people become more and more detached from their inner souls and spirits, and instead become robotised, using drugs and alcohol to fuel their failing mental health. If financial theories and systems fail to capture the side-effects and irreversible damage caused by the institutions then they cannot help sustain life on earth.

There are whole towns which have been turned to employment deserts as a result of outsourcing, or the closure of large industries, disrupting social and communal life severely, without any care or concern by business or finance (Jaffe, 2021). Many corporate jobs today cause and spread insecurity in society, subverting culture. Routinised environmental pollution is rarely priced or punished by financial markets in spite of the scale of their damage, like the activities of the oil multinationals whose share prices continue to rise. Trillions of dollars are spent every year in the war industry, and finance science is silent about the significant anxiety and fear created by such a large machinery of violence. Our incentives and models have failed severely in restraining direct expropriation of society and natural resources – often they have done the very opposite.

Re-culturation of Financial Knowledge

Instead of deculturation of finance, we urgently need re-culturation – culture's role, importance and nuances need to be understood. We need to analyse cases of corporate financial waste through individualist cultures, and the betrayal of trust that shareholders place in the managers, which often subverts the entire culture and future of a corporation, shaping an immoral economy of fraud (Whyte & Wiegratz, 2016). Even systems of accounting and accountability, which are ostensibly designed to improve transparency often fail to do so, and can hide financial mismanagement or fraud for years, in spite of auditors and regulators overseeing financial reporting. In elite institutions all over the world, finance has divorced itself from accounting and almost overpowered it, with a strong assumption that accounting is merely information for capital markets, who will ultimately interpret it for purposes of share valuation. For a long time, the critical role of accounting in shaping what is measured and what is excluded was not given importance.

There is a need to reclaim and re-evaluate the ontology and belief system which underpins modern finance, and make it plural and inclusive of indigenous wisdoms (DePuy et al., 2022; Shrivastava, Ivanaj & Persson, 2013). It is important to expose the deeply buried cultural assumptions and unpick them for their lack of diversity or universality. These beliefs shape our global eco-system of understanding and have a strong bearing on how finance is experienced, analysed and interpreted by humans and communities all over the world. When we do so, we will discover the significant diversity of financial beliefs all over the world, and the difference in customs, practices, trustworthiness and accountability that prevail. We will start to explore the cultural nuances and implications of financial markets, institutions and practices. These decisions and structures have real world implications in terms of jobs, opportunities, professional lives, careers and grounded industries like food and agriculture or water systems and air quality.

The ground of micro-finance in terms of beliefs, trust and relationships ought to be revived and given the importance it deserves (Prahlad, 2019). Anthropologists and geographers are doing pioneering work in this area, especially on indigenous cultures (Beliso-De Jesús & Pierre, 2020; Poyser & Daugaard, 2023; Short, 2010). This will help lay a very different foundation to the science of finance and its methods of research and analysis. Voices and beliefs which have hitherto been marginalised, ignored or trivialised will come back to the fore, and find spaces to be heard, respected and trusted even. Researchers need to write case studies of the varieties of finance practices all over the world, including the vast diversity that exists even within countries and communities.

Universities in different parts of the world need to transform their incentives and appointment processes to grow such research. This plurality will encourage and enable a much deeper investigation of the foundations of finance, and its relevance to human sustainability. It will also become a valuable resource for diversity in education and training. Subjects ignored or abandoned such as animals, forests, rivers, air quality, farming or communities and religion will now find space in the business classroom. These should not be seen as objects to protect for human use, but as the foundations for all life, without which humans fail in their stewardship and trusteeship.

One example of deep cultural difference with the west lies in the timeless Indian culture and way of life (Dalrymple, 2024). There is a very different approach to risk, enterprise and money (Pattanaik, 2015). Belief is all important, and steers the leader, who also values family, community and belonging. Money (like the goddess of wealth, Laxmi) is seen as whimsical and a flow, rather than something to be accumulated, and the aim of enterprise is to serve society, with growth coming from beyond the material – growth in knowledge or wisdom often given a higher status. *Sanatana Dharma* – a timeless science of sustainable living, is critical to the belief system, which also helps Indians cope with risk and uncertainty. There are tens of thousands of temples, mosques, schools, hospitals, community centres and other charitable institutions all over the country, and they continue to receive voluntary support and regular donations. *Seva*, or selfless service, is written into the code of the culture, and often helps remind people of higher purposes in life.

While the philosophy is very deep, it is never separated from everyday life and there is constant reflexivity about behaviours and actions. Time and performance are often tempered by patience and fulfilment – there is no rush to make money. In fact, there is a very large 'contented' economy in India of small entrepreneurs, like tea sellers, samosa makers or fruit retailers, which is often ignored. A businessman or woman starts the shop with a prayer in the morning – such is the profound importance of faith and ritual. Family and community are very important, and a lot of key discussions and meetings happen around the sharing of food, with little or no separation between home life and work life. Prayer helps entrepreneurs engage with their conscience, and also limit taking too much personal credit for their success – it contains the ego. Finance is always a part of a much larger whole, and not separated, siloed or overly prioritised.

Holistic Finance: Diversifying Theories and Methods

All this calls for an urgent need for our knowledge systems to embrace a much deeper and wider understanding of the role and impact of finance on our societies and economies. Context matters. It shapes how finance works in different industries and in different parts of one country, and different parts of the world. Urban finance is different from rural finance. *Kikuyu* finance is different from *Marvadi* finance. Finance in China operates differently from finance in

America. We need to abandon our desire to *impose* our theoretical dogmatism on diverse cultures and societies. The denial of culture and context may make theories and mathematical models more convenient to the scientists, but it displaces truth and imposes fiction.

Interpretive field studies of finance, which have a qualitative component, have been virtually abandoned and ignored by the discipline, even though they are prevalent and valued in subjects like psychology, sociology and anthropology, where finance is increasingly seen as a major influence on human behaviour and cultures (Lagoarde-Segot, 2015). When different disciplines come together to talk about their frameworks and evidence relating to finance, they help open a much wider dialogue and debate process, where alternative methods and perspectives engage with one another (Tett, 2021).

The finance discipline has strayed away from the wide toolkits and methods available to social scientists like interviews, case studies and surveys (Brooks et al., 2019). Such dialogues should unravel commonalities and differences of understanding, new potential sources of evidence and perspectives on finance, and unleash the voices of the marginalised, which have hitherto been ignored. The jargon that finance has developed without engaging with its meaning and relevance can be questioned through such encounters, helping everyone get to the bottom of the truth.

The advantage of field studies is that they help broaden the outlook of the researcher at a very early stage in their career. Depending on which field they choose to study, they will be able to see the wide range of factors which influence actions, consequences, networks and behaviours relating to finance. If they choose to go to foreign countries, they will directly experience the diversity of customs and traditions around money and see a variety of factors which influence enterprise and risk-taking. Without knowing local languages and customs, they can mis-interpret or mis-represent the truth, so care needs to be exercised. The training required prior to field research ought to incorporate case studies and examples from diverse fields like geography or cultural political economy to help them understand the varying environments and impacts of finance in different parts of the world. Conducting good field studies requires a range of skills, and their writing and evaluation is also much more challenging than quantitative research. Given their virtual extinction from finance, it is important that even descriptive studies of finance practice (without explicit theories and frameworks, which often are also European or American) are allowed and published to enrich global understanding of the vast real-world diversity of its practice.

Students of accounting and finance would also need to be trained in qualitative research methods. Examples of these would include field observation, communication, interview and survey techniques, ethical dilemmas, triangulation of evidence, and the nuances of obtaining permission and access in different contexts and regions. Where they are primarily brought up in a neo-liberal, capitalist and materialist society, the criticality of discussing cultural diversity, and the variety of worldviews and perspectives about freedom, happiness, religion and belief and community need to be taught and discussed.

Students need to understand the depth of diversity in practice and allow different cultures and communities to speak their own truths without judgement bias by the researcher. When they have not experienced strong family and community bonds, and a deeper role of faith in everyday life, they may find such field studies alienating and disturbing even. This is why good quality prior training, including international travel and education, can be very helpful. Restricting research outputs to papers and journals is also a parochial practice, preventing depth and breadth of analysis – in so many disciplines, a research monograph is a must for promotion, but not so in finance. In fact, it would be seen as a disadvantage and waste of time. This has saturated and narrowed the disciplinary growth and critique.

With the rise of digital transactions and fin-tech, the importance of trust and relationships may not be easy to identify and may also be reduced through secure but distant money transfer mechanisms. The resulting externality and damage that this removal of the need for human trust creates is unknown. There may be repercussions from this which need to be observed and documented in terms of their impact on behaviours, families and social life. The political and economic climate for enterprise and jobs also needs to be carefully documented to help understand the comparative context in which finance operates. The environment in which local systems and structures of finance operate needs to be documented and understood before evidence is collected or analysed. This process can take time and may require a combination of primary and secondary research, including directly living in the field communities in the way anthropologists operate. An ability to speak local languages can be a significant advantage in building trusted relationships and collating reliable evidence.

Documenting and Mapping Finance Culture

Just as air and water have been taken for granted by finance, so are culture and trust. The concept of culture is virtually deleted. A culture of individualism and selfishness is assumed, encouraged and incentivised even. Trust is instead placed on contracts, transactions and markets, even to the extent that markets know best about where and what resources to allocate at what price. Many scholars are so obsessed by free market fundamentalism that social and environmental protections and inter-generational equity and fairness are also in their eyes best left to market mechanisms, rather than human judgement, culture or politics. There is a chaotic mix of ideology and science, and selective use of evidence to justify such prejudice.

Culture also varies from cities to towns and villages, and even within the same city, where there may be a significant diversity of population. It takes time and patience to understand culture, and document it on its own terms (Thomas & Inkson, 2017). Anthropologists undergo a lot of training to do this. In addition, they can spend years learning the local languages and customs, which help increase the depth and sophistication of their research and analyses. It is telling that one of the most pioneering and widely cited books in finance in the last decade has been written by an anthropologist who was not trained in economics or finance – David Graeber (2014).

To map finance culture, scholars and scientists can recruit anthropologists to conduct such detailed fieldwork given their training and supervise them to ensure that the finance research objectives are also fulfilled. Meyer (2016) explains through case studies how important and challenging it can be to decode culture across business borders. The English language can mislead people into thinking that methods of persuasion or trust-building are the same across cultures who speak English, but this is rarely true. Whilst American culture can be performative and time-conscious, Brazilian or Indian culture would prefer longer lunches and time devoted to relationship-building, without any specific agenda or mission.

Scholars who themselves come from diverse cultural backgrounds, may already know the languages and customs of their subjects, and have significant social and trust capital to undertake a deep study of finance. Migrants often have this inter-cultural advantage of risk and assimilation. The cultural diversity of finance scholars should be seen as an asset in such circumstances, and not avoided or neutralised by superficial ideas of technical objectivity, meritocracy and colour-blindness.

Our modern-day obsession with theory has also narrowed and colonised many disciplines, as particular 'white' theorists like Marx, Foucault, Giddens, Latour or Derrida keep getting cited again and again. This makes disciplines like Sociology, which ought to be the epitome of diversity and inclusion, very difficult to decolonise, as PhD students have to be trained using one of these acceptable philosophers and theoreticians (Meghji, 2021). To open up disciplines to diversity, initially it ought to be acceptable for scholars to conduct descriptive research about different cultures and belief systems and use this evidence base to engage with pluralities of finance. If instead, we keep emphasizing the requirement of explicit often western theories as the only benchmarks for new insights, we will not be able to break the deep cultural silos in our knowledge systems.

The inter-mingling of faith and culture is complex and nuanced, and not easy to discern for students of no faith or those with little experience of old cultures and traditions. However, its understanding and analysis is crucial for a qualitative study of finance customs and practices. Even though Erin Meyer is a world authority on culture and its influence on business, she avoids discussing faith and belief altogether in her famous book (Meyer, 2016). In this sense, her 'scientific' prejudice prevents her from seeing the entirety of cultures and influences, avoiding a very significant component. In terms of self-regulation of conduct and behaviour, faith can be an important silent force, shaping honourable conduct. At times, faith can create close bonds of trust and community, but also be exclusive of outsiders. Members of faith communities may trust one another too much and lose from any finance partnerships, thereby reducing trustworthiness in the community.

It is possible that at very high levels of financial decision-making, trust has been built over generations (see e.g. Shah, 2022), and the importance of honour and reputation is such that very large financial transactions are undertaken by a handshake. The savings in terms of legal costs, imperfect contracts and low likelihood of dispute can be very significant for economic efficiency and development. Furthermore, local methods of dispute resolution can be very powerful as they are culture-sensitive and much less costly. Much more research is needed on how finance disputes are reserved globally, and the diversity of these processes and methods.

Rituals, community gatherings and festivals can be the subliminal physical banks and reservoirs of trust capital. Here relationships are cultivated and reinforced on a routine basis. Indigenous cultures have unique strengths which can help transform modern understandings of economy (Fenelon & Alford, 2020; Poyser & Daugaard, 2023). These may seem outside the normal field of commerce or finance, yet can be very relevant to it. Even trusted knowledge and information can be shared in communities during mealtimes or at weddings, which can have a significant influence on commerce and enterprise. Risk can be managed much easily where there is good information, and an ability to swiftly respond to unforeseen events with the help of relationships and networks. Specific traditions and communities can be deep mutual reservoirs of trust, and when they specialise in finance, like the Jains or the Jews, these groups can develop knowledge and expertise which is deep and lasting, and ethical too.

Inter-cultural Trust: Embracing Human 'Biodiversity' in Finance

The profound monotheism and fundamentalist universalism of the modern social sciences means that there is deep resistance to inter-cultural dialogue and pluralism. The possibility that different cultures may have different understandings of truth, including finance, and society needs to find ways to bridge humanity in an increasingly global and inter-connected world should be sought. Superficial tolerance is not sustainable. We need to invest in mutual respect and understanding and accept different ways of working in business and finance.

Globalisation and travel have brought cultures closer together, yet their importance and the nuances of inter-cultural practices and understandings of finance are largely unresearched and suppressed. Researchers of cross-cultural dialogue show how stereotypes prevail, with serious consequences for failing business deals and implementation (Thomas & Inkson, 2017). There are ways to be more culturally aware, mindful and adaptable, but these require training and practice, and an acceptance of the profound cultural differences across the world. The rise of technology as an intermediary for communication can mean that there is even more misunderstanding as senior managers rarely meet in person.

Given the hegemonic power of the West, and the dominance of the English language globally, we have a serious challenge in cultivating respect and mutuality. If in addition, the financialised world is obsessed by measurement and currency, then culture and tolerance are ignored, misunderstood and often dropped by the wayside in the rush to make a deal and show the numbers. In fact, the combination of a quantitative financialised mindset with western hegemonic power can lead to a misunderstanding of 'foreign' cultures, arrogance, misrepresentation, and significant losses in productivity and efficiency as a result. Numbers and targets can be useful ways of ignoring and suppressing cultural differences, creating a common measurable narrative, even when it leads to low morale and stress among international workforces.

Given the criticality of trust, such instrumental leadership can breed mistrust, betraying the important relationships needed to make an international operation work. Performance and productivity require respect and motivation, otherwise talent will migrate, and a hollow shell remains after an acquisition or merger. As we have seen, there are plenty of examples of such devastating corporate failures, leading to losses of hundreds of millions of dollars from large deals. There is increasing research explaining the need for cultural intelligence and sensitivity, and models have been developed to improve co-operation across borders and time zones. However, these findings need to be applied, and leaders also need to be able to think beyond a euro-centric mindset, and the arrogance that often comes with it. Very different ways of thinking and operating will need to be merged in a way which does not compromise efficiency and productivity, and instead enhances mutuality and opens up new domains of growth for the international business.

Through inter-cultural training and dialogue, new domains of understanding in finance and plural theories can be developed which work side-by-side to enrich the science and cultivate a mindset which is not egocentric. We also need to discover new ways of framing finance away from the anthropocentric thinking which is so ingrained in Euro-centric leadership. This process would require dialogue, travel, patience and an investment in time and field visits to understand different contexts of businesses and their local realities and diversity. Investments will need to be made in inter-cultural trust and relationship building. It also means that marketing leaders would need to speak to finance leaders, and both of them need to learn about human rights and the urgency of abandoning arrogance and ignorance. Technology and mediated communications may not to be put aside for whole-person meetings and dialogues to grow trust and make the financial investment truly long-term and sustainable.

Elite Finance Networks of Expropriation

Deculturation disables us from seeing how in the real world, it is people and their cultural assumptions and behaviours which influence leadership, management and investment decisions and deals in finance – research on financial fraud processes exposes this well as we have already seen. If we were to rely on conspiracy theory, we might think that the real-world master's in finance actually want the academy and intellectuals to side-track and confuse society, actively wishing its ignorance and illiteracy. The elite 'gangs' can then continue their sophisticated pilfering under the cloud of free markets, competition, efficiency and skill. When things do go wrong, and on a large scale, they know the state will bail them out. They have successfully managed to use financial systems for their own private benefit, using money to make more money.

Whatever the motive, it seems politically convenient for finance academics to ignore culture and networks in finance. This can then remove research focus from the reality of the shady dealing that goes under big global brands and financial institutions like international banks and the Big 4 accounting firms. There is an active cognitive dissonance which is completely unjustifiable given the predicament of billions of people. There has been a political capture of business and science research by large corporations (Monbiot, 2000), undermining our exposure of truth, fairness and injustice.

Knowledge factories (like universities) and research institutions have the resources to dig deep and spend time analysing truth and wisdom. If instead they become trapped in certain ideologies, and compete for excellence from within these frameworks, they get captured and remain trapped in their pursuit of colonial versions of truth (Bhambra, Gebrial & Nişancıoğlu, 2018). Politically, they become incapable of raising any deep critiques of powerful financial institutions, markets or leaders and influencers. Instead, they legitimate bad behaviour, such as maximising profits at any cost, or focusing on wealth creation, without using their scientific training to see the wider social and environmental implications of such conduct. The significant power and influence of their truth claims is prevented from any reflexivity precisely because of their refusal to admit this as editors of top finance journals, or deans of elite business schools. The knowledge network of finance has become partial and elitist in the last fifty years, without admitting to it from within or engaging with its critics at an intellectual level.

The environment of finance is dominated by the activities of large multinational financial institutions, global fund managers and investors, networks of professional firms of lawyers, accountants and tax avoidance experts (Empson, 2017), and traders in financial and currency markets who facilitate large financial flows. Whole countries like Britain, have become 'Butlers to the World' (Bullough, 2023), hosting and enabling global networks of financial expropriation, yet there is no mention of this in the finance classroom. Whilst the total amounts are very large, in the billions and trillions, the actual number of people involved in the transactions and movements of money is relatively small. The City of London Square Mile in Britain is one of the highest concentrations of financial power in the world. Geography also influences economic might (Kaiser, 2018).

Research shows that they cooperate and closely work with one another, and often the actual pensioner or investor is very remote from the process of decision making and asset allocation (Brooks, 2018; Lewis, 2010; Prins, 2014). Hoang (2022) shows through meticulous interviews how spiderweb capitalism operates through shadow networks of trust – yes even deceit requires professionals to collude and cooperate. Furthermore, while these networks play a crucial role in shaping the environment of finance, they are hardly mentioned in the theories or textbooks, and thereby assumed to be irrelevant or unworthy of study. Bankers and their networks can be critical oxygen providers to needy organisations, and also rain makers in terms of facilitating large complex mergers, acquisitions or transactions like government bond issuance and public financial management (Mazzucato & Collington, 2024).

Networks and relationships shape the financial culture of economic practice (MacKenzie, 2005), and where they are between powerful elites, they can have significant influence on many aspects of public life, including laws, regulations and social or environmental responsibility and accountability. There is absolute silence on the existence or importance of these in finance textbooks – eminent investigative journalists show how thieves and crooks are the real rulers of the finance world (see e.g. Brooks, 2018; Bullough, 2018; Lewis, 2011; Lewis, 2014). If the science of finance ignores this power and influence, or the cultural factors and incentives which directly impact market prices, interest rates, exchange rates and investment allocations, then it is a significant failure of knowledge. This deliberate illiteracy actively disempowers experts to ask critical questions and probe the real and lasting influences on finance practices. For leaders and practitioners of high finance, the learning of the ropes happens on the field, in clubs, bars and private gatherings, and this process too can be highly selective and partial. The discussions are not recorded on any computer platforms or voice machines, but they are often very powerful and significant (Lewis, 1989; Lewis, 2010; Lewis, 2011).

The nature of the mutual relationships between different finance leaders and experts, and the potential for conflicts of interest, given that they are often managing other peoples' money, is significant. States and governments often get looted and exploited by such professional collusion which is in the private interest. It can be highly convenient for the academy to ignore such practices, as to actively research and challenge them would be to discourage the consulting fees and kudos they could earn from elite endorsements and sponsorships. The capture of finance knowledge can itself be a function of the abuse of political power and economic discrimination, and can exacerbate these inequalities over time. Tax avoidance is a classic example of this behaviour (Brooks, 2014; Murphy, 2015), where corporations are able to choose the taxes they pay and the locations where they pay them with their access to legal and accounting experts, something which most ordinary people would be unable to accomplish even if they wanted to. Finance science encourages tax avoidance, without having any debate or discussion on the implications for society of such systemic behaviour – deliberate cognitive fences are erected and policed.

Nature's Wisdom

Nature seems innocent to collusion, deceit and elite power or control – indigenous cultures have known and respected this (Williams, 2012). That is why it has never charged for air or water, and the sun shines for free 24 hours a day, nourishing the planet with energy and vitality. In truth it has a monopoly over these items and knows that we humans cannot survive without oxygen, water or food, which come only from its generosity and selflessness. Nature's own 'systems of knowledge and understanding' have been nurtured over millions of years, and built through evolution and adaptation. In terms of equality, it does not even know how to discriminate as to who gets air or water or the benefits of the sun and its warmth. Its wisdom lies in its actions and is beyond words or language. However, in finance, we do not even acknowledge this, let alone celebrate it or be thankful.

Species have given birth, experienced death and extinction or evolved and adapted over time to changing climates and needs. However, man (or particular types of men from specific cultures) has somehow managed to use their own knowledge systems to exploit and expropriate nature and forget to maintain or even replenish its interdependence. Through technology, man has learnt to overpower and control the environment and at times even overwhelm it, for the pursuit of materialistic human welfare. The profound spiritual wisdom and intelligence of animals and our ecosystem have been dismissed, denied or suppressed by science and modernity, leading to a profound irreversible moral, animal and species catastrophe.

In many cultures, cosmology, seasons and astrology influence trade and financial decision-making (Armstrong, 2006; Pattanaik, 2015; Sacks, 2010, 2003; Dalrymple, 2024). The positions of the planets, the days and times when big decisions are made, or new account books opened, can affect risk-taking behaviour and perceived outcomes. I have seen many times street hawkers in India thanking God for their first morning transaction, and even starting the day with prayers. Here there is an acceptance of the significant powers of the cosmos, and a respect for wider forces and influences in business success than simply one's own efforts and outcomes. This practice also breeds humility and calmness, and avoids rash decision-making. In finance research, cosmology is completely ignored and seen as superstitious and unscientific.

The accumulation and concentration of finance, with its emphasis on material consumption, fossil fuels and industrialised killing of soil and animals, has been at the front line of the attack on nature (Monbiot, 2017; Whyte, 2020). Collusion between experts, and incentives to profit and expropriate natural resources, including the chemical waste of fossil fuel refining, has led to devastating ecological harm. To reform our planet and reinvigorate it with clean air, water and spiritual harmony, we have no choice but to examine in detail the knowledge, networks and technologies used by finance to overwhelm the environment. Religions and traditions which have long called for balance and protection of animals and nature ought to be revived and celebrated even, to help us reform our habits, behaviours and technologies. The very ideology which defines our sense of meaning and purpose in life ought to be of central interest to finance.

The theories of finance which encourage mass manufacturing and reckless consumption, or a separation between man and animals, or the active attempt to reap from natural resources without replenishing them, ought to be re-examined in the light of our urgent need to protect the planet. They can no longer be ignored from the curriculum of finance research and education or celebrated by it given our modern crises. If such ideologies are deeply buried inside the unstated assumptions and the abstract equations, it is our job to resurface these moral presumptions, debate and question them given the evidence of the damaging consequences of financial markets and institutions.

Knowledge and its influence are rarely visible to the naked eye. Nature's wisdom is not stated in any universal written language, but cultures all over the world have in different ways and at different times tried to decipher this wisdom and live with a deep respect and sense of awe. They have often carved limits to human activity and consumption, and used prayer and meditation to cultivate active peace-building among humans, and between humans and other species. Very often these profound scientific and cultural introspections have been driven by the experience of human death and mortality, another fact which contemporary finance science is in denial of. Simple questions like 'If we are going to die, why were we ever born?' have led to a range of different moral traditions and cultures, none of which advocated mass consumption and wastefulness, or industrial scale oil exploration or animal slaughter. In the past, death was common and happened at a younger age, disrupting whole families, making them even more vulnerable. This is still true today in many parts of the developing world. This experience makes them cultivate a belief and use it to develop resilience in hardship. Alternatively, when finance creates the myth of human immortality, it fuels an egregious culture of recklessness and irresponsibility to the planet and other life forms.

Social Harmony

For society to survive, it needs to be harmonious, peaceful and cohesive – desirable qualities which are not even discussed in finance research. If such qualities do not exist, humans need to cultivate them with patience, humility and perseverance. This must be a precondition of our systems of money and finance, and reinforced by them. Just as a variety of instruments and musicians need to come together and perform with skill and cooperation to produce harmony, financial markets and institutions also need to learn how to serve society in order to harmonise it and generate sweet music. Who is the conductor of the finance orchestra, and what are the different musicians who come together, to produce the harmony we seek? Who is the composer of the music and creator of the melody?

Unfortunately, the science of finance has detached itself so much from human society and cohesion, that it is unable to even think about harmony, let alone compose it, conduct it and produce it. This detachment is deep and conscious, regularly celebrated by the experts, who spend all their time fine-tuning their knowledge rather than consider its environment, impact and the extent to which it produces melodies or disrupts and destabilises. Financial hubs like Wall Street or the Docklands in London are concrete jungles with large towers of arrogance and hubris, and artificial in their construction, far removed from green spaces and grounded designs. They (experts, bankers and traders) never perform in any public concerts, choosing instead to hide behind their private wealth and mastery, in secret offshore jurisdictions, not caring about the impact of their knowledge on others, be they near or far.

Experts who are committed to harmony need to regularly meet to study and discuss the limitations of their science, the knowledge pollution it creates, and the externalities in terms of unemployment, poverty, farmer suicides, environmental exploitation and public health and well-being. They need to be sensitised to world suffering instead of becoming fenced off from it. Economics is by far the most powerful of social sciences (Raworth, 2018), and this power needs to be acknowledged and counter-vailed by deliberate acts of humility, soul-searching and invitations to debate and challenge the knowledge claims and research methods. It needs to take direct responsibility for the knowledge environment it shapes and influences and invite critique from other experts, whichever discipline they may come from. Listening is not the same as affirming or agreeing, but it opens the ability for different sources and types of evidence to come together and help clarify the wider social and natural environment influenced by economic models and institutions.

Economists need to remind themselves of the history and politics of money, its corruption by powerful interests, and how its movement and ownership shapes inequality, war and cultural demolition. The study and research in financial history needs to be urgently revived and taught. Otherwise, new generations of scholars will not learn from the experiences of older economic storms, booms and busts and may end up repeating the same mistakes. Politics should not be feigned but recognised and analysed to ensure financial power is not allowed to corrupt and exploit current and future generations. Critical political economists already do that – for example, the *Review of International Political Economy* publishes excellent articles on these themes. Technologies created and financed by money ought to be stripped to help unravel their costs and benefits at a macro level to decide whether or not they should be licenced to damage society and turn children into innocent addicts of social media. Finance should withdraw its power to fund organisations which disrupt our fragile harmony, and understand its deep responsibility and accountability to society.

Just as an orchestra needs a variety of instruments, experts also need to come together from a variety of disciplines to understand and interpret the social and environmental implications of finance customs, practices and institutions. Medical doctors who help drug addicts or those dependent on opioids and pain killers, should be able to express their understanding of what is killing their patients, and how medicine fails to prevent it. Anthropologists and sociologists can collate evidence from the ground about the ways in which the presence or absence of finance is transforming our social fabric.

Psychologists can bring to the table the behavioural transformations that they see in their patients, and marriage counsellors can explain firsthand what is happening to the modern family. They should be permitted to share their findings on the deep links between personal debt and mental health, and how this corrodes whole families and communities. Criminologists can discuss their findings on white collar crime, and the role of money laundering in facilitating international expropriation and wealth extraction. The results of these encounters may not immediately produce music, but it would start a rehearsal process which can ultimately lead to a public concert, where human knowledge systems and instruments come to perform together to help shape social and ecological harmony.

Planet earth knows how to help produce beauty and cooperation, whilst maintaining silence and a state of constant meditation. We can learn from these principles and values and be reflexive about our thinking and impacts, by having an openness to listen and learn from everyone, and to reflect at a deeper level about how science is transforming society for both good and bad.

Cultivating Plurality in Finance

Cultural diversity is key to widening the orchestra and embracing a truly global diaspora of sound and belief. The denial of this diversity in finance can only be rectified by the collation of case studies and evidence from different parts of the world about ways in which money influences and is influenced by a variety of social customs and cultural practices. Ignoring this diversity cannot produce the planetary harmony we seek. There will be commonalities and differences in the sounds and rhythms, and opportunities to learn and grow through communication and questioning. Often it is only when we encounter very different cultures that we come to understand fundamental assumptions and values of our own.

When we dig deep into different cultures, we will unravel the depth and breadth by which the universalism of finance science has tried to ignore and suppress human diversity. This understanding is crucial to its reform – we cannot build harmony by suppressing or denying difference, or creating currencies and institutions which ignore social and cultural traditions and suppress or disrupt them for short-term gains. These inter-cultural dialogues can enrich our knowledge and understanding, taking it to levels we did not even know we could reach. The opposite can also be true – the more insular and parochial our cultural hubris, the more likely it is that we dig a deeper and deeper hole for ourselves and instead of reforming society, we end up harming it irreversibly.

When we engage in such dialogue, we may find our conventions of science such as rational argument and critique to be limiting. Different cultures have their own methods of knowing and narrating, and customs and practices which reinforce their values and morality. They also have their own languages which cannot all be translated into English without losing the nuances and meanings. This means that such dialogues will require patience and perseverance, travel and observation, respect and tolerance. Even people who may look backward or indigenous, living remotely in the forests, and those who have in the past been seen as uncivilised, will need to be respected and listened to, as they may hold secret keys for a finance respectful of nature and forest.

The universalist approach to finance has sub-consciously removed itself from inter-cultural evaluation and critique and become much poorer as a result. When we admit this pluralism to finance, we open it to much deeper analysis and investigation then is done to date. This can help the world to really get to the bottom of the truths about the vast experience and memory that underlies human transactions and exchange. It can reveal layers of assumptions and presumptions that we never knew we were making, and open interdependencies and connections which we would never have thought to influence finance practices. This depth of understanding is urgently needed given the evidence of the significant power, inequality and disarray caused by finance knowledge.

One of the keys to this dialogue is the criticality and centrality of morality to a vast range of faiths and cultures all over the world, which is the foundation of their social and public life. As Finance has detached its science from morality, it needs to unlearn and reground itself, transforming its language, equations and institutions, and such cultural engagement will help significantly in doing so. By their nature, communities of people which are based on faith and principled living, have cultivated long traditions of knowledge and wisdom about ethical behaviour and its importance. Not only do they shape and encourage private conscience and reflexivity, but they also have a deep social conscience where the behaviours and actions of whole groups of people is regularly questioned and cajoled towards responsibility and accountability. This makes finance a servant of morality, and actions like charity and philanthropy, practical ways in containing greed, accumulation and inequality.

Cultures speak in different languages and hold different beliefs. Hitherto, the world of finance has seen this as a nuisance and a handicap, trying to universalise knowledge, calculations, equations and institutions. This has led to the growth in globalisation, financialisation and the capture of national laws and regulations by powerful elites and expert networks. It has also meant that people have lost control of money and debt, and have become overwhelmed by it instead of feeling supported and in control of this elixir of economics. This level of global cultural diversity is consistent with the biodiversity of our planet, and finance needs to discover ways of respecting and working with this diversity instead of overpowering it and attempting to standardise society. The more that systems of money and finance resonate with local cultures and belief systems, the more likely it is that society will be at peace and contented, and this will also have positive benefits for the natural environment.

Pluralism in finance cannot be cultivated overnight. It requires research on the vast diversity of finance customs and practices around the world, and the different ways in which they each convey principles of sustainability and equality. Case studies of small and large businesses, and the varieties of public and social enterprises which help shape trust and relationships need to be mapped out, to illustrate this economic diversity. Different belief systems and practices related to money also need research and analysis to help inform economic policies. The evidence will show that instead of developing new technocratic and autocratic solutions to climate change such as net zero emissions, working with indigenous cultures and knowledge systems is likely to be much more effective in the long run. As an example, faith communities already have large networks of knowledge sharing and dissemination, and these are trusted. Through these groups, the culture and behaviour change required for sustainable living can be transmitted much more efficiently and effectively. The outcomes of this engagement are likely to be longer term and consistent over time.

A practical way of embracing plurality in finance wisdom is to move academic workshops and gatherings to different places where the experiences of finance are raw and natural. At present, most of these conferences are held either in hotels or universities, with very little variation in the location. A hotel is a place where strangers are passing through every day – there is no human settlement or permanence. Conference venues could instead be an outdoor retreat centre for a workshop on environmental responsibility; a temple or mosque for a discussion on ethical and spiritual finance; a community centre or social hub for an exploration of how finance impacts marginal communities or people; a multi-faith or multi-cultural museum for opening shared and respectful dialogues on pluralism in finance, and how it can help cultivate inclusion and harmonious financial institutions and markets. In such spaces, feelings and emotions are allowed to surface, and the artificiality and commercial nature of hotels, and often universities too, is bypassed and cooperation and dialogue are encouraged.

Owner-managed Enterprise and Financial Reflexivity

In contemporary finance science and education, the universalist approach is obsessed by big business and standardisation, and assumes without explicitly stating it, that the same theory is applicable across all sizes of business and all products and services. This is very far from the truth, and also ignores the diversity of ways of doing business and leading and managing them. There is little discussion about access to finance, and an assumption that finance is always available for good businesses irrespective of size, reputation or networks.

In this theoretical world, floods of money are available, and growth at any cost is encouraged to maximise returns to investors (Stiglitz, 2019). The possibility that finance could flood an organisation and drown its productivity and efficiency is rarely considered, even when it happens often and with devastating consequences for large corporations and financial institutions. The length of personal experience in financial management, or even the quality of leadership is irrelevant in this theoretical dream world, when we know from history that this is very far from the truth. For large businesses, poor leadership can drive well-known companies to the wall in a very short time, destroying jobs, skills and reputations with them. It is so important that the climate for enterprise is diverse and inclusive, and allows small businesses to grow and flourish organically.

People work hard when they have incentives to do so, and the opportunities to realise their ambitions and dreams. Small businesses are critical to the life blood of most countries all over the world, providing very important goods and services that are locally needed and consumed. Their advantage is versatility and adaptability, and they often possess a sense of contentment and patience rather than greed and arrogance. They know from direct experience that if a customer is unhappy, they will not come back, and they want to please their customers so that they keep coming back. Relationships are often personal and they matter – which in turn leads to social cohesion and mutual respect.

All too often today, big businesses have become global, standardised and transactional, and have little or no relationship with the customer or even the suppliers or lenders. They are increasingly materialistic and selfish, and grow their power and size so that they can build monopolies and reduce choice for the customers. Finance science has very little to say about such hubris, and has actually encouraged growth and profit maximisation at the expense of social responsibility and cohesion. How can this ever be sustainable? Also, large businesses are not agile or adaptable, and often through branding and marketing try to 'standardise' the customer rather than engage with their diversity. Leadership, a subject which has attracted nearly 75,000 books and authors, has been banished from finance training altogether. There are hardly any books on good leadership in finance and what it looks like. The theoretical presumption is that leadership in finance is irrelevant to the science – markets will decide between good and bad leadership!

The ecosystem in any country for small businesses is critical to sustainable development. Small businesses need to have a climate where credit is available, trust and relationships are encouraged and not undermined, and market information, skills and training are also accessible. They bring with them a spirit of risk-taking, hard work and customer service which is rarely possible to cultivate among the employees of large or global companies. When things go wrong, they have to take the blame personally and have nowhere to hide. Entrepreneurs have direct skin in the game, and that spirit is very critical if we are to create a sustainable financial system.

Risk should be experienced, not just delegated or hedged, for society to develop and progress. This raw 'experience' of risk should be researched and debated, and ways in which financial systems allow societies to engage practically with risk debated. The cushioning of risk through insurance and hedging is not always desirable or perfect, and this is rarely analysed in a meaningful way. Through risk taking, entrepreneurs come to feel personally the opportunities and consequences, and this can be very empowering. Small businesses are bred by a diversity of skills, services and knowledge and often help spread and sustain this diversity through their imagination, creativity and spirit of enterprise. Competition is real and leads them to work harder and better to sustain themselves or grow. In a vast country like India, for example, the ecosystem for small businesses is huge and there are millions of one-man or one-woman enterprises which help feed whole families.

Small Business Finance and Accessibility

All small businesses struggle to obtain finance in the early days, as they have no track record or safety net to borrow from. They also learn very quickly how prudence and cash flow are critical to their survival, and extravagance and the easy availability of finance, detrimental to their success. In fact, they often generate finance organically, and are reluctant to borrow from outsiders who may become a burden when times are hard. Instead, they prefer to grow their own finance and invest within a manageable scale. However, where there is availability of micro-finance and startup support for small businesses, combined with coaching and mentoring for business management, the chances of sustainability are significantly improved.

Over the last century, in many parts of the world, big businesses have grown in size, market power and reach. Small businesses have increasingly been pushed aside, marginalised or wiped out from whole sectors such as tailoring (replaced by standardised manufactured clothes) or even restaurants, where brands, franchises and chains are taking over. This reduces the diversity of commerce and industry and increases society's dependence on standardised goods and services. The global growth of Amazon as a supplier of a wide range of products for all households has meant that small businesses have no choice but to be their supplier, paying a fat margin on every sale, and losing that direct relationship with the customer. Not only is Amazon a platform distributor, it has also become a market-maker, and uses the knowledge gained to promote its own products to gain higher margins. Small businesses feel more and more squeezed over time, and have no recourse for their complaints. Access to finance for owner-managed businesses should be an important topic in the finance curriculum. The wider social and ecological contribution of micro-businesses and their critical presence in rural communities, should not be ignored. Without them, rural villages would disappear altogether.

For the finance environment to encourage small enterprise, it is very important that the growth of monopolies is tightly controlled, policed and regulated. Big business, including big banks, should be severely punished if they are found to directly attack and undermine small businesses, and abuse their power and scale in order to do so. It is equally important that small businesses are encouraged and supported in their survival challenges, and not forced to go bankrupt every time they hit a temporary buffer – which is often what big banks are doing today to their small business customers. More generally, transactional cultures in business and leaders who act purely for short-term profits and fast-paced growth at any cost, should not be allowed to fester. The record of big business destroying whole towns and cities when they relocate, outsource or go bust is significant, and the burden always falls back on the state to pick up the pieces. When small businesses go bankrupt, their social and economic impact is much smaller and localised.

Every farmer knows about risk and directly experiences it – with climate, sun and rain being their biggest unpredictable factors, with soil quality and resilience not far behind. Similarly, the food prices they will fetch in the market are unpredictable, and if the food buyers are monopolies, they can squeeze the farmers so hard that they often go out of business. Just as small businesses are important to a sustainable finance ecosystem, so are small farmers to our sustainable land management and food supply. They have skin in the game to look after the soil, and cultivate crops which will nourish society with good health and well-being. Risk experience for all citizens is important, and should not be cushioned by a welfare state which discourages them to study or work. The experience of risk will strengthen citizens and help them to learn about effort and resilience, and manage their finances within their means, and not become wasteful or extravagant. Every finance class should have some discussion and debate about human experiences of risk, and the consequences of this, positive or negative.

Size and Scale of Knowledge *Framing*: Encouraging Financial Intimacy

When students are trained from the outset to think big and focus their knowledge on large global organisations and markets, they fail to see or understand the small and the local. They begin to take abstraction for granted, and see finance models as truisms rather than simplifications – the fall into the trap of the 'fallacy of misplaced concreteness' (Whitehead, 1979). So entrenched do they become in learning about multinational corporations and global financial markets, that they fail to see any potential wisdom or foresight among the near and dear. This is disempowering for students from diverse backgrounds.

Even when they shop from the local store, or buy at the market, they lack the imagination to think about accounting or finance at this micro level. At undergraduate level, they have little life experience, and are very easy to persuade, especially when they are birthed in a world of deep competition for quality jobs. They become obsessed with getting good grades and appeasing their professors than to question them or even engage with the deeper foundations of finance knowledge. This pedagogical approach is both impersonal and de-personalising, burying the experience they may have from family, community and tradition. The education is likely to make them unable to practically manage their own finances, let alone advising others about it.

If, instead, we started our teaching by talking about micro-politics, micro-finance, home economics or family attitudes to morality and belief about money and possessions, we could help them better understand their own assumptions and values (Shah, 2018). Open dialogues with other students will also help them discover the differences in experiences and perspectives varying students bring, and sometimes unlocking finance wisdoms which they did not even know they had. More importantly, it awakens their personal engagement with the importance of finance education and training, rather than simply learning it to get a job or build a career, in a transactional and functional manner. It empowers and engages learners from the very beginning.

In class, I often start by asking students to share their own experiences of finance, and a student once shared a story from Mauritania about his Bedouin uncle, who lives a nomadic life. It was such a unique and memorable story that the whole class was surprised to hear it, and the student even discovered a new confidence in finance which hitherto he had not expressed. Nomads, by definition, have little need for money, as they can rarely go to a forest to buy fruit, or a river to pay for bottled water. Yet he said his uncle was very strong, deeply spiritual, and majestic in his candour and composure. His was a life of the eternal moment, and when they left an oasis, it was as if they were never there – so light was their social and ecological footprint. This is the kind of 'raw' finance story which can really empower students about the nature and limits of money and become memorable too.

When our finance ecosystem values deeper and meaningful education and training, we can hope for a big boost to sustainable development in society. In such pedagogical approaches, the understanding and linkages start from a foundational level, rather than being superimposed much later (if at all) after all the deculturation has already happened. This can sometimes be too late or counterproductive, with students thinking that ethics knowledge is something to pass an exam with, rather than a theme which is critical to the whole of the professional career. With recent evidence of exam cheating by partners in top professional firms, we see how embedded and damaging such attitudes have become.

With size and scale, impersonality, anonymity and transactionalism can become norms without students even realising it – a subconsciously selfish culture is valorised. To students, it can mean that this is a dog-eat-dog world, and there are no ethics in finance, and all that matters is how much one can earn and what they can get away with. Any deeper level of reflexivity is discouraged and may even feel very uncomfortable, with no one to share one's concerns with. Evidence of this often comes out during interviews of whistleblowers who find themselves alienated and destroyed (Heffernan, 2011). This is true even when they are trying to really support an organisation by avoiding significant financial losses and excessive risk-taking. No one seems to want to hear or help them.

Growing the Thirst for Wisdom and Meaning

To combat our environmental crisis, we need to shape a thirst and hunger for learning and the urgency of embracing sustainable wisdom. This requires an active engagement with land, water and forests, with field trips where leaders facilitate deeper questioning and reflexivity. At present, deeper questions about life, meaning and purpose are avoided in a standardised, impersonal and utilitarian education system. However, this separation from the personal subjectivity of learning and growth and the inner spirit to learn and assimilate is unsustainable. In reforming finance, we have no choice but to awaken this deeper questioning at the earliest stage possible. This needs to be done for both scholars and students alike.

As we have seen, the present approach and language of finance science disables this completely, so to rebuild it will be hard and take time and patience. Baby steps can be taken easily through such field trips, which could also include temples and churches, places where prayer and reflection are woven into the architecture and rituals. This will create raw and deeper experiences about the human spirit, its direction and destiny, and how work, professions and productivity affect the soul. Over time it is likely to give people a deeper sense of purpose and meaning about their lives and what it is that makes them fulfilled and at peace. Such actions are also likely to improve mental and physical health and shape a deeper sense of confidence which cannot easily be shaken or displaced.

When learners experience this wholeness, their approach to nature is bound to change and is likely to be deeper and more long-lasting than any external rule, law or principle. They will start asking critical question of their finance models and theories, when they see the disconnect with nature and society. When finance practitioners and leaders come from this spirit, they are less likely to want to be greedy or selfish or to acquire and possess for the sake of it. It is possible that they will set aside some time every week to read and reflect, instead of just working and running their lives materially. Experts and practitioners are more likely to ask questions and seek solutions which have a longer-term orientation and operate in a win-win way where trust is nourished rather than depleted. Leaders' lives and actions will then be an example for others given the kindness and selflessness they see – sustainable approaches to finance will ripple out. At present, this is rare to see among finance practitioners, and change is urgently needed.

In many parts of the world, the finance classroom is extremely diverse, especially in globally renown Universities which attract international students. Many of these students are going to be future finance leaders and policy makers. By avoiding the engagement with this diversity, a significant opportunity is lost. Sub-consciously the message is that a student's own understanding and experience of finance is irrelevant. They may come from family businesses or entrepreneurial cultures – in fact, that is why they are in class as they can afford the international fees. The bank of knowledge and experience they have can become a resource for finance discussion and a dialogue on the variety of its perspectives and practices. This opportunity should be seized positively and pro-actively, and the responsibility that comes from educating future elites who will go on to shape society and nature taken seriously.

Chapter Summary

We have examined the ecosystem of finance knowledge as it is key to shaping thought and behaviour. The modern-day exclusion of morality and culture from this has become a key source of our Anthropocene, given the significant power and authority accumulated by financial institutions and their leaders. The abject denial of the responsibility and accountability that come from this power has become a chainsaw on current living systems and present and future generations. If we are to reform finance, we need to get to the roots of this displacement, and understand the limits of laws and regulations in transforming human conduct and behaviour.

We discovered that not only has finance excluded and denied the important role of culture in human affairs and public policy, it has used science to authorise a mythic counter-culture which sees humans as utilitarian consuming actors, driven by selfish material goals. Finance has been altogether de-cultured and removed purpose and meaning from society and its practitioners. The academy has woven irresponsibility and un-accountability deep into the fabric of personal life, and incentivised it as the right way to live for economists and households too. The power accumulated from such a worldview has been disguised within jargon and equations, and denied through knowledge silos and specialisation. Whole markets and institutions have been designed to encourage profit maximisation and wealth accumulation at the expense of society and nature, yet this is not even acknowledged by the hard-core economists. Evidence from behavioural research shows that it is rare for humans anywhere in the world to behave in this way, and material rationality is overcome by emotions, wants and desires.

To transform finance knowledge, we need to understand this deculturation, and play an active role in re-culturation, by re-examining the basics of trust and relationships between humans and nature, and among one another. Academics need to uphold and celebrate public values, and practice eco-consciousness. The separation between research and teaching is fundamentally unsustainable. Pedagogy and reflexivity are critical to the transformation of finance knowledge and practice. We need to enable pluralism and diversity in our science, research and teaching, and use this to challenge the universalist assumptions and biases of modern finance knowledge. This change will have to start from the classroom in our methods of training, where students are encouraged to bring their own stories and experiences in finance, and engage with their personal values and ambitions. A new way of recalling the roots of trust and relationships needs to be practiced, and money and materiality temporarily set aside in helping learners discover their purpose and meaning in life. Research has shown that materialistic behaviour confuses our priorities and cultivates insecurity and unhappiness.

There is a significant biodiversity of finance wisdom that will be uncovered once we explore more deeply the profound linkages between finance and culture. Solutions and techniques which we never thought relevant would emerge through deeper inter-cultural dialogues, and ways in which communities build financial resilience unearthed. The role of trust and relationships in finance will be reignited rather than assumed away or alienated by law and contracts. Sustainability will be seen as woven into cultural behaviours and norms, and to transform finance, these behaviours will need to be understood and acknowledged as being a part of the problem. A richer understanding of the nature and limits of money will become apparent, helping shape different models and institutions to build long-term harmony between man and nature.

This engagement and reflection may appear discomforting at first, especially for those people who have never been encouraged to do so. It can be done through various methods like field trips to natural spaces, or class discussions and workshops, including sessions on mindfulness or guided meditation. The location and environment of expert gatherings and conferences need to change – forests or nature woods, rural villages, community centres, cultural hubs, could all be used to provoke a different dialogue, one which provokes reflexivity instead of suppressing it. What will result is a deeper feeling of awareness and awakening, and an understanding of the need to develop one's own methods of questioning and reflection in the journey to becoming a finance practitioner and leader. Such approaches will help build a grounded finance knowledge ecosystem, and reduce its distance from deeper truths and purpose. These meditations need to be regular and continuous to help make finance harmonious with soul, society and the environment.

References

Aggarwal, R., and Goodell, J. W. (2014, 1 May). Culture, Institutions, and Financing Choices: How and Why Are They Related? *Research in International Business and Finance* 31: 101–111.

Armstrong, K. (2006). *The Great Transformation: The World in the Time of Buddha, Socrates, Confucius and Jeremiah*. USA: Atlantic Books.

Beliso-De Jesús, A. M., & Pierre, J. (2020). Special Section: Anthropology of White Supremacy. *American Anthropologist*, 122(1), 65–75.

Bhambra, G. K., Gebrial, D., and Nişancıoğlu, K. (eds) (2018). *Decolonising the University*, illustrated edition. London: Pluto Press.

Brooks, C., and Schopohl, L. (2018). Topics and Trends in Finance Research: What Is Published, Who Publishes It and What Gets Cited? *The British Accounting Review*, 50(6), 615–637.

Brooks, C., Fenton, E., Schopohl, L., and Walker, J. (2019). Why Does Research in Finance Have so Little Impact? *Critical Perspectives on Accounting* 58, 24–52.

Brooks, R. (2014). *The Great Tax Robbery*. One World.

Brooks, R. (2018). *Bean Counters: The Triumph of the Accountants and How They Broke Capitalism*. London: Atlantic Books.

Bullough, O. (2018). *Moneyland: Why Thieves and Crooks Now Rule the World and How to Take It Back*. Profile Books.

Bullough, O. (2023). *Butler to the World: How Britain Became the Servant of Tycoons, Tax Dodgers, Kleptocrats and Criminals*. London: Profile Books.

Burrell, G., Hyman, M. R., Michaelson, C., Nelson, J. A., Taylor, S., and West, A. (2022). The Ethics and Politics of Academic Knowledge Production: Thoughts on the Future of Business Ethics. *Journal of Business Ethics* 180(3), 917–940.

Chen, J. Z. (2009). Material Flow and Circular Economy. *Systems Research and Behavioral Science* 26(2), 269–278.

Choat, S., Wolf, C., and O'Neill, S. (2024). Decolonising Economics and Politics Curricula in UK Universities. *Studies in Higher Education* 49(9), 1504–1518.

Clark, G. L., and Wójcik, D. (2007). *The Geography of Finance: Corporate Governance in the Global Marketplace*. New York, Oxford: Oxford University Press.

Dalrymple, W. (2024). *The Golden Road: How Ancient India Transformed the World*. Bloomsbury Publishing.

Deckard, S., Niblett, M., and Shapiro, S. (2024). *Tracking Capital: World-Systems, World-Ecology, World-Culture*. Albany: SUNY Press.

DePuy, W., Weger, J., Foster, K., Bonanno, A. M., Kumar, S., Lear, K., Basilio, R., and German, L. (2022, 1 June). Environmental Governance: Broadening Ontological Spaces for a More Liveable World. *Environment and Planning E: Nature and Space* 5(2), 947–975.

Dodd, N. (2014). *The Social Life of Money*. Princeton University Press.

Egan, M. (2021). Diversity, Inclusion, and the Opportunities for Accounting Research. *Social and Environmental Accountability Journal*, 41(3), 201–207.

Empson, L. (2017). *Leading Professionals: Power, Politics and Prima Donnas*. Oxford University Press.

Engelen, E., Ertürk, I., Froud, J., Johal, S., Leaver, A., Moran, M., & Williams, K. (2012). Misrule of Experts? The Financial Crisis as Elite Debacle. *Economy and Society*, 41(3), 360–382.

Fenelon, J., & Alford, J. (2020). Envisioning Indigenous Models for Social and Ecological Change in the Anthropocene. *Journal of World-Systems Research*, 26(2), 372–399.

Ferguson, K., & Petro, P. (2016). *After Capitalism: Horizons of Finance, Culture, and Citizenship*. Rutgers University Press.

George, S. (2013). *Whose Crisis, Whose Future?*Polity.

Ghio, A., McGuigan, N., Stewart, O. J., Tharapos, M., & Wood, L. I. (2023). Diversity, Equity, and Social Justice in Accounting Education. *Issues in Accounting Education*, 38(1), 1–5.

Goodell, J. W., Kumar, S., Lahmar, O., & Pandey, N. (2023). A Bibliometric Analysis of Cultural Finance. *International Review of Financial Analysis*, 85, 102442.

Graeber, D. (2014). *Debt: The First 5000 Years*, 2nd revised edition. Melville House Publishing.

Hampden-Turner, C., & Trompenaars, A. (1993). *The Seven Cultures of Capitalism: Value Systems for Creating Wealth in the United States, Japan, Germany, France, Britain, Sweden, and the Netherlands*. Currency Doubleday.

Hoang, K. K. (2022). *Spiderweb Capitalism: How Global Elites Exploit Frontier Markets*. Princeton University Press.

Heffernan, M. (2011). *Wilful Blindness: Why We Ignore the Obvious at our Peril*. Walker.

Jaffe, S. (2021). *Work Won't Love You Back: How Devotion to Our Jobs Keeps Us Exploited, Exhausted and Alone*. C Hurst & Co Publishers Ltd.

Kaiser, A. (2018). *The New Oxford Handbook of Economic Geography*. Oxford University Press.

Keucheyan, R. (2017). *Nature is a Battlefield: Towards a Political Ecology*. John Wiley & Sons.

Lagoarde-Segot, T. (2015). Diversifying Finance Research: From Financialization to Sustainability. *International Review of Financial Analysis*, 39, 1–6.

Langley, P., Anderson, B., Ash, J., & Gordon, R. (2019). Indebted Life and Money Culture: Payday Lending in the United Kingdom. *Economy and Society*, 48(1), 30–51.

Lewis, M. (2011). *Boomerang: The Biggest Bust*. Penguin Books.

Lewis, M. (2014). *Flash Boys: Cracking the Money Code*. Penguin.

Lewis, M. (1989). *Liar's Poker: Rising through the Wreckage on Wall Street*. London, New York: W. W. Norton.

Lewis, M. (2011). *The Money Culture*. London, New York: Norton.

Lewis, M. (2010). *The Big Short: Inside the Doomsday Machine*. London, New York: Allen Lane.

Mackenzie, D. (2006). *An Engine, Not a Camera: How Financial Models Shape Markets*. MIT Press.

MacKenzie, D. (2005). Opening the Black Boxes of Global Finance. *Review of International Political Economy*, 12(4), 555–576.

MacKenzie, D.. (2011, May). The Credit Crisis as a Problem in the Sociology of Knowledge. *American Journal of Sociology*, 116(6), 1778–1841.

Mazzucato, M., & Collington, R. (2024). *The Big Con: How the Consulting Industry Weakens our Businesses, Infantilizes our Governments and Warps our Economies*. Penguin.

Meghji, A. (2021). *Decolonizing Sociology: An Introduction*. Polity.

Meyer, E. (2016). *The Culture Map: Decoding How People Think, Lead, and Get Things Done Across Cultures*. PublicAffairs.

Monbiot, G. (2000). *The Corporate Takeover of Britain*. London: Macmillan.

Monbiot, G. (2017). *How Did We Get Into This Mess? Politics, Equality, Nature*. London: Verso.

Montgomerie, J. (2008). Bridging the Critical Divide: Global Finance, Financialisation and Contemporary Capitalism. *Contemporary Politics*, 14(3), 233–252.

Muniesa, F. (2024). *Paranoid Finance*. Polity.

Muradoglu, G., & Harvey, N. (2012). Behavioural Finance: The Role of Psychological Factors in Financial Decisions. *Review of Behavioral Finance*, 4(2), 68–80.

Murau, S., & Pforr, T. (2020). What is Money in a Critical Macro-Finance Framework? *Finance and Society*, 6(1), 56–66.

Murphy, R. (2015). *The Joy of Tax*. Transworld Publishers.

Ortiz, H. (2017). A Political Anthropology of Finance: Profits, States, and Cultures in Cross-Border Investment in Shanghai. *HAU Journal of Ethnographic Theory*, 7(3), 325–345.

Pabrai, M. (2007). *The Dhandho Investor: The Low-Risk Value Method to High Returns*. Wiley.

Paik, P. Y., & Wiesner-Hanks, M. (2013). *Debt: Ethics, the Environment, and the Economy: Vol. 6*. Indiana University Press.

Pattanaik, D. (2015). *Business Sutra: A Very Indian Approach to Management*. Aleph Book Company.

Poyser, A., & Daugaard, D. (2023). Indigenous Sustainable Finance as a Research Field: A Systematic Literature Review on Indigenising ESG, Sustainability and Indigenous Community Practices. *Accounting and Finance (Parkville)*, 63(1), 47–76.

Prahlad, C. K. (2019). *The Fortune at The Bottom of The Pyramid*. Pearson Education.

Pretty, J. N. (2002). *Agri-Culture: Reconnecting People, Land and Nature*. London: Earthscan.

Prins, N. (2014). *All the Presidents' Bankers: The Hidden Alliances That Drive American Power*. Hachette UK.

Raworth, K. (2018). *Doughnut Economics: The Must-Read Book That Redefines Economics for a World in Crisis*. Random House Business.

Renner, A., Daly, H., & Mayumi, K. (2021). The Dual Nature of Money: Why Monetary Systems Matter for Equitable Bioeconomy. *Environmental Economics and Policy Studies*, 23(4), 749–760.

Reurink, A. (2018). Financial Fraud: A Literature Review. *Journal of Economic Surveys*, 32(5), 1292–1325.

Reuter, C. H. J. (2011). A Survey of 'Culture and Finance'. *Finance*, 32(1), 75–152.

Rifkin, J. (2001). *The Age of Access: The New Culture of Hypercapitalism, Where All of Life is a Paid-For Experience*. Jeremy P. Tarcher.

Sacks, J. (2010). *The Persistence of Faith: Religion, Morality and Society in a Secular Age (the BBC Reith Lectures)*. Continuum Compact Series.

Sacks, J. (2003). *The Dignity of Difference: How to Avoid the Clash of Civilisations*. Continuum Books.

Sandel, M. J. (2013). *What Money Can't Buy: The Moral Limits of Markets*. Penguin.

Schulz, J., Bahrami-Rad, D., Beauchamp, J., & Henrich, J. (2018). *The Origins of WEIRD Psychology*. https://ssrn.com/abstract=3201031

Shah, A. (2018). *Reinventing Accounting and Finance Education: For a Caring, Inclusive and Sustainable Planet*. Routledge.

Shah, A. K. (2022a). *Inclusive and Sustainable Finance: Leadership, Ethics and Culture*. London: Routledge. doi:10.4324/9781003164746

Shah, A. K. (2022b). Reform Lessons from Investigative Journalism. Review Essay of 'Beancounters' by Richard Brooks. *The British Accounting Review*, 54(3), 101069.

Short, D. (2010). Cultural Genocide and Indigenous Peoples: A Sociological Approach. *The International Journal of Human Rights*, 14(6), 833–848.

Shrivastava, P., Ivanaj, S., & Persson, S. (2013). Transdisciplinary Study of Sustainable Enterprise. *Business Strategy and the Environment*, 22(4), 230–244.

Stein, M. (2011). *A Culture of Mania – A Psychoanalytic View of the Incubation of the 2008 Credit Crisis*. Organisation.

Stiglitz, J. E. (2019). *People, Power and Profits: Progressive Capitalism for an Age of Discontent*. Allen Lane.

Stiglitz, J. E. (2024). *The Road to Freedom: Economics and the Good Society*. Allen Lane.

Tett, G. (2021). *Anthro-Vision: How Anthropology Can Explain Business and Life*. Random House Business.

Thomas, D. C., & Inkson, K. (2017). *Cultural Intelligence: Building People Skills for the 21st Century: Surviving and Thriving in the Global Village*, 3rd edition. Berrett-Koehler Publishers.

Toledo, V. M. (2022). Agroecology and Spirituality: Reflections About an Unrecognized Link. *Agroecology and Sustainable Food Systems*, 46(4), 626–641.

Trompenaars, A., & Hampden-Turner, C. (2020). *Riding the Waves of Culture: Understanding Diversity in Global Business*, 4th edition. Nicholas Brealey Publishing.

Turner, A. (2015). *Between Debt and the Devil: Money, Credit, and Fixing Global Finance* (illustrated edition). Princeton University Press.

Valentinov, V. (2021). Sustainability in Classical Institutional Economics: A Systems Theory View. *Sustainable Production and Consumption*, 28, 1500–1507.

Whitehead, A. N. (1979). *Process and Reality*. Free Press.

Whyte, D. (2020). *Ecocide: Kill the Corporation before it Kills Us*. Manchester University Press.

Whyte, D., & Wiegratz, J. (eds) (2016). *Neoliberalism and the Moral Economy of Fraud*. Routledge.

Williams, J. (2012). The Impact of Climate Change on Indigenous People: The Implications for the Cultural, Spiritual, Economic and Legal Rights of Indigenous People. *The International Journal of Human Rights*, 16(4), 648–688.

Zingales, L. (2015). Presidential Address: Does Finance Benefit Society? *The Journal of Finance*, 70(4), 1327–1363.

Zuboff, P. S. (2019). *The Age of Surveillance Capitalism: The Fight for a Human Future at the New Frontier of Power: Barack Obama's Books of 2019*. Profile Books.

5   Inner Growth

Nature grows, and it has seasons, and all the time, living beings, including plants, insects, animals and humans, are born and die in its embrace. The cycle of birth and death is a part of the rhythms of nature, and for thousands of years, even man understood and accepted it, even though it was often painful and there were no pensions. In the Jain culture, it is believed that man is the most evolved of all species, with the highest levels of consciousness, and as a result has the elevated responsibility to protect other living beings and be a steward and trustee of nature. Five decades ago, we were warned of nature's 'Limits to Growth' and in particular, the systemic problems caused by a fossil fuel-dependent economy and the damage to public health and pollution resulting from it (Meadows et al., 1979). This report was supported by the United Nations and had global impact.

However, over the last hundred years, economics and finance have come to ignore this inter-dependent reality, and instead pursued an ambition of perennial growth without any limits. A dream-world of unending money and credit has been created, where material prosperity is privileged. Consciously and deliberately, human death and nature's entropy are being forgotten and denied. The mechanised killing of animals on a scale much larger than our human holocausts, has been routinised and justified as *efficient, productive and competitive* food agriculture and manufacturing. Their pain and cries have been siloed away in our factory farms and finance knowledge industries. Even oil extraction or commodity mining have become routinised as sources of wealth creation and necessary for human prosperity and growth. That they are direct attacks on tens of thousands of years of nature's conservation, or poison the air and water when they are extracted, is a mere externality to our economics. In finance, growth is described in anthropocentric material and financial terms, separating means from ends. In fact, the subconscious assumption is that the ends of growth justify any means towards achieving it.

At the same time, we have multiplied our human population, increased our urbanisation, and used industrialisation to create jobs and mass production all over the world. This has uprooted people from rural communities into cities and factories which force them into labour camps and insecure housing. The promised prosperity of economics has increased inequality, and led to displacement,

DOI: 10.4324/9781003534532-5

third world poverty and rising human health and mental crises. The externalities of growth have not been allowed to upset the equations of economics and finance, nor the incomes and rewards of their experts. In fact, even among a benchmark of social or physical scientists, finance and economics experts come out superior – such are the reward structures they have built for themselves.

Nature has ways to control population and species survival, and that is why it is rare to see excessive populations of wildlife anywhere in the world. Access to food and water limits populations of animals, and interdependence helps maintain a deeper balance if there is no interference from humans into the forests and wetlands available to wildlife. We can view the Anthropocene as nature's defence mechanism to correct the overwhelming population growth, arrogance and violence of the human species on the balance of our multi-billion-year-old ecosystem. From this perspective, it is OK for the human species to become extinct, as it has overgrown its shelf life and forgotten its duties and responsibilities to planet earth. After humans are gone, nature will renew itself and survive like it has always done. However, at present, all humans are paying the price of this exploitation, even when the systems, processes and institutions are designed and benefit a select few, mainly in the western world. There is deep ecological inequality (Armstrong, 2024).

Finance and economics have made growth a defining mantra and made material prosperity a primary focus. The disciplines have not allowed any doubt to creep in, and we still hear politicians all over the world scrambling for more and more growth. While social and environmental responsibility are attracting increasing attention, there is also a backlash, and an ESG spin factory, which is form overriding substance (Buller, 2022; Jäger & Dziwok, 2024; Macey, 2022). Even business schools all over the world have introduced courses in business ethics, but these sit uncomfortably with what is taught in economics and finance (Burrell et al., 2022). The primary institutions of finance, banks and financial markets, have been crafted to maximise growth and shaped by measures and incentives such as profits, share options and stock indices to remove all challenges to the overwhelming priority of economic prosperity (Foroohar, 2016; Ott, 2011; Soukup, 2021).

In this chapter, we explore the nature and limits of growth, and ways in which its measurement and obsession can actually restrict us from embracing true freedom and liberation. Entropy limits growth of all living beings, but is denied by compounding in finance. Corporations often become masters unto themselves, forgetting that growth is not always sustainable or worthy as size and complexity can be unmanageable. Even knowledge growth should aspire to embrace the limits of performativity and measurement and leaders should explore aesthetic and spiritual growth to embrace their own limitations and weaknesses. Organic growth can come from within, and be controlled by management who prioritise quality and service instead of endless profits and expansion.

Nature of Growth

If we allow finance and economic priorities to define growth, we limit ourselves from the endless possibilities of human ingenuity and peaceful, harmonious living. Given the unique human capacities for language and imagination, and the ability to create enough food and shelter, we can have infinite growth of our creative and spiritual natures, including our knowledge. Material growth limits our lives, breaks our marriages, and destroys our mental health as a result of addiction and insecurity. These 'externalities' of finance are never discussed in the curriculum, but real, lasting and highly damaging to personal well-being and social harmony (Marquis, 2024).

For humanity, real and sustainable growth is far beyond the material, and unless this is recognised, we will not build a peaceful, cohesive and responsible society, accountable to nature instead of being exploitative of it. This perspective will also help us embrace social and environmental responsibility, as we begin to see ourselves fundamentally as a part of nature rather than apart from it. In fact, we will shift our focus from our needs, desires and greed to one of duties and self-discipline, where freedom comes from overcoming the fear of death, or the obsession with possessiveness. Creativity and spiritual potentiality will be encouraged and seen as central to growth and cohesion. No longer will reason be separated from imagination.

The mindset of finance science needs to change, and for this, we need to reconnect finance to human morality, spirituality, imagination and duty. The current financial hubris we see both in the behaviours of finance leaders and markets and institutions stems from a very corrupt and unsustainable way of thinking about society and nature. In earlier chapters, we have elaborated on the need for a holistic theory and science of finance, which is plural and multi-disciplinary, and acknowledges the need for finance to be in the service of the planet, instead of its master.

Growth needs to be revisited from this plural and inclusive context. There is a large and expanding literature on de-growth (see e.g. Hickel, 1982). One of the first conclusions from this reflection is how limiting it is to allow money to overwhelm human life. Experts need to engage in deeper dialogues and debates about the fundamentals of growth, and how institutions and markets can be designed so as to encourage and incentivise humans to control and limit possessiveness. The deeper security which comes from self-discipline and not owning, wanting or desiring, and an acceptance of death as a reality and not just something that happens to other people, is critical to how de-growth (in a material sense) gets crafted into the heart of finance science. Case studies of entrepreneurs and financiers who have experienced wealth, and moved beyond it, can be analysed and shared widely to help increase and deepen reflexivity in finance science (see e.g. Astrachan et al., 2020, 2020; Bell et al., 2021; Bhatnagar et al., 2020).

So steeped is the contemporary finance academy in materiality and possessiveness as the only route to 'rational' happiness, that they may find this alternative analysis of growth very disturbing and dismiss it outright as fluff and impossible. It is likely that they have themselves become detached from imagination and spirit to such an extent that they cannot even see its potential, let alone experience it. What society and expert professions will need to do in such circumstances is to engineer an alternative approach to finance. They will need to engage with policymakers and professional bodies at the highest levels to help them see the potential of such a revised approach for sustainability to prevail. Leadership, a subject hitherto removed from finance textbooks, needs to come back in and made central to a new moral and responsible finance. The growth mindset of these leaders should make the opening chapters to such a curriculum.

Growth Beyond Money and Finance

For growth to be sustainable, every human being needs to understand the limits of money, not just intellectually but also experientially. Otherwise, growth will always be stunted and can even be severely damaging, as it spreads greedy and selfish behaviours in society. This is an area in which the discipline of finance has failed miserably, and continues to do so as it has tried to depersonalise finance even when it is deculturing it knowingly and actively.

The intellectual understanding of the limits of money can come by examining what money can and what it cannot do (Nesvetailova, 2012). An analysis of basic human needs like love, compassion, food, family, community, belonging, health and well-being and inner peace will quickly show where money spoils the equations of happiness and fulfilment. Research evidence can also show how surplus money ruins many of these basic needs, and instead of bringing satisfaction and a deeper sense of meaning, it shapes and creates more and more insecurity. Simple things like trust and relationships become coloured by money and confused by it. This research evidence is widely available from fields like psychology and behavioural science, and sociology and anthropology have plenty of case studies where cultures and communities often thrive with very little money. These findings should be taught and discussed in a finance classroom as they sit centrally within its theoretical framework. The analysis will show that if we make the science inter-disciplinary from the beginning, we can change attitudes to materialism and utilitarianism and promote sustainable living.

To provide experiences of life outside money, students would need to go into small markets, or farmer stores where they have direct dialogues with the producers of food or merchandise. Many small entrepreneurs value independence and freedom and are content with their profits – they have different goals than wealth creation – they are happy to provide a good product and service. Just as we have raw food, we need to increase student experience and engagement with 'raw' finance. Here there are few middlemen in the chain of production, and they are able to see and experience raw finance through narratives and conversation. What motivated them to go into farming, how do they earn a living, how much do they have to repay the sun, soil and the rain for the produce could be questions asked to farmers. Market traders could be asked about the risks and returns they make, and why they choose to trade in person than to take a job or trade in the stock market. What is it that gives them satisfaction from the small business? Visits to public institutions like schools and hospitals could help them see the varieties of public service, and the different motivations by which people choose to work here instead of the corporate world. They could be guided in understanding the efficiency of public provision of basic services like energy, water, road transport or even healthcare as compared to private provision.

Experiences are memorable and transformative. Equations and classrooms provide abstractions, and, if we are not sensitive, these abstractions become the reality for many students, who end up thinking that finance is a gamble or trade, rather than a living cultural practice. Abstractions can make them feel desensitised to feelings and emotions, and even heartless and more and more selfish. There would result deeper personal alienation alongside material prosperity, and this is deeply painful let alone unsustainable. Finance classrooms can easily 'convert' people into the religion of materialism without their permission, and with the authority of science. The wider footprint of this can make whole societies unsustainable.

Art and creativity are other ways of helping students experience the limits of money. Stories and narratives could be discussed in class about deeply financialised leaders having nervous breakdowns. There are many such true stories, but normally, false narratives are pedalled, and true ones denied. Paintings and plays depicting the nature and limits of money could be shown and debated in class, helping students imagine different futures for themselves. Pictures of different cultural and religious practices around money, and stories of nomadic communities, could help them see the variety of attitudes to finance as part of the larger canvas of humanity, rather than being ignorant or backward in any way.

Unless students can experience the limits of money through field trips, dialogues and narratives, they are going to get brainwashed into seeing materialism as the only goal in life. They also need to be permitted to share their own personal and family experiences with money for everyone to understand how varied these are, and to see that money cannot cure cancer, or replace a departed member of the family. Love and kindness can be selfless acts which are priceless, and their value should not be removed from class but reinstated into learning and education. This is how the reality of sustainable growth in finance can be transmitted to future generations. They need to see living examples of caring finance by visiting public hospitals or care homes.

Knowledge and expertise in finance catapults students and professionals to positions of power and influence. When this power is exercised irresponsibly and undemocratically, we will increase organisational and economic unsustainability. To shape a sustainable mindset, it is equally important that this arrogance and influence is discussed in class, and examples and case studies used to highlight hubris and its wider implications on jobs, households and society. Financial hubris overpowers animals and nature, given their inability to fight back, and the dangers of this ought to be exposed while the professional minds are being moulded. The earlier we can help students understand the wider impacts and implications of finance practice, good or bad, the more sensitised they will be to being concerned about the outcomes of their actions. Furthermore, if they understand the power and influence they are likely to command, and the ease with which hubris can set in, they will be more likely to use it responsibly.

Respecting Seasonality in Finance

Just as there is spring, summer, autumn and winter, all in one year, we need to find ways of embracing seasonality in finance. While spring and summer represent growth, autumn and winter lead to decay and renewal. This is not a denial of growth, but an acceptance of its seasonality. In finance, interest rates make a significant impact on the pricing of credit and are compounded as if there is no limit to how much lenders can make from borrowers. Loans are designed to deny death, and made immortal by financial markets and institutions, to serve their own interests. Seasonality is ignored, and endless borrowing is justified in so far as corporations can earn higher rates of return, irrespective of how these returns are earned. Borrowers can end up paying several multiples of the original amount, and still be in debt, and this is true today for many third world countries who are steeped in a perennial cycle of very costly and unaffordable interest obligations. Whole countries and societies are ransomed and blackmailed by finance. The equations of finance defy nature deliberately, thereby making it more difficult to incorporate nature into the calculations. We have a whole engine of growth for its own sake, promoted by politicians and corporations, with little regard to motive, purpose or consequences.

When growth is financed by perennial interest claims, and investors also expect constant surplus returns, we structure an economy of endless material extraction unless there are checks and balances relating to social and environmental equality. There is no choice but to generate more and more profits, or for states in debt to charge higher taxes, sell valuable assets and infrastructure, and deflate their currencies just to repay the interest on the loans. Whole economies and countries are then materialised and enslaved in the name of rational and efficient finance. The result is deepening inequality, urban explosion, growth in crime and declining literacy and public health. Such financial mechanisms end up destroying whole nations and their political, social and cultural stability.

Such violence and expropriation of whole nations is not allowed to create any discomfort for the experts or the scientists of finance. The removal of the equations from personal morality and values, and the measurement of the wider social and ecological implications of return on investment, or leverage, becomes very 'convenient' to the science and the scientists. There has been significant critique of the term 'externalities' in economics, even from the experts from within the disciplines. However, its use and deliberate disciplinary silos have continued to grow and flourish unabated. When plunder become a norm, the science and laws over time are designed to justify it. What we urgently need to do is to expose the plunder that is often disguised as growth and stop it from happening. The deaths that are natural, and the lives which need nourishment, should be respected in the cycle of economic growth. Interest growth irrespective of its externalities, needs to be capped to allow society to find its balance and equality.

Micro-enterprise often Poisons Less and Gives More

For small businesses and enterprises, growth is rarely over-powering or insatiable. Often it is contained within limits of resources and scale, and designed to prevent excessive debt burdens, avoid bankruptcy, and help future generations to survive, by prudent and responsible business practices (see e.g. Bank, 2020; Bischoff, 2021; Nguyen et al., 2020). Capital when it is needed is generated from within, so as not to become obligated to external stakeholders who may demand returns and payback. Entrepreneurs prefer to have their own skin in the game, and control their own resources and manage-ability. For minorities and immigrants, race and language barriers mean that entrepreneurship is the only hope to work and feed the family – it is the default, and they are willing to work all the hours to make a start.

History shows that certain cultures and communities have developed particular skills in finance, and managed to retain this growth and success over many generations. Other communities have learnt to stay contented and use finance for sustainable growth, without becoming greedy or selfish. They have all wanted to nourish their cultural and spiritual institutions, and seen in these wisdom sciences, a deep sense of meaning and purpose which drives their enterprise. Profits are often reinvested in building temples, mosques, gurudwaras to help sustain the community, maintain identity, and provide mutual support and encouragement.

Many of these leaders understand from their own traditions, the nature and limits of growth and are able to live within their means and minimise their debt burdens because of this wisdom. In many cultures, there is a direct engagement with death through regular attendance at community funerals and prayers. This helps entrepreneurs experience the limits of money. In contrast in so many western cultures, the breakdown of family and community means that either death is denied, or it is a very lonely and depressing experience. Simply talking about death becomes impossible. The insecurity of loneliness can also lead to greed and materialism as a coping mechanism, a temporary form of stability, power and security.

A large number of small businesses in any country help make a sizable impact on economic growth, and widen its distribution and resilience. They also collectively learn to adapt and change with the dynamic nature of markets and opportunities, especially to serve the local consumers where they operate. They help cultivate deeply personal economic relationships and trust, as opposed to the transactional nature of big business. Where they make excess or surplus profits, many small businesses play an active role in local philanthropic projects relating to education, healthcare or public and environmental welfare.

Local presence helps them see the local needs, and exercise the social responsibility that comes from citizenship. This can also mean that growth is not at the expense of society but alongside it, and there may be many inter-dependencies and inter-relationships which are directly experienced by such local businesses. For example, their children may attend a charity school, or the customers may be trustees of a local housing association, providing shelter to the needy. Medical supplies may be sold to local nursing homes, run by caring people, including faith groups, and the charges for this would recognise the good public service they are providing.

When entrepreneurs are not driven by greed, they can see the wider social and political implications of their actions. They also see in charity work a way of enhancing purpose and meaning, and showing the local community that they care and are not just selfish. Their personal networks would be enhanced through such involvement, giving them pecuniary benefits to grow their business and expand their customer base. This virtuous circle helps them see the bigger picture of enterprise and they may not need rules or codifications to persuade entrepreneurs to act responsibly. They may discover that there is no other alternative and are able to comfortably sleep at night having done a good day's work. By its very nature, locality creates transparency and accountability at deeper level than we would otherwise get from big businesses.

Corporate Expropriation and Offshore Extraction

Corporations have become the major engines of 'growth' in modern economies all over the world, and governments and politicians routinely support and encourage their contributions, irrespective of their real impacts in terms of society and environment (Baars & Spicer, 2017; Lazonick & Shin, 2019). This growth is highly financial and financializing. Global multinationals have an even more enhanced degree of power, as they can now pressurise governments to compete for 'their' business, through attractive incentives such as grants and reduced taxes. In the western world, corporate growth is assumed to be the major method of economic growth – the public sector is there to collect taxes and provide public services only. There are few incentives for pro-social corporations or pro-environmental large enterprises. As to the direct and indirect attack by large corporations and monopolies on micro-enterprises, there is virtual silence and policies and politics are captured by big business.

The law and powers given to corporations are alien and alienating, the more they grow in size and influence. They have become highly influential impersonal creatures, making little effort to shape harmonious growth, inclusive of nature and society. They refuse to account for the costs of social and environmental responsibility, and often make profits from expropriation of those very fundamental saviours of our ecosystem. Oil, air and water pollution is financed and driven by large multinational corporations on a global scale, and fuelled by stock markets and global financial institutions without restraint. Their activities directly attack life on planet earth and is legitimated by experts in finance and the theories of finance.

All multinational corporations have links with offshore secrecy jurisdictions and tax havens – islands where they can hide their financial transactions, and subvert not only tax payments but also financial transparency (Bullough, 2018; Palan, 2003; Shaxson, 2012). This undermines accountability to their own investors and shareholders, let alone nation states or the environment. Here again finance science chooses not to discuss this topic, making it an externality to their education syllabi. Given the scale and volume of transactions going through tax havens, this is a further example of the growth in fictious education about the true nature of corporate conduct. Offshore tax havens are the 'black holes' in finance theory which ought to be analysed and broken if we are to achieve our UN sustainable development goals.

The fact that human society has chosen to delegate growth to such 'alien creatures' as multinational corporations, ought to be examined carefully. Their size and power, not just at a national but a global level ought to generate a cause for concern, and should not be ignored by the equations and calculations of corporate finance. This power has a direct bearing on their behaviour, and is wielded actively and deliberately to undermine regulations which force them to be more sustainable and accountable. The Big 4 accounting firms have themselves become multinationals, who use their regulatory knowledge and corporatised greed and conflicts of interest to assist global corporations from public and ecological accountability. They often help their 'clients' design structures of extraction and regulatory arbitrage (Shah, 2015a; Shah, 2015b). When this power is avoided from questioning by scientists, they deliberately want to delude society from the hubris and conduct of multinationals. For Business Schools who benefit from corporate executives and their largesse, this capture helps them generate large revenues, irrespective of truth or wisdom – some argue they ought to be bulldozed (Parker, 2018). Growth in the corporation and growth in business education may be parallel, but they end up regressing society, not advancing it.

Inside the corporation, there are real people who lead and manage the activities and resource allocation, shaping the incentives for employees to behave and make executive decisions. Good culture then becomes critical, and the structures ought to be designed in such a way as to promote care and compassion towards all living beings. However, the reality is that these organisations are deeply materialistic, and the culture is universalised and instrumentalised in the service of these goals. Financial institutions, who ought to be the epitome of global power and responsibility, constantly fail to cultivate good culture or prevent hubris and excess. They carry a moral hazard where risqué behaviour always ends up getting bailed out by governments, with no personal punishment, such that their irresponsibility is encouraged.

If corporations are the role models of economic growth, they fail miserably to learn from nature. Nature is beyond materiality, often selfless and generous, and operates with humility and responsibility. Trees remain local and fail to globalise. Forests host whole communities of wildlife, and encourage interdependence, helping to protect our soil, soul and society, bringing rain and protecting the ozone layer for human survival. They often do best without human interference, and suffer when corporations exploit them for profit. Forests ebb and flow with the seasons and try to work within nature's limits, shedding leaves in the autumn and growing them again in the spring. They selflessly provide shelter in the heat, and fruits for the inhabitants, without even thinking of revenues or profits. In spite of this unconditional giving, trees continue to survive and sustain themselves if humans choose to leave them alone. Forests don't need external loans or capital to fund their growth and expansion, and thereby remind us of the limits of finance – it is not always and forever the panacea for growth and human prosperity.

The diversity of cultures of the world, and their varying perspectives on growth are not only ignored, but suppressed and marginalised by global corporations. Even the simple fact that they need to operate differently in different countries, and respect local laws, customs and regulations, is very difficult for them to accept. Given that their finance comes from global capital markets hubs, multinational corporations focus their efforts on appeasing those investors and markets, who are often themselves alienated from diverse local cultures and communities. The universalisation of corporate mentalities, structures and policies facilitates centralised extraction, but damages global human diversity. Outsourcing often means that manufacturing is done in cheap labour countries, where the cost minimisation can be implemented from a distance. The externalities caused by such working conditions and brainless work, kills the imagination and spirit of developing countries population's unapologetically and aggressively.

The same attitude applies to environments – operations are sourced where such laws and restraints are weak or compromised, and the damage is then 'foreign' rather than in the host countries where the senior management are based. Carbon trading encourages this behaviour – there is no need to change existing systems and processes as carbon credits can be bought on the open market (Blakey, 2021). Despite the fact that global corporations have a direct stake in protecting the global environment and its sustainability, their actions are often the opposite and driven by short-term materialism and ecological degradation. As lenders and investors also become globalised and controlled by large fund and asset managers, this concentration of power and control becomes embedded in the very heart of finance.

Job Creation or Job Destruction? Questioning the Soul of Financial Growth

Jobs provide the tentacles for finance and enterprise, and fuel business growth and prosperity. They give corporations the ability to expand and grow by delegating work and distributing it to improve productivity and efficiency. Jobs are human, and often provide the critical economic support to whole families, who in turn are able to play their role in civil society as responsible citizens. Large-scale manufacturing and production have given rise to jobs and a middle class, with the promise of social upliftment for one and all. Not everyone can or wants to be an entrepreneur – they may not want to take the risk, or lack the culture of enterprise and the hunger to create and harness commercial opportunities. Jobs can be either public or private, and vary in their nature, qualifications and experience, and so do the wages and rewards of employment.

In neo-liberal economies, politicians routinely use job creation as a proxy for economic growth. Often, in the media, corporations use the narrative of job creation as a proxy for growth and their contribution to the economy. However, finance sees jobs as a cost, and one to be minimised in order to maximise profits and wealth creation. Furthermore, the humanity of jobs and the need to give importance to skills, training, motivation and culture, is very low on the priority list, as it would likely increase cost. Getting the most out of workers in terms of productivity and efficiency is a higher priority than to give a good living and purposeful life to employees. Humans have been turned into numbers and burdens for the organisation, by accounting and finance. The calculations eliminate soul, spirit, family, culture and community entirely.

The ownership of corporations is primarily given to large investors and wealthy shareholders, with employees, irrespective of their stakeholding in the company, given little ownership or voting power. Contemporary finance science is not interested in who owns the company, or widening employee share ownership, except when it comes to senior management, who must be incentivised to act as the best agents for their principals. In modernity, the move towards mechanisation and robotics is seen as a progression, as it does away with the need to follow labour laws, dealing with trade unions, or working with different shifts of labourers. Technology can reliably work 24/7 so why not minimise labour cost and labour pain?

Modernity has also created bullshit jobs, which occupy layers of bureaucracy in large companies, and are often meaningless and highly political (Graeber, 2019). Workers in such roles often become politicised and use their roles as ways to manoeuvre power and prestige, and keep others out. Such work can actually reduce productivity and efficiency, but the jobs are not easy to remove in large organisations. They spread the growth of meaningless middle management, and the pursuit of power for its own sake. The importance of work as a means of providing security and stability can be undermined by the actions of such middle managers, who like growth for its own sake, create work for its own sake. Also, jobs are often urban, leading to a lot of displacement, and precarity when technology takes over or employers go bust or transfer to another country (Fleming, 2014).

In the public sector, job quality can be different and there may be better security of tenure, even though wages may be low. There is also a chance of greater job satisfaction – an opportunity to live by public purpose. A teacher or nurse working for the government is likely to be satisfied with a purposeful salaried lifestyle, and even attracted by the public non-commercial values espoused by their employers. It is possible that the families brought up by such public professionals have a more rounded and less materialistic outlook on life, and espouse a greater sense of contentment and fulfilment. Incentives for work are different, and customers like parents or patients may be less demanding or more humane in their engagement. However, neo-liberalism has created a very insecure climate for such jobs, with the public sector regularly being seen as the enemy of free markets and enterprise, and incapable of providing efficient and reliable public services. The discipline of corporate finance completely ignores public sector work or jobs altogether as being irrelevant and unimportant to the pursuit of corporate growth and expansion.

The ignorance of job quality, humanity and job security by corporate finance is disturbing and unsustainable. The importance of employee stakeholding in corporate performance ought to be recognised and incentivised equally for all workers, whether they are on the shop floor or the middle management or executives (Baddon et al., 2017; Driver & Thompson, 2018). Such incentives can give all workers skin in the game, and an opportunity to benefit from the good performance that they bring to the firm. They can create a deeper and more engaging workforce, leading to a better culture and loyalty from employees. There are financial benefits from seeing workers as stakeholders, but these are often given lip service in the theories and the science.

When jobs are routinised and made repetitive and meaningless, there are wider social repercussions for society which corporations cannot ignore. These externalities ought to be internalised, and employee satisfaction valued and respected. The health of workers – both mental and physical, is important to productivity and society too. Furthermore, the standardisation of work can also increase turnover and replaceability, as the costs of training or the benefits of experience are minimised. In many cases, work is designed to be standardised such that it can be easily controlled, monitored, fired, rehired and expended when the demands change. Where this standardised culture is applied globally for large multinationals, the damage can be globalised too, creating wildfires of uncertainty and dependence.

Where large businesses encroach on small businesses and their local goods and services, they make it very difficult for entrepreneurs to thrive and operate sustainably. Often, the small enterprise ecosystem is destroyed entirely by big business creating significant social consequences. This makes immigrants and minorities more and more precarious, and forces them to look for marginal jobs. Farming is another example of a small enterprise which has been ruined by corporate power and muscle, resulting in a lot of farmer insecurity, and future generations wanting to work in jobs rather than struggle with the risk, breaking rural communities and societies altogether. This can also cause displacement as workers are forced to move to cities for jobs, and family links and rural support mechanisms are broken, creating social upheaval. If this is labelled as growth, then it has failed to count the full price of rented, insecure, mentally disturbing and soul-destroying work.

Growth Measurement: Income and Value

Nature does not measure growth, nor does it trade it. It is not obsessed by growth either – it simply adapts and moves with the seasons. The same applies to trees and wildlife – they may expand and grow in some years, and die and whither in others, depending on availability of food and water or pasture for grazing. Nature has no strategic policies for growth – what it knows is about symbiosis and interdependence – creating a climate and atmosphere where different species can thrive together with minimal violence. Man has interfered with all this, and one of the key features of this attack on nature has been the obsession with growth, defined in a particular anthropocentric way.

Finance has learnt to ignore the complexities of growth, and instead simplify it using what it knows best – numbers. And the two key numbers of growth are income and value, and finance is obsessed by those numbers, and persuades society that growth in those two key numbers is the panacea for all evils and pains. This is simplistic and highly convenient for the experts and masters of the discipline, but it is a fiction to which we give power and authority (Hines, 1988). It gives business leaders an authority in both calculation and politics – each time we are concerned about growth, we need to speak to them. The fact that both the calculations are highly subjective, inaccurate and incomplete, often manipulated by corporations and governments, is put aside and ignored.

A myth is created around profits and share prices as proxies for performance. Intangibles like culture, social cohesion, kindness and compassion, are critical to sustainable development but ignored by the experts simply because they are hard to measure. There is an unstated assumption that income and value summarise and encapsulate all aspects of growth, material and intangible, and are keys to unlocking its mystery and tapping its power to progress society.

Let us take the animal manufacturing industry as an example. Here there is no question in finance about the sentience of animals, or the need to be kind and caring rather than cruel and manipulative (Turner & D'Silva, 2006). They are beasts for human consumption, and we ought to focus on expanding the food supply, even though in terms of energy, water and pollution, the environmental impact is 1,000 times more per calorie of food then what we would get from growing vegetables. In spite of all the evidence of the Anthropocene, there is no change in attitudes to animal agriculture. The industry has turned animal lives into products and feedlots, subject to large scale battery farming and unnatural impregnation, all for the pursuit of human consumption. Numbers hide cruelty and pollution and turn wasteful energy into a cost to be minimised rather than a problem to be resolved. Workers in animal factories often suffer from health problems and mental breakdowns as a result of the pain they witness and the conditions in which they are forced to work.

Even human language has been changed to distance 'those' animals from pets and other types of animals. The norms of income and value maximisation are used to hide the cruelty even when on a macro level the numbers do not add up. These numbers help generate the large amounts of finance needed to pursue factory farming on an industrial scale. The manufacturers and meat are traded in markets which have become soulless – there is profound epistemic violence in how finance shapes animal narratives (Christensen & Lamberton, 2022). The finance experts do not see nature as a teacher, nor a permanent asset which needs to be cared for and replenished through kindness, humility and a light footprint.

Markets are not sacrosanct or all knowing. They, too, go with the tide, and are happy to use subjective and incomplete income numbers to decide on values and financial investment decisions. Often experts keep dancing and trading until the music stops, as they did in the 2008 global financial crash, when there was a sudden correction in valuation due to fraud in the housing and securities markets. As history and experience are not taught or valued, these market and financial crashes keep recurring, and governments keep bailing them out. The crash in knowledge and science that is required as a result of such events also gets postponed and bailed out. Even researchers and academics keep dancing until the music stops, with the Anthropocene very far from view given the toolkit of their training, and the deculturation they experienced in the PhD training.

Multiple measures and proxies may be difficult to collate, but are needed simply because they comprise the holistic aspects of income and growth, and incorporate sustainability which ought to be our primary focus (Laine, Unerman & Tregidga, 2022). Nature grows in a variety of ways, and encourages cooperation and competition, helping species to learn from each other and adapt to changing circumstances, without any need to claim credit for doing so, or measure the success of its strategy. Even after man has become extinct, nature will find a way to recover and rebuild, though the damage will be very long-lasting. The science of finance needs to take responsibility when it is a cause of the Anthropocene, and be willing to plead guilty and transform its ways.

Knowledge 'Growth' and its Consequences

In economics, micro-economics deals with households and firms and macro-economics focuses on governments, markets, global trade, interest rates and currencies. Not only are there knowledge silos between disciplines, but some are also created within the same discipline, which should raise our suspicions. Corporate finance has become a further 'branch' of micro-economics and does not take an interest in how inflation arises, or how interest rates are set, nor the politics and power of financial institutions or corporations. Corporate finance does not even care whether or not financial markets promote equality and sustainable development, focusing instead on how to maximise income and value for corporations. The reality is that many corporations have become so powerful that they can influence governments and markets, especially large global financial institutions. The separation of micro and macro finance is another way in which specialisation and silos are dug to hide wider understanding, and prevent larger truths from hurting the equations or theorems. The politics of the education and training in finance is hidden from view.

If income grows at the expense of state and society, it is not a problem for corporate finance science. In fact, it is often encouraged and rewarded, as we have seen with tax avoidance. From a nature perspective, this dualism in finance is a further way of ignoring the structural, cultural, social and ecological residues of corporate conduct and behaviour, whilst at the same time legitimating them scientifically. Society is regularly influenced and transformed by corporate conduct in a number of ways which are very far from sustainable. This situation cannot be allowed to continue unchallenged.

Prioritising corporate income and corporate value creation knowingly and deliberately avoids larger questions about corporate purpose and behaviour, and the non-dualistic reality of finance and its wider implications (Shah, 2018).

The growth in business schools all over the world has led to a parallel rise in academic finance jobs, much larger than jobs in economics which have been declining. This has resulted in more and more journals in finance, and globalisation of the narrow-mindedness, silos and specialisation that comes with the baggage. The growth of the discipline and its wider educational influence has become a major part of the problem of modernity, and this has real world influences and many adverse consequences (Fleming, 2017). The mindsets that are certified and graduated by business schools all over the world often end up managing or even leading businesses and corporations, and the more materialistic and utilitarian they are, the greater the chance they have of adversely influencing the whole culture of the organisations they choose to work in. We need much deeper reflexivity on the role and responsibility of the finance intellectual in modern society (Said, 1996).

The unchecked and uncontested growth in the technocratic science and expertise of finance, including the financialisation of other business disciplines like marketing or management, needs to be challenged and questioned because of its seriously damaging influence. Its monotheism has wide-ranging unsustainable consequences, and the footprint this has in the production of future finance managers and leaders cannot go unquestioned. Whitley (1986) predicted the perils of this trend very early on. To expect any radical change from within the science is unrealistic, given the hold it has and the conservative nature of academic change and evolution.

Professional bodies, who expand this intellectual footprint, have been all too happy to work within the technocratic expert framework, and their own growth in membership and revenues has been significant, cushioning the need for any radical curricular changes (West, 2003). Notions of public interest protection have been abandoned. Knowledge growth and its footprint are hampering sustainable development on a global scale. Given the power and influence of finance experts and managers in their own organisations, this training is leading to greed and aggression as opposed to sensitivity and kindness, values required for reversing the Anthropocene.

When a powerful discipline – whose authority derives from its very focus on finance and fundamental relevance to material social life – grows and expands its reach nationally and globally, and universalises its knowledge base, society ought to be on high alert. This materialistic curriculum should raise critical questions and a deeper reflexivity about the knowledge and its sustainability. It is causing severe decay, and using the narrative of growth to hide the underlying values. Not only has corporate finance ignored the reality of political power and influence, it has managed to prevent the questioning of its own disciplinary power and influence through its tight control of intellectual output and production. Its theories and methods should be made subject to public scrutiny, and critiques be used to transform the curriculum to help shape sustainable development. The criticality of this knowledge, and its wider global economics and social footprint requires society to question its assumptions – and this 'trial' should not just be held by the experts speaking their own jargon.

When knowledge and power come together, they cannot be allowed to grow unchecked if we care about sustainability of all species on the planet.

Biodiversity of Finance Knowledge

In nature, growth is not just about one species and its ability to flourish and survive. The nature of growth is bio-diverse and inclusive, and different species are created to give balance to our fragile ecosystems and create variety and paint the creative canvas of the planet. As we have already examined, there is significant diversity within the human species and this can be respected for its natural characteristics and not made extinct simply because of human ignorance, arrogance and abuse of power (Armstrong, 2024). If human diversity is a natural phenomenon, then just as we are trying to protect our ozone layer, we need to understand and value this human biodiversity and see it as a critical part of our growth and resilience on this planet. Cultural diversity also means a diversity of knowledge and theories about finance, and even 'growth' will mean many different things to different cultures and peoples. Suppressing these voices just because they lack power, or are different and marginalised, or simply because they cannot speak our expert tongue, is a recipe for planetary anguish and even conflict. Finance research needs to diversify much more to open the range of truths and perspectives that really underly it (Lagoarde-Segot, 2015).

We need to carefully examine our knowledge institutions to see how it is that we have come to endorse this discrimination and ignorance and deny such marginal yet important voices to help shape our planetary sustainable development. We also need to build active strategies to recreate diverse finance knowledges and share them both in the research laboratory and the classroom. Such cultural arrogance stunts growth in wisdom and handicaps us from shaping a truly bio-diverse humanity. It also prevents questioning and critique of our knowledge systems from alternative experiences and perspectives, something which we urgently need if we are to develop an inclusive science which respects planetary human biodiversity.

In reality, the biodiversity of the planet is a deep source of wisdom for all our sciences and we have forgotten to acknowledge and respect this in economics and finance. In hindsight, the ways in which we have eschewed culture and severed it from finance seems foolish, ignorant, colonising and violent. It appears to be an extension of empire, where foreign cultures and nations needed to be 'civilised' and enslaved to our way of thinking and behaving. The discipline of finance has done this in very subtle ways and through the pretence of objectivity and universalism.

Growth has been actively and deliberately stunted by such thinking and many countries have been enslaved by perennial debt through control of oil reserves and the penury of compound interest, making it very difficult for them to grow and nurture their own finance theories. Even when they get into a trouble, they are put into special measures by the World Bank and IMF where indebted nations have to implement culturally insensitive structural adjustment policies dictated by the materialist and greedy Western nations. Instead of encouraging their independence, nations have been forced to become dependent on western finance and currency regimes. The profound social and ecological consequences of structural adjustment are ignored and make these countries even more displaced and unequal. Where they do not wish to 'grow' in a model defined and forced by these powerful lending institutions, they are not given any choice but to submit to a particular materialist view of growth. As an example, 'cash crops' (like tea, coffee and pyrethrum) were forced upon many countries so that they can earn foreign exchange to repay their sovereign debt, making it difficult for the local farmers to feed their own families when the market prices of these cash crops collapsed. Subsistence farmers could not subsist by eating tea or pyrethrum, but then who really cares?

When we allow the biodiversity of finance knowledge to grow, we acknowledge its cultural context and allow alternative perspectives to prevail harmoniously at the same time. Different species of birds will sing or fly alongside one another, recognising that there is enough space for everyone, and even when it comes to food or water they never fight in spite of their differences or the scarcity of food. When nature allows lions to kill and eat gazelles or zebras, there is no inter-species war or rebellion, just an acceptance of the laws of nature. The fact that a zebra cannot eat meat, nor does it want to, is simply seen as its own deeper nature, and there is no attempt to force it to eat meat or to kill just because other animals may kill it. Zebras, lions and gazelles have developed their own cultures of living and surviving, and these are different and allowed to stay different, and never suppressed or undermined by 'higher' knowledge systems or experts.

We ought to prevent finance science from becoming an arbiter and judge of alternative cultural truths and ways of living. Even religion, which has long been a major influence on human belief and character (Barrera & Amore, 2024) – even capitalism was shaped by it – has been banished by finance science as dogmatic, fundamentalist and unworthy of any respect. If elements of religious belief and practice promote sustainable and ethical finance, what is wrong with that? The history of capitalism is littered with religious influence and this has been a major finding in research, yet all this evidence is denied simply because it is inconvenient to the new 'corporate' finance. The more we examine the trajectory of growth of finance science, the more we see its universalising and expropriative tendency, cursing society whilst at the same time overpowering it. The evidence seems consistent with a science designed to plunder society and our fragile ecosystem, to feed some cultures' desperation for power and control over others be it soil, animals or humans. Knowledge has been the new frontier after empire, with finance its driving force.

A Growth Mindset

Accepting that knowledge needs to be at the centre of growth, and this knowledge needs to be inclusive and respectful, we have the opportunity to build a radical new ecosystem of finance wisdom. Given our significant historical weakness in accepting the role of culture and belief in shaping this diversity, and the variety of understandings that already exist and are respectful of society and nature, we need to make a start in this direction to grow our knowledge. This transformation requires both new 'local' research, and adapted methods of education to be sensitive to local culture and at the same time bring about holistic change towards sustainable lifestyles.

Research programmes from different parts of the world could be set up to document the variety of views and practices around money and finance, and the ethics and beliefs which sustain them. History and political economy should not be ignored but instead documented. The variety of institutions and influences on finance in each country, the relative size and impact of small family-owned businesses and the degree to which financial structures are influenced by external events and currencies, could help us with a deeper picture of the national context of finance in each country. Local scholars in these countries could be empowered to document their own understandings, rather than be forced to put finance into an external global neo-liberal, standardised free market straightjacket. We need much more research on small business finance, and its diverse global ecosystem – this is often the neglected frontier of sustainable enterprise.

Such knowledge could become a vital global resource in the diversity of understandings of income, growth and wealth, and the variety of political and historical contexts in which they operate. Not all this evidence will be ethical or sustainable, but it will help shape our understanding of the knowledge gaps, and opportunities for reform of education and financial institutions. We need to accept the variety of beliefs and practices within one country and document these, rather than ignore or suppress them in pursuit of a macro-national story. This evidence could then be compared and contrasted to help build a deeper understanding of society and the financial innovations which influence and incentivise behaviour. Universal knowledge about how to make finance a servant of society can then be built from the ground up. A taxonomy of different attitudes and beliefs about animals and nature, and the importance of sustainability could be developed to detail the vast diversity of finance cultures in the world. This is a critical first step to the transformation to a globally sustainable finance.

Standardised content and methods of education lead to standardised outcomes, which are often insensitive to local beliefs and traditions, and dismissive of them consciously or subconsciously. Given the criticality of culture to sustainable finance, cultural reforms are needed to ensure sustainable behaviours and attitudes to money are critical to national and global transformation. In the classroom, culture needs to be taught and discussed, and modified if necessary to bring about transformations towards sustainable development. This means that each child should be empowered to understand the nature and limits of money and be able to prevent becoming overwhelmed and overpowered by finance.

These pedagogies should take a bottom-up approach rather than be a top down *dictat*. Development of these methods of teaching, and the revision of the content of the education materials, would also require investment and training of teachers, and changes in the school curricula globally. These reforms are not just about numeracy or financial literacy, but about helping the world put money in its place, and prevent it from subverting culture, trust and human relationships. It is also about empowering children and young people to cultivate good habits in finance during their formative years such that they can live purposefully and be comfortable managing their own finances. Unless these goals are achieved, sustainable development will remain a chimera.

One outcome of this transformation will be the cultivation of a growth mindset among children and young people which is not obsessive about money and is able to see beyond it. It will value the understanding of history and traditions, and religion and belief will not be banished from the classroom. Growth will be seen in a much larger canvas of human development, rather than a narrower and limiting mindset of income and wealth maximisation. If pupils are able to see this from a young age, and exposed to alternative lifestyle choices and outcomes, they will become much more confident citizens. A lot of this education can be delivered on the field, in the communities, gardens and forests, with elders explaining history and traditions, and mindfulness meditations about money and its opportunities and limitations.

A growth mindset will encourage children and young people to think forward rather than simply study the subjects to get a qualification. It will help them understand better and more deeply their own skills, preferences and abilities, helping to cultivate a deeper and more lasting self-confidence. Rather than feel powerless about the environment, they may become more hopeful and see in the classroom a variety of different abilities and aspirations which could co-operate to bring about positive change. The joy of belonging and community will not just be academic, but directly experienced through the different pedagogies and field trip experiences. Silos between subjects will be broken by interdisciplinarity and placing the students mind, body and spirit at the centre of a new growth and sustainability mindset.

It is critical that we remodel and reshape the culture of growth and set good behaviours from a young age which are respectful of people, animals and nature through a variety of materials and narratives from diverse cultures of the world. Arts and creativity can play a central role in this change process, and children from a young age could be empowered to dream alternative futures and aspirations for an inclusive, harmonious society. Some of this may be challenging to local customs and traditions, but if this challenge is ignored, then sustainable transformations that are urgently needed will not happen. If done sensitively with respect to local norms and behaviours, this growth mindset will become more deeply embedded and therefore longer lasting.

Visions of Macro-spiritual Growth

When humans and society understand the limits of money, they will focus on deeper values like peace, community, mutuality, creativity and meaning. In many parts of the world, such people, groups and communities already exist but are often marginalised because of their 'strangeness' or 'belief systems'. However, when we close in on their lifestyles, characters and generosity, what we realise is that they have actually understood the limits of money and learnt to operate beyond it. They are contented, sharing, caring and peaceful, using hard work and enterprise to maintain their values and educate and inspire all around them. They are rooted in the land and not uprooted from it, and respect elders and traditions, doing their best to protect their cultural inheritance. The simple lifestyles mean that their footprint on the ecosystem is light, and future generations are nourished and inspired to continue to live gently, compassionately and generously. The material world is there to be adapted to, rather than become drowned in.

When money is put in its place, even our language changes – time is no longer money, but a gift and resource for hope and community. Social work is seen as a duty, not a choice, and there may even be competition among volunteers to serve and help in times of need. For finance leaders, volunteering is a very importantly practical way of keeping their feet on the ground and staying connected with people from all walks of life, rich and poor, healthy and disabled. It's a humbling act. Children would grow up in a world where people make things rather than buy them, and where imagination is not dulled by ready-made entertainment, but inspired by creativity in the school curriculum, and colourful rituals and festivals at home. Elderly care no longer needs to be contracted out or left to the nursing home, but instead done in the home and the community. Age is given the highest respect, and people regularly gather to hear the stories of the olden days, making the old feel young again.

Nature will be routinely celebrated for its vastness and beauty, and even the thought of 'caring' and protecting it will have dissolved as our knowledge and education will no longer separate it from human life. Interdependence will be deeply woven in our science and philosophy, and encouraged and respected in our laws and customs. There will be no rush to expand at the expense of our friends and neighbours, and growth will be viewed as a collective endeavour, like a rising tide which lifts all boats. Competition will be overcome by cooperation, and excellence will depend on aspiration and imagination rather than brawn and muscle. Technology will be crafted and designed to serve society and prevented from becoming its master. The flows of money will be regulated, and limits placed on its egregious accumulation or wasteful uses. War machines will be dismantled, and peace industries will be funded instead.

Spirituality, the space where belief and hope are ignited, and meditation and inner peace are cultivated, can potentially become a source of immeasurable growth and deep compassion for all living beings. It will come to show human mastery over the body and its sensual desires, and ignite a deep search for learning and wisdom, even overcoming the limits of words and language. In our history, this was a living reality in many parts of the world and at various times – we had progressed, and have now regressed. Whilst each soul will have to seek within through their own efforts, education methods and practices such as yoga and silent reflexivity in the forests, rivers and mountains, will help people discover the ocean within. Music, poetry, theatre and craft will grow from these deep experiences and nourish the growth of whole communities and nations.

Chapter Summary

In this chapter, we have reflected on the nature of growth, and seen how deeply it has been defined by society in a materialistic language, which is also profoundly selfish and anthropocentric. It has been seen as an objective good, even when its real understanding and impacts may be deeply unequal. Finance and its science have profited from this version of growth because it has helped extend the materialistic view of the world, and deepened the power and dominance of its expert practitioners. The promised security that comes from more and more income and wealth, has failed to materialise. Instead we have rising inequality, anxiety and devastating climate change.

In nature, growth is seasonal, and also not always guaranteed. Death is accepted as the flip side of life, and not denied or postponed, whilst finance tries to falsely create immortality through its obsession with future cash flows and material growth. Nature has a lot to teach us about growth, and how money has no place in it. If money has been created to help society build trust and relationships, growth should be a servant to this trust instead of coming to replace and overpower it.

Our finance knowledge content and methods of transmission and certification need to dramatically change to embrace the profound ontological shifts that our understanding of interdependence has shaped. This change will not happen by relying on elite institutions or euro-centric worldviews, even when these institutions have the potential to provide renewed leadership through a paradigm shift in finance. The deep disconnect from life and nature that has been practiced and encouraged in the discipline, needs a complete reversal. Students need to be actively sensitised to the meaning of sustainable growth, and the need to engage with the grassroots of society and observe raw finance in action. Personal meditation and reflexivity are central to a new and urgent reformation in finance education.

Lasting sustainable growth comes from understanding the nature and limits of money and overcoming them. Corporations have come to expropriate nature and society through their growth engines fuelled by finance, and are now doing this not just on a national level but on a global arena. Whilst micro-enterprises are often local, flexible and contented, large businesses accumulate power and hubris through finance, and become unaccountable to society, often capturing regulatory and political processes through their size and influence. Society needs to find ways to put money in its place and seek different types of growth which is more lasting and non-material.

Humans are not just bodies but souls and spirits too – and like all living beings, experience growth and decay. However, the imagination and spirit can continue to rise and glow, enriching the quality of life and helping to build peaceful sharing relationships and communities of kindness and compassion.

Science and education can help encourage this type of growth, and finance can become an engine for cooperation and simplicity, encouraging creativity, health and well-being as key measures of growth. Strategies which enhance trust and relationships in society should be encouraged by finance, and this will in turn boost interdependence and sustainable development.

When we start to imagine growth beyond the material, we realise that a lot of it is already hiding in plain sight, but we have been looking in the wrong place due to our obsession with money. Religion and belief structures often inspire deep contentment and sharing and build communities of hope. Techniques like yoga, meditation and silence help human beings develop a deeper respect for nature and come to see the vastness of their own inner nature, and its growth potential. Our businesses and industries could be designed to value these types of growth and the peacefulness and reflexivity they create. In many cases, finance is not needed and should step aside and overcome its own limitations and malpractices. Lasting meaning and security come from within, rather than the accumulation of more and more objects and wealth. In our concluding chapter, we examine forests, and what they can teach us about a harmonious and blended financial ecosystem, where there is respect and tolerance for biodiversity. We then conclude with the lessons learnt from this extended holistic meditation and develop a new organic framework and theory of finance, which can transform both the science and the professional training.

References

Armstrong, C. (2024). *Global Justice and the Biodiversity Crisis: Conservation in a World of Inequality*. Oxford University Press.

Astrachan, J. H., Astrachan, C. B., Campopiano, G., & Baù, M. (2020). Values, Spirituality and Religion: Family Business and the Roots of Sustainable Ethical Behavior. *Journal of Business Ethics*, 163(4), 637–645.

Baars, G., & Spicer, A. (2017). *The Corporation: A Critical, Multi-Disciplinary Handbook*. Cambridge University Press.

Baddon, L., Hunter, L., Hyman, J., & Leopold, J. (2017). *People's Capitalism? A Critical Analysis of Profit-Sharing and Employee Share Ownership: 1*. Routledge.

Bakan, J. (2004). *The Corporation: The Pathological Pursuit of Profit and Power*. Free Press.

British Business Bank (2020). *Alone, Together: Entrepreneurship and Diversity in the UK*. Oliver Wyman and British Business Bank.

Barrera, A., & Amore, R. C. (eds) (2024). *The Oxford Handbook of Religion and Economic Ethics*. Oxford University Press.

Bell, E., Winchester, N., & Wray-Bliss, E. (2021). Enchantment in Business Ethics Research. *Journal of Business Ethics*, 174(2), 251–262.

Bhatnagar, N., Sharma, P., & Ramachandran, K. (2020). Spirituality and Corporate Philanthropy in Indian Family Firms: An Exploratory Study. *Journal of Business Ethics*, 163(4), 715–728.

Bischoff, K. (2021). A Study on the Perceived Strength of Sustainable Entrepreneurial Ecosystems on the Dimensions of Stakeholder Theory and Culture. *Small Business Economics*, 56(3), 1121–1140.

Blakey, J. (2021). Accounting for Elephants: The (Post)Politics of Carbon Omissions. *Geoforum*, 121, 1–11.

Buller, A. (2022). *The Value of a Whale: On the Illusions of Green Capitalism*. Manchester University Press.

Bullough. (2018). *Moneyland: Why Thieves and Crooks Now Rule the World and How to Take It Back*. Profile Books.

Burrell, G., Hyman, M. R., Michaelson, C., Nelson, J. A., Taylor, S., & West, A. (2022). The Ethics and Politics of Academic Knowledge Production: Thoughts on the Future of Business Ethics. *Journal of Business Ethics*, 180(3), 917–940.

Christensen, M., & Lamberton, G. (2022). Accounting for Animal Welfare: Addressing Epistemic Vices During Live Sheep Export Voyages. *Journal of Business Ethics*, 180(1), 35–56.

Driver, C., & Thompson, G. (2018). *Corporate Governance in Contention*. Oxford University Press.

Fleming, P. (2014). *Resisting Work: The Corporatization of Life and Its Discontents*. Temple University Press.

Fleming, P. (2017b). Wreckage Economics. In *The Death of Homo Economicus* (Vol. 1, p. 40). Pluto Press.

Foroohar, R. (2016). *Makers and Takers: How Wall Street Destroyed Main Street*. Crown.

Graeber, D. (2019). *Bullshit Jobs: The Rise of Pointless Work, and What We Can Do About It*. Penguin.

Hickel, J. (1982). *Less is More: How Degrowth Will Save the World*. William Heinemann.

Hines, R. D. (1988). Financial Accounting: In Communicating Reality, We Construct Reality. *Accounting, Organizations and Society*, 13(3), 251–261.

Jäger, J., & Dziwok, E. (2024). *Understanding Green Finance: A Critical Assessment and Alternative Perspectives*. Edward Elgar Publishing.

Lagoarde-Segot, T. (2015). Diversifying Finance Research: From Financialization to Sustainability. *International Review of Financial Analysis*, 39, 1–6.

Laine, M., Unerman, J., & Tregidga, H. (2022). *Sustainability Accounting and Accountability*, 3rd edition. Routledge.

Lazonick, W., & Shin, J.-S. (2019). *Predatory Value Extraction: How the Looting of the Business Corporation Became the US Norm and How Sustainable Prosperity Can Be Restored*. Oxford University Press.

Macey, J. R. (2022). ESG Investing: Why Here? Why Now? *Berkeley Business Law Journal*, 19, 258.

Marquis, C. (2024). *The Profiteers: How Business Privatizes Profits and Socializes Costs*. Hachette UK.

Meadows, D. H., Meadows, D. L., Randers, J., & Behrens, W. W. (1979). *The Limits to Growth: A Report for the Club of Rome's Project on the Predicament of Mankind* (new edition). Macmillan.

Nesvetailova, A. (2012). Money and Finance in a Globalized Economy. In R. Palan (ed.), *Global Political Economy*, 2nd edition. Routledge.

Nguyen, M.-H., Pham, T.-H., Ho, M.-T., Nguyen, H. T. T., & Vuong, Q.-H. (2020). On the Social and Conceptual Structure of the 50-Year Research Landscape in Entrepreneurial Finance. *SN Business & Economics*, 1(1), 2.

Ott, J. C. (2011). *When Wall Street Met Main Street: The Quest for an Investors' Democracy*. Harvard University Press.

Palan, R. (2003). *The Offshore World: Sovereign Markets, Virtual Places, and Nomad Millionaires*. Cornell University Press.

Parker, M. (2018). Why We Should Bulldoze the Business School, *The Guardian*.

Said, E. W. (1996). *Representations of the Intellectual: The 1933 Reith Lectures*. Vintage.

Shah, A. (2015a). Systemic Regulatory Arbitrage – A Case Study of KPMG. www.academia.edu.

Shah, A. (2015b). The Chemistry of Audit Failure – A Case Study of KPMG. www.academia.edu.

Shah, A. (2018). *Reinventing Accounting and Finance Education – For a Caring, Inclusive and Sustainable Planet*. Routledge.

Shaxson, N. (2012). *Treasure Islands: Tax Havens and the Men Who Stole the World*. Vintage Books.

Soukup, S. R. (2021). *The Dictatorship of Woke Capital: How Political Correctness Captured Big Business*. Encounter Books.

Turner, J., & D'Silva, J. (2006). *Animals, Ethics, and Trade: The Challenge of Animal Sentience*. Earthscan.

West, B. (2003). *Professionalism and Accounting Rules*. Routledge.

Whitley, R. (1986). The Transformation of Business Finance into Financial Economics: The Roles of Academic Expansion and Changes in U.S. Capital Markets. *Accounting, Organizations and Society*, 11(2), 171–192.

6   Forests of Hope

Forests are reservoirs of wildlife, turning the sun's energy into a supermarket of food and shelter, even bringing rain and absorbing carbon dioxide from the atmosphere. They never even think about charging for their food supply, or carbon capture, nor do they want animals to suffer in the heat – they create a canopy for them selflessly, not expecting any payment in return. They are proof that nature knows about community and interdependence, even without attending university or conducting any research in a controlled experiment. Our neo-classical economic failure has been *not* to recognise this wisdom and understand its prescience for the benefit of all species, including humans. Instead we have discriminated against it and even destroyed it through Empire. In this chapter, we will learn from this wisdom, and explore how finance can create ecosystems of hope, opportunity and shelter and become a real rainmaker rather than a selfish extractor. In particular, we will see how interdependence can be encouraged and nourished by finance, and the kinds of institutions, markets, nations and communities can help nurture and sustain it.

One of the saddest realities of successful forests, is that they survive best without any humans nearby and within its canopy. They prove the Anthropocene's reality through their history, courage and resilience. For millennia, humans have lived alongside forests, and some of the wisest teachers like Buddha, Mahavira or Rama have found refuge and wisdom through meditation in the canopy. It is a fact that 'wildlife' including tigers and leopards, prevailed in those same forests and yet refused to harm these saints – even the animals recognised long ago the importance of preserving that which does not harm anyone. Humans in many parts of the world saw this wisdom, and developed stories and cultures about forests and their vast communities, and sought to protect them, taking only that which they needed. Today's hamburgers come from animals grazing the land regained from chopped forests and are damaging human health globally. The finance behind this violent operation is hidden but significant. In chopping the trees, we focused on the wood and land, and did not understand that we were disturbing a vast ecosystem. And now that we are dying, we start turning green. Indigenous cultures, in contrast, know how to live alongside and in harmony with forests.

The air, water, music and canopy of forests are ideal places to host a seminar on global finance. Scholars should come here to meditate and speak only after

DOI: 10.4324/9781003534532-6

they have experienced the bounty and generosity of the forest. If they cannot find a voice as a result of the whole experience, they should choose to stay silent and allow the forest to calm their mind, body and spirit instead. Trees may have no language that we can understand, but we can choose to respect their silence. We can tune into the forest music to deeply reflect on the nature of money and finance and feel the pain that it has caused in the planet through its widespread and out of control reach and influence. By undergoing this inner journey, we will be renewed and rejuvenated to control the excesses of finance, and ensure it does not deplete trust and relationships, and if anything nourishes our social and environmental capital. Far away from concrete jungles of our cities, and under a forest canopy, we are better able to rethink financial markets and institutions.

In this chapter, we use the forest metaphor to explore the principles and values of an inclusive finance, which like forests, respects interdependence, and shapes harmony under its canopy. Rather than judging the different species, a forest is happy to welcome one and all, and share its resources, canopy and fruits. It is not ambitious about growth or expansion, but organically grows if and when nature permits. Even climate is not controlled but embraced, and both the rough and smooth are accepted with equanimity. Values and principles like tolerance, kindness, generosity, calmness and patience are used to imagine what such finance can look like. Forests are a living community of different spirits and sustain themselves without needing money or finance. Purpose, meaning, roots, culture, groundedness and biodiversity are explored as critical elements in a moral finance. At the end of the chapter, there is a summary of the principal contributions of the book, and implications for future research.

Banks of Tolerance and Kindness

Forests are institutions shaped by nature to build communities and sustain them through the ups and downs of life. They have had no coaching or training in doing so, but have somehow learnt over time to tune into nature's seasons and rhythms, and to accept the cycle of birth and death. They are deeply rooted in the ground for generations, and do not yearn to fly or travel just so that they can explore, or relax and get a sun tan. Even though they are 'local' they seem far from parochial, and embrace change through humility and acceptance. We know from recent research on mycelium that through the roots network underground, they share nourishment sometimes even going hungry so that they can support younger trees and plants (Ostendorf-Rodríguez, 2023). So much of their wisdom we still do not know or understand.

Forests prevent trees from being selfish, individualist and utilitarian – they are communities by nature, and sharing and caring becomes their norm. When we immerse ourselves in a forest, we experience the music of nature in all its harmony, without the need for any conductor or rehearsal. In a forest, all living beings go about their daily business and experience the risks and opportunities nature provides. Forests do not market insurance policies to protect animals from danger, or sell food in supermarkets – wild animals and birds have to fend for themselves through trial and error, and coaching from elders. There is a rawness of experience which is magical, and something we have forgotten to value in modernity, preferring instead to super-market our food, or to insure against risks rather than to experience them. Forests make great laboratories of learning for our society, and it is wrong that modern finance chooses to do all its learning through technology and data rather than raw engagement with nature.

As we have explored in previous chapters, many human cultures of the world have had a deep respect for nature and are now labelled 'indigenous'. Many have withered or died along the way (often as a result of empire and greed), or if they survive, they are on the fringes and margins of society. When we think a bit more deeply about, for example, the few Amazonian tribes who profoundly understand the forest, but are shrinking and dying because of human exploitation, we diminish their wisdom through our prejudice and ignorance. We forget that their survival comes in spite of finance as they need very little money and have no intention of ever being rich or powerful. Amazonian tribes are, in fact, playing a significant role and taking big risks in protecting the rain forests which we are destroying, with very little capital or technology to support them. Just as the silent work of the trees and forests was not respected by finance and actively destroyed by it over the last few hundred years, are we doing the same in terms of our diminution of indigenous cultures and their wisdom today? This is certainly true today if we look at global textbooks in finance – just as forests are not in the index, even when they have been sacrificed to print the books, indigenous cultures are also missing from any finance discussion. Context matters deeply in finance and needs to be resuscitated.

The timeless virtues of tolerance and kindness can be learnt and passed down the generations. It does not require rocket science for humanity to understand that peace for oneself comes from giving peace to others. The same applies to love and kindness. It is nature's law that somewhere somehow, the peace and love will come back, and we do not need a formal transaction to seal the promise or the reciprocity. They can be taught through living example, and the opposite is also likely to be true. If we teach selfishness and violence in the home, then it will ripple out into the wider society, as children learn from the examples around them, just as trees have done from their neighbours over millennia.

Finance cannot teach selflessness or generosity, nor can it broadcast the virtue of tolerance and kindness. However, it can certainly recognise and appreciate it, and develop models and theories which show the world what can happen when a family and community are founded on such pristine principles. Public funding, social enterprise, entrepreneurship and corporate finance should be taught alongside one another for students to understand the vast diversity of living finance practices. If instead the theory chooses to stay positivist and detached, and claim no duty or responsibility to create a better society or a healthier planet, then we have every right to call it out for its profound act of vandalism. Its experts are deliberately destroying humanity, and should know better given their education and training. The last example they should give our dying world is how to stay greedy, violent and selfish, and then call it freedom and liberation. That is deliberate and knowing unsustainability, shaped by experts who ought to be tried for the planetary harm they are causing.

When there are whole communities shaped by kindness and tolerance, like rainforests, they can not only preserve and conserve society, they can reinvigorate our social environment. Just as banks concentrate finance and capital, communities concentrate culture and regularly renew and reinvigorate it. Banks have a lot to learn from forests how to build and grow communities, and given that they are creators and pillars of our modern money system, one of their top priorities ought to be how they *grow* trust and not deplete it. Mechanisms for monitoring and accounting for trust should be developed so that banks who are given the licence to influence and shape our financial system ought to be trustworthy and obligated to be planters and multipliers of trust in society. Their globalisation and power can and often does act to overpower and overwhelm communities, but this is unsustainable behaviour. Forests rarely try to control or overpower nature, and in fact protect it and enable diversity and inclusion.

Citizens from community and ethical groups can do more and reach out to absorb the pollution in society, and then become role models of peace and hope. When such communities exist, they should be protected and not plundered, celebrated and not discriminated or marginalised, and asked to share their principles and wisdom with wider society, such that the good culture ripples out. Their bank of morality should be on every high street, not to preach or convert but to be open and available should people have questions and those who are curious to learn more about trust and relationships, by saving and investing. This will not be at the expense of profits, but greed and excess would be curtailed, and marketing costs will be reduced as word would soon spread that the bank genuinely cares and advises what is in the best interest of their customers.

Time is *Not* Money

Given the reality and finality of death, the temporality of money and materiality is not dependent on any rocket science. Sadly, rocket scientists who work in powerful positions in finance are in denial of this reality. In fact, there is a whole knowledge industry of denial which has been authorised by science. Through markets and financial instruments, the industry has managed to collapse the future into the present and enable people to 'cash in' on the future, leading to inter-generational inequity, structured in the very heart of our financial system. We need to find ways of reallocating such capital gains so that future generations are not exploited and their needs protected.

Given our prowess at data and analysis, information systems which collate the inter-generational implications of such practices should be developed to make the impacts visible to the decision-makers. Boards with the power to monitor and allocate resources need to capture such information and provide leadership to ensure that the power over money is not abused, and the hubris curtailed by humility and active compassion for all living beings. The methods of doing so could be through training, incentives and setting good examples and becoming generous and humble role models for their employees. A culture which embraces the temporality of money and its related power is critical to the sustainable transformation of business organisations.

Forests are incapable of owning and accumulating timber, or even the fruits they painstakingly produce in wholesale. Instead they use their ability to patiently and selflessly convert solar energy and water into food to help nourish life. They overwhelmingly live in the present so do not understand time nor are they preoccupied with the rush to accomplish life goals. Instead of constantly trying to become or be someone, they enjoy just being in the now, without fear or anxiety. There is a profound sense of acceptance and acknowledgment of the generosity of nature, and a willingness to accept death if and when it comes. When they get cremated by nature's fires, we cannot hear their screams because they simply accept this fate.

Time is like the wind which forests allow to pass through their leaves, quietly allowing its flow, just as the birds and animals that depend on them are helped to live. We have so much to learn from this patience and flow, and indigenous cultures who lived inside the forests understood it very deeply. They developed stories, poetry and songs to show their respect for the forests, and pass this culture to future generations to enable sustainable living. They were overwhelmed by the silence and generosity of the forests, and embraced this wisdom in their own behaviours and lifestyles. We need to rediscover ways of locating our finance hubs inside rain forests so that such wisdom permeates deep into our decision-making – locating headquarters in urban cities encourages the dissonance from nature, making us cold and calculating instead.

The Roots of Finance: Recognising and Valuing Cultural Depth and Wisdom

Just as the roots and heights of different plants differ in their length, depth and breadth, so does culture in human society. Long-established rain forests are likely to have very strong and deep roots, and a heritage of mutuality and interdependence. The same applies to communities, even those which have been put today in the margins like Native Americans or Aborigines. These very deep cultures have instead been 'imprisoned' in modern reserves, so that society can hide its violence and inhumanity and still feel good about it. We have not only severed rain forests, but deep historical cultures too, and have little understanding of their value and wisdom. It appears as if those cultures which do not comply with our modern neo-liberal worldview are confined to the margins and discriminated against *because* of their heritage. Modernity has learnt to actively destroy and subvert culture in the name of science. Indigenous knowledge, experience and wisdom has been eliminated by 'epistemic' violence. It is no coincidence that just as European cultures went on a rampage against 'backward' or 'uncivilised' people all over the world, expanding the scope and power of material science and weaponry, the planet went into an irreversible Anthropocene.

The sustainable finance promoted in this book appreciates wisdom and its history and depth, and encourages society to value and celebrate it.

This is a significant rewriting of the equations of money and economics. Knowledge is deeply entwined with belief and heritage in many indigenous cultures and communities all over the world, and very few seek material power or dominance over nature and society – they are contented to recall their songs and narratives and live in tune with the animals and the land. Elders are highly respected and cared for in these communities and so long as their basic needs are satisfied, time is spent on festivals, ritual and the continuity of traditions. Jobs were not needed or created in these cultures, peace was valued much more than prosperity and, in many cases, greed was banished altogether. Money was not allowed to tarnish everyday social life.

A material and materialist culture, and related institutions and norms, comes to diminish the importance of history, memory and tradition and instead turn people into consumers and servants of distant markets for clothes, cars, homes, jobs, food and leisure. This change may appear temporarily attractive, but the more it seeps into our habits and routines, the more it alienates us from trust, relationships and community. Forests have never been materialistic, nor have they been forced to succumb to it, except when man has decided to see them as clusters of wood, and occupiers of land from which money can be made. In such cases, the history of the forest, its vast ocean of interdependent life, is suddenly turned worthless, and hundreds of years of biodiversity are destroyed overnight. In a similar way, the cultural 'rain forests' all over the world, sometimes labelled 'indigenous cultures' have been decimated by a new materialist and fundamentalist economic wisdom, which has no value for community or kinship or even trust and tradition.

When value trumps values, the depth and scale of the moral harm to society is profound and cannot be ignored in our drive towards sustainability. We have forgotten what culture and kinship even mean, and are now pretending that technocratic fixes like ESG or Net Zero will save humanity, and we can then carry on behaving as normal. Even in our universities, the importance and value of humanities has been disappearing very fast, as students choose to pursue more practical and 'valuable' subjects from which they can get well-paid jobs to service the high student debt they have accumulated.

A subtle but significant cycle of cultural demolition has become normalised and routinised, and we are happy to romanticise about culture in our museums but unable or unwilling to see it alive in various communities all over the world. In fact, those groups which are able to retain their traditions and beliefs, do so against this utilitarian tidal wave, and should be saluted and celebrated for their bravery and resilience. Instead of museums, we should attend their festivals and rituals to understand the traditions and customs, and see how it is that they have survived for so long and sustained themselves. We need to enable cultures to speak their own truths on their own terms. Through these experiences, we may begin to cultivate future cultural rain forests of hope.

Selfless Science: Nurturing Generosity

Forests do not make speeches about their wisdom, nor do they create markets for their products or services. They speak through their actions, one of which is selflessness, as opposed to selfishness. Finance has turned selfishness into a science which is profoundly unsustainable. Communities and indigenous cultures all over the world have cultivated experiences of sharing and selflessness similar to forests, and developed the wisdom to enjoy it and pass it to future generations, through art, rituals and narratives. Finance today is being forced to think in terms of equality, fairness and meeting the needs of future generations, all without compromising the bounty of nature. Our current predicament *forces* finance theory to value the opposite of what it has assumed so far – the criticality of sharing, caring and community. Even when there is plenty of evidence of selfishness, materialism and greed, especially in the Western world, where the forests of finance theory are headquartered, it needs to urgently find a new language and model reflecting interdependence.

The denial of history and tradition needs to be rooted out, and inter-disciplinarity and diversity, which forests routinely practice and host, need to be central to the reform syllabus. The roots of finance need to be exhumed from a bio-diverse perspective, and the fact that for thousands of years, human communities lived largely in harmony with nature celebrated. Just because many indigenous cultures have become extinct or marginalised today does not mean that their knowledge should also be made extinct. If forests are teachers through their actions, so should finance professors become those teachers, actively embracing an open and inclusive science. There is a unique opportunity to provide such humble and respectful education to students from all parts of the world, and remove any desire to standardise and materialise the false objectivity and impersonality that has become its mantra.

We need to reinstate the criticality of responsibility to education. Unfortunately, experts committed to their materialist theories have long embraced this framework in their everyday lives, such that everything is a transaction, including students and teaching. Their lives have become steeped in selfishness and materialism. Finance trees (professors) need to take an active responsibility for their models and theories and face the devastation that they have caused directly. This may involve pain and grief, but we need to face this and experience the catharsis for us to help shape sustainable futures. *Feeling* the anguish and the harm caused by our science is critical to making the necessary changes – we simply cannot assume that our knowledge can be changed without experiencing the suffering we have caused. No longer can we sustain an irresponsible attitude to our students, nor should we abandon the love and care required to bring about genuine change among the future leaders of finance.

There are over a hundred quality academic journals in accounting and finance, which have become the forests of expertise, paradoxically killing trees to spread their science. However, their agenda and framing has been very narrow and siloed. If we are to marry soil, soul and climate, in order to create and sustain forests which absorb carbon, then this holistic approach should also apply to the roots of our science. There is an urgency to re-examine our scientific branches, and prevent the colonisation of other business disciplines to the service of a neo-liberal materialist finance. The media we use to communicate our science also need to be re-evaluated for their ethics and morality, and any methods which deny our communitarian and life preserving roots, should be scrutinised and actively reformed. Given the significant power of finance, we have an academic duty to avoid hubris and arrogance, and enhance our responsibility and accountability to the biodiversity of all life on the planet. Just as the United Nations had created a global convention on biodiversity, we need to convene a global dialogue of experts on how to shape an inclusive morality where money once again becomes the servant of forests, rather than its chainsaw.

The knowledge catharsis that will be required is not being underestimated here. It implies a changing of the content and approach to PhD programmes in finance and business, and an active engagement with a whole approach to science where the criticality of interdependence is made central. The obsession with evidence and materialist objectivity needs to be directly addressed, and an inter-disciplinary training curriculum drawn up to shape the transformational knowledge that will be required. Students need to be taken on field trips to communities where money is put in its place and not allowed to overwhelm social trust and relationships. Similarly, rainforests can be studied and experienced before the models of finance are theorised and standardised for the whole planet. Post-visit discussions and dialogues about the possibilities and meanings which can be drawn from such field immersions need to be central to the training. Even meditations and reflections should be encouraged to awaken the spiritual depths of each student. The silence of trees shows how long they meditate, with stoicism and equipoise, and finance experts need to 'unlearn' the ignorance of this wisdom.

Purpose and Meaning

Forests appear to have a clear sense of purpose and meaning – they group together to provide shelter and food for wildlife, and also help absorb carbon from the atmosphere. They are not afraid of death, nor obsessed by life – there is a deep contentment without a desire to grow and conquer nature. There is a symbiosis with the elements, where forests are a combination of soil, soul and sunshine – and they do not act as if they have forgotten their roots or mutuality.

Modernity has 'discovered' that for sustainable leadership, we need to ensure that humans have a clear sense of purpose and meaning and are able to live in harmony with this essence. Given that finance has divorced itself from any deep sense of reflexivity, we need to acknowledge the simple fact that if such experiment were to be conducted, many leaders would immediately feel very uncomfortable, and choose to use their power to avoid it altogether. However, this need not be true of young minds and future leaders, who are open to persuasion, and concerned about their own future, with Greta Thunberg as a unique radical role model.

Finance trainees need to be asked to reflect on purpose, and science can be used to provide the evidence base for the destruction caused by contemporary economics and its resource expropriation engine. If they are shown how money is a social, political and cultural construct, they are likely to want to explore this topic further and dig deep into the roots of money. This journey could then help them consider their own interpretation of finance, and how this need not be irrelevant, but is critical to unleashing their motivation to become an expert guide to sustainability. It is critical that from an early stage, we play an active role in 'personalising' finance and explaining the role of contentedness, the limits of growth, and how intellectually, there is unlimited possibility for growth beyond the material. Like forests, we can encourage them to experience the joy of giving and the violence of taking, and help them through this personal journey.

This reflection cannot be done without examining the role of the Finance professions and the Business School and their own purpose and meaning. The institution and incentives frame and influence what is taught and how it is taught, so this also needs to change radically given the deep conflicts humanity faces today. When forests are chopped and profits made, humanity finds ways to avoid the injury and pain temporarily, but the long-term consequences are significant. Similarly, the environmental and scientific footprint of the business school and its institutional model ought to be re-evaluated, using nature as a resource of wisdom and enlightenment. If students are asked to find purpose and meaning in an environment where they have to pay tens of thousands of dollars in fees, they are likely to already be self-selected for material returns on their training (Parker, 2018). The selflessness of forests, and the ways in which they protect nature for free, should provide us important lessons on how we structure and incentivise our financial education and training systems.

Cultivating Structural Conscience

Trees work quietly and behind the scenes. They may not have brains or the intelligence we prioritise, but seem to be wise beyond their years – and contented with their lot. In finance, we have banished conscience and reflexivity about our actions and character. In fact, we actively seek dissonance and have shaped our institutions to be impersonal and cold, rather than emotional and sensitive to the needs of humanity. Conscience is a deeper and quieter method of facing the facts with honesty and sincerity, and has a wholeness to it which does not separate mind, body and spirit. Like intuition, it is an early warning system for when we are doing something wrong, and modernity has dulled this reflexivity especially among corporate leaders, who are likely to be frightened by the prospect of facing their inner selves.

Organisations need to find ways of monitoring and engaging with their conscience (Hawken, 1994; Shah, 2022; Stiglitz, 2024). They should not take their mission and purpose for granted, or assume that their products and services are sustainable, without allowing challenge and introspection. Just because profits and performance are good, and the stock price is up should not mean that an organisation is sustainable – in fact it can have the opposite effect of creating a false sense of accomplishment. This comfort blanket can remove it from deeper questioning. Modern accounting and reporting systems are deeply transactional and impersonal, and have no role for subjective frameworks such as corporate conscience. They are in denial of emotion or intuition, and obsessed by measurement and facts, without understanding how even evidence can be deeply biased.

If concern for nature and environment is accepted, then conscience can help create reporting systems which are outside law and standards, but help leaders to understand the depth and extent of their impact on other living beings. By definition, laws and regulations take time to implement and be standardised so may not be universally applicable. They may even create measurements which are misleading for the industry that a corporation is working in. The knowledge and systems required to create this information require an understanding of the products and services provided by the organisation, and need to be adapted according to the methods available to measure and monitor the impacts of these on society and the environment. New methods can be developed with the help of expert professionals who understand the industry very well. Such processes can help organisations dig deeper into their own minds and spirits, and engage employees to introspect about genuinely sustainable ways of operating.

Law and Regulation

Do forests own the land on which they stand? Does the soil own them? Should they charge for the carbon absorption that is so vital to protecting the ecosystem? In so many ways, we have shaped the laws and regulations which have attacked forests, and found ways to separate this structural harm from our scientific study. Corporations are alien beasts, fuelled by finance, who then develop a global power to practice irresponsibility through plunder, without accountability or even fair tax payments. Forests only deal with living elements, and do not know much about laws, rules and regulations – they just live and die, naturally or under the human axe. Society should not allow corporations to get out of control, or plunder culture and nature at will, without accountability in the courtroom of the forest.

We urgently need to re-examine our systems of property, land ownership, resource extraction and legalised natural expropriation to suit human ends – which have in practice led to the end of humanity as we had known it. Our break between law and indigenous culture, and the desire to standardise and make ideas like fairness and rights uniform all over the world has led us to the lowest common denominator of ethics. We have industrialised our plunder of knowledge, tradition and nature. The protection of animals and nature ought to be central to our systems, and, as far as possible, violence should never be authorised. Such ideals can help shape the philosophy of our justice system, which has hitherto been deeply anthropocentric and encouraged greed and wealth creation through injustices against minority cultures and the environment. It is critical that we recognise the unsustainability of this legal framework, and understand how reform is needed at its very root.

Alien corporations are able to raise finance in global markets, helping them to expand the scale of their plunder with very little local or cultural accountability. Their political role and influence are entirely ignored by finance even when it is central to their wealth extraction. This behaviour should not be supported by our legal systems, nor should they be allowed to practice regulatory arbitrage between countries to minimise their environmental restrictions, or employment costs and inhumanity, away from the 'western' eye. We need to be very careful with market-based solutions like carbon-trading or green finance, which are often disguised by spin machines and rarely transparent in their conduct. Just as forests stay grounded throughout their lives, we need to find mechanisms to ground corporations and reduce their social and ecological harms without proper control and accountability.

As laws are human constructs, we need to find ways of reclaiming them, rather than suffering under their weight. Global loopholes create a race to the bottom, and pose a relentless threat to nature, where poverty and inequality is used to pump and dump pollutants without recourse to the culprit mega-corporations. At present countries are often forced to compete against each other to invite corporations on their lands and give incentives to attract them. Supply chains have become increasingly complex, and are often used to suppress the pollution and the violence committed by them (Fleming, 2014; Klein, 1970). They have become hidden weapons of mass expropriation – even corporate structures are constructed such as to hide the malaise and make it difficult for society to follow the money trail. Audit and investigation professionals should have the independence and authority to report this abuse and be allowed to challenge multinationals without fear of capture or reprisal.

Forests survive without laws and regulations. Nature sets the rules, and they are exposed to the laws of nature, which can include disease, forest fires, heavy rain, storms, drought and even attack from commercial loggers. They also grow and nourish wildlife, and create canopies of hope and community. While we need laws to govern our lives, we need to question their efficacy and effectiveness, and be ready to change them if our risks and priorities change. At present, we seem to be captured by existing laws and legal systems, creating minefields of new legislation, fuelling the demand for lawyers. In the meantime, we feel paralysed as a society to reverse the devastation of our natural systems. The positivist discipline of finance ought to take an active role in studying the impact of our financial laws towards nature and society, and understand the criticality of normativity, if we are to preserve human life on this planet. A whole systems perspective needs to be adopted to understand the macro implications of financial markets and institutions, and this means multi-disciplinarity. Where the laws and incentives increase greed, inequality and natural resource extraction, they should be called out, reformed or thrown out by governments.

Beyond Materialism

As we have seen our theories in finance are based on neo-liberalism and utilitarianism, where nature has been assumed to be abundant and non-living or inanimate, a servant to our limitless material ambitions. Evidence shows that when young innocent students study this economic science, often in prestigious Universities, they become converted by its assumptions, and begin to embrace materialist ideals and selfishness as the root of their lives (Gerlach, 2017). Their own culture and values get subverted, and they carry this mindset into the organisations they enter, and even end up leading or managing them. Cold calculation, and rule by profit maximisation becomes the norm, and the short term becomes the only business horizon, especially when it comes to managing people and performance. We have financialised our organisations and, in the process, subverted human cultures too.

If the scale of this thinking were local, it would be easy to control and contain even. Sadly, this ideology has been globalised, such that even in India, the land of deep culture and faith, the thousands of business schools there teach finance from an American model. This actively depresses the local culture and beliefs, and subverts it in ways which may seem temporarily seductive, but in the long term are very damaging. Its licencing by prestigious global universities, which attract high calibre students from all over the world, adds to the problem, exporting the forest of materialistic finance all over the world. This allows the inequality and resource extraction to be justified, and cold calculation to take over without any connection with local contexts, diversity or the criticality of protecting natural resources. Concepts like the triple bottom line, and corporate social responsibility or even ESG have become overpowered by materiality and greed and subverted to suit corporate greed agendas.

Instead of learning from the calmness and inclusivity of forests, we have done the opposite – chopped up their wisdom and even uprooted their history and heritage in the name of progress and science. We have undervalued the quality and depth of human cultures, and instead made them look and feel the same, assuming that everyone is selfish and ought to be so. Our illiteracy on faith, and the vast diversity of its influence on human character and community, has been supreme – we have completely ignored their historic and continuing influence on financial behaviour and decision making. This is gross ignorance and shameful given the significant awareness and knowledge we have about diversity today. Faith and culture overlap to different degrees, and faith is an important self-regulator of conduct and behaviour, something which no legal system can achieve. Faith enhances the quality and depth of trust and relationships in society, and often weaves the harmony in ways akin to the behaviour of rain forests. Many faiths are plural in their outlook and respect people of other faiths, and trade with them, because they see the spiritual similarity in their culture and aspirations.

Professional bodies in accounting and finance, have become the wings of these materialist forests, spreading their religion far and wide. They are secular, even when we know for a fact that the roots of chartered accountancy in the UK nearly 150 years ago were strongly based on faith and ethics. They are also standardised and universalist in their syllabi, assuming a common thread of knowledge applicable to the whole world, licencing professionals to think and operate in this way. Ethics are now commonly discussed and examined, but in a secular, technocratic and transactional form, such that once the exams are passed, they are abandoned. The criticality of whistleblowers to large organisations are off the professional syllabi, even when finance holds the key to fraud and hubris, and ought to challenge it in a timely manner to avoid large losses for employees and shareholders. Even teamwork and culture are taught to serve the profit engine, and tax avoidance is celebrated in accounting rather than actively challenged. Such certified forests of education and training are unsustainable.

Environmental Aesthetics

As science has evolved and progressed, it has focused on reason and evidence, with a strong emphasis on materiality and the measurable. This has suited the growth of finance even when the evidence has been partial, and the reason has become subverted to a particular neo-liberal secular ethic of rights and fairness. The chapters in this book have exposed that if we acknowledge nature, we learn to revere it, and see the wisdom in animals and trees, their contentedness and inclusivity. Science has shown the depth and breadth of knowledge about the land and agriculture in indigenous traditions, although this has been separated from the study and teaching of finance. In some cultures, it is even believed that the land owns the people – so entwined and rooted they are to the locality and community. By externalizing nature and culture, finance has damaged and uprooted society, making ethics and sustainability harder. I have no doubt that there are many finance academics who don't believe in sustainability at all.

We urgently need to find ways to grow the aesthetics of finance and enable it to embrace the breadth and depth of human-nature relationships, and the limits of materiality. Poetry is one way of revealing and discussing the aesthetics of nature and help people understand its complexity, humility and kindness too. Music and stories are also powerful in taking us into the soul and rhythms of nature and explore life beyond the material. It is only when we truly understand the nature and limits of money will we be able to transcend it. Living experiences of charity and volunteering can be very helpful in understanding the joys of life outside a money economy. Such knowledge cannot come from equations and analysis alone – something else must be opened and experienced for students to see the limits of measurement and evidence and search beyond it.

As scientists, we value this quest for truth and understanding and share the thirst with our saints and poets. We now need to find ways of talking and listening to one another and engaging in open dialogues which are pluralist and seek to overcome the boundaries that have been set in our learning. There needs to be a commitment to change, and a feeling for the pain and anguish suffered by nature, to help us find ways to reform our science. Forests are great spaces for the awakening of such aesthetic sensibilities, but not the only ones.

The disconnect we have created between objective finance and subjective human life is also a steep challenge to overcome. In forests, trees are subjective but have no qualms about acting selflessly – behaving as if they understand the interdependence of all life very profoundly. A finance class which discusses and debates the mycelium evidence from forests could become an important way of engaging with the reality of interdependence, and the urgency to abandon our views on selfish independence. Debates and discussions with students and scholars from other departments like ecology or agriculture and forestry or theology can help break some of the silos and enable students to see the wider depths and breadths of knowledge needed to tackle our environmental crises.

Book Summary and Contributions

This book has used the method of grounded and natural reflexivity to generate possibilities for a sustainable finance which is humble, responsible, accountable and above all, stays rooted instead of expropriating nature, animals and humanity. Opening any finance textbook will instead tell you the opposite – that there is no room for reflection, and calculation and measurement are the real truths. The soul is actively detached from the body and made irrelevant to the science. Money, life and fact have been commodified. Context, biodiversity, and culture – the real canvases which operationalise finance – have been removed from research and analysis such that the science can be *imposed* on society, which is forced to fit into the equations. In the research, the disciplinary silo moulded and policed by finance has been broken, and a wide range of perspectives relevant to finance from disciplines such as natural sciences, sociology, political economy, theology, anthropology, geography and philosophy have been included.

The abstraction that is rife in finance, and amplified by it, has been critiqued from the very beginning. This abstraction is central to professional finance education and training systems all over the world, without any reference to the reality. The scholars help to construct a new fictitious and damaging reality, and call it science, with all the attendant power and authority. Indigenous cultures and wisdoms are plundered by the equations. Money itself is an abstraction, and finance experts today are *terrified* of addressing the fundamentals of its nature, beliefs and limitations. However, our climate emergency gives us no choice or alternative. We are forced to abandon our hubris and domineering philosophy of life and psyche of conquest over humans, animals and nature. To reimagine finance, we need to abandon existing theories, techniques and methods, as they are built on individualistic, utilitarian and materialistic principles which have been proven to be unsustainable.

As an alternative, we have shown what non-anthropocentric finance can look like – nature is not dumb, but intelligent, inclusive and lives with interdependence. Neither are indigenous cultures and traditions illiterate, especially in relation to debt and finance. Even if humans disappear from the planet, nature will evolve. Euro-centric empire cultures have chosen to rule and expropriate the world and control its financial systems for their own private material benefit. The result is a nightmare of greed, violence, anxiety and social upheaval. This needs serious repair, and it starts from the ground up and not from a particular neo-liberal, materialist, and hyper-specialised technocratic theory down.

We have exposed the unsustainability of this worldview, and resurfaced the beliefs and culture hidden behind the equations of finance. Given that money and finance are nothing but systems of belief and human construction, we have the capacity to rewire our knowledge and institutions to shape sustainability. The least we could do is to *not* deny the vast diversity of perspectives, practices and wisdoms of finance that already exist in the world. Whilst embracing diversity has become fashionable, engaging with diverse theories and philosophies is still in its infancy. Indigenous philosophies enshrine contentment as a means of attaining higher levels of purpose and meaning, far beyond vacuous and anxious materialistic happiness. As Graeber and Wengrow (2021) demonstrate, there has been a lot of imagination and innovation in human history then we give credit for. Progress has never been linear. To simply focus on a materialist and universalist theory of finance as the only hope is to betray our ancestors too. It is moral regression, damaging cultures and communities in its wake.

Graeber's call for a moral, grounded and communitarian finance, which understands the importance of trust and relationships, and instead of subverting and expropriating land and society, learns to take responsibility, is heeded in this book. The cultural genocide caused by empire, financial markets and institutions is exposed, and the resulting unsustainability articulated. When finance destroys culture, the damage is long-term and material. Soil, seed, growth and soul, the roots of our connection with one another and the wilderness, are discussed extensively. These are themes rarely if ever found in a finance textbook or curriculum, including research and PhD training. Many of the silos created by contemporary finance have been broken and replaced by possibilities of deeper learning and transformation. This is not an exhaustive study of world cultures and their perspectives on finance, nor does it comprise or analyse all different moralities and ethics about money and finance. The book opens different ways and perspectives of moralizing and grounding finance in peace, inclusion and sustainability.

Belonging to an indigenous culture (Jain) and having had the opportunity to live and train in the West has helped me develop inter-cultural experience. My timeless tradition has given me the tools for plural intellectual curiosity where the pursuit of knowledge and wisdom is revered, and money is prevented from corrupting the motives. The Jains have a long experience of reflection on the nature and limits of money and even today live with this understanding, helping us see the flaws in our financial system. Even within India, the Jains are a 'high context' culture, having had a significant impact on its cultural, economic and financial history. This has helped me to see how finance can be enriched by a very different cultural and ontological framing, which starts with a perspective of respect and compassion for all living beings, not just humans. In this sense, Jain science is grounded yet deeply plural and inclusive, something very rare in modernity.

I have used my creativity and imagination to write this book, even though this 'subjectivity' has long been banned from finance. The research method adopted in this book draws upon both knowledge and experience, and participation in international conferences, dialogues and professional conversations about the depth and breadth of challenges in accounting and finance. Belief has been incorporated into the analysis, even when social scientists and economists deny it. I am hopeful that this approach will encourage more creativity and diverse voices who care deeply about the planet and its future, and go against the tide of positivism, empiricism and technical complexity for its own sake.

Whilst decolonizing the curriculum, the importance of embracing human diversity is currently being encouraged and celebrated, although the methods and techniques for doing so in finance are largely unknown. Furthermore, the rebellion is often deeply anthropocentric, when the climate crisis is calling for much more kindness and humility to *all* living beings in our sciences and institutions. In this sense, this book is constructive and draws upon diverse wisdoms to shape a caring and responsible science. It helps remove the prejudice normally practiced on 'native' populations through equations and fundamentalism and shows how hope can come from respecting all living beings.

The abject removal of history and reflexivity on the techniques of learning and education from scientific pursuits has been exposed as core to epistemic violence – as finance is nothing but an idea and human construct. It is a belief system and ideology, just like religions and faiths. The defensive silos which have been constructed and regularly policed by top journal editors have been exposed for their vacuity and irresponsibility, exposing the highly political nature of the science and its prophets. Significant insights from other disciplines like geography, anthropology, sociology, economic history, critical accounting, psychology, theology and philosophy have been cited in these pages to expand and enrich our understanding of the wide varieties of finance in the world. On reflection, it is clear that the silos created by finance stem from a deep insecurity of the experts, and the need to hold onto positions of power and influence instead of facing truth and justice.

One of the deepest silos that have been created in finance is the distance between the science and the teaching methods and effectiveness. There is virtually no reflexivity or importance given to professional training and the underlying ethics and impact on students and society. In this book, pedagogy has been reconnected to knowledge in finance and given the deserved importance – graduates and professionals are the field force of financial ideology, and the wrong training can have devastating social and ecological impact. A new way of framing and teaching finance has been opened, showcasing wisdoms which have long been hiding in plain sight. A diverse set of research findings and literature has been revealed, which can help open the mindset of finance scholarship, shaping its inter-disciplinarity, and enabling greater responsibility and accountability of its knowledge and pedagogical processes and systems.

Context matters significantly in finance – the silences over the purpose and meaning of products and services supplied by markets, and their abject attacks on humanity, animals and nature, are not avoided in this book. Existing research on 'cultural' finance is primarily euro-centric and uses narrow techniques of analysis which are therefore limiting in the critical insights they can provide. The deep cultural differences between nations should not be papered over or misrepresented by selfish western superiority and materialism. There is a profound fallacy of misplaced concreteness, and distancing from the social and ecological outcomes of the equations which is unsustainable, when numbers are the sole measure of performance. Even memory and lived 'experience' have been abolished from finance, completely antithetical to the social and cultural nature of its practice. Culture has a strong influence on financial decision-making, and inter-cultural nuances are complex but worth learning to avoid breaking trust and relationships.

The ESG greenwashing is part of a much deeper intellectual and structural hubris in the science. This book shows what happens when we change our perspective to one which is multi-disciplinary and grounded in nature, interdependence and human communities. Denial of culture, belief, history and context have been a convenient tool and ideology, not disconnected from the wide-spread looting and racism of empire. Europe deliberately and actively used prejudice and violence towards humans, animals and nature as a weapon of wealth creation, principles whose cultural residues are framed today in economic science and institutions. This book re-instates ethics, morality, tradition and belief at the heart of finance science.

The complex multi-layered supply chain of finance distances and buries morality, responsibility and accountability. The science refuses to engage with this repression and instead legitimates complexity. By going back to first principles, this book has shown that for many people in the world, finance was not allowed to overwhelm their lives, and trust and relationships mattered crucially. They did not want or create complex finance networks or institutions due to their focus on a life beyond the material, and one imbued with faith and belief in nature, family and community. Many of these cultures and communities still survive today in spite of the sweep of materiality and individualism. Studying them closely can reveal the varied ways in which finance is made a servant and prevented from becoming a master. This would produce organic knowledge about finance. Instead of the theoretical universalism that is preached, we urgently need to revive the living diversity of finance and its purpose and meaning.

A word which appears throughout the book is community. This word is missing from finance textbooks. There are communities all over the world which have different degrees of selflessness, trust and social capital, practices antithetical to mainstream finance. Like forests of trees, many people have an experience of being part of a collective and this changes their attitudes to money and finance. For them, meaning and purpose are instilled from childhood, and even for those members who choose to go into business, their approach to profits and wealth can be very different as a result. Sustainability requires us to preserve communities, and build them where they are missing.

Forests of Hope 175

The least finance science could do is to research, unpack and celebrate communities which are large banks of trust and cooperation.

An organic theory of finance is plural, not singular, and makes culture, ethics and values central to the language and framing of lending, borrowing and investing. It is not profit maximising, but allows growth to be organic and manageable, with many firms choosing contentedness and remaining small in scale. It is non-materialistic and gives importance to customers, service, quality and relationships. Trust is a critical currency of organic finance and highly valued. Families, communities, plants, animals and land should all be considered in the way knowledge is designed and articulated. Dualistic and materialistic ontology has no place in a sustainable finance future. While power, violence, greed and monopoly are central to finance and its 'growth' agenda, this book has shown an alternative perspective which is based on a deeper understanding of the nature and limits of money. It encourages moral reflexivity of finance leaders throughout the business journey and exposes the unsustainability of growth and accumulation for its own sake. The complexity of financial instruments ought not to be used to exploit the ignorant or the weak. Growth should be within manageable limits, with borrowing controlled to ensure relationships, trust and honour are protected and not undermined. Short-termism and transactionalism are discouraged throughout.

When trust and relationships are a key currency, nature puts money in its rightful place, as a servant of society. In such an environment the outcomes of finance are very, very, different. Instead of depleting community, the culture and belief system enhances and reinvigorates it. Whilst the multiplication of money can reduce trust in society, the opposite is true for belief communities – they are multipliers of trust. Information, mentoring and social capital are critical to the financial system within such groups and diasporas, and when faith communities globalise, such relationships also take on a global dimension. Finance on its own, either through its science or teaching, cannot build or nurture society. Faith and belief systems have done this throughout history, for good or bad, but the fact still remains that traditions have resilience and their rituals and festivals reinforce the spirit of community. For a sustainable future, we need to recognise the importance of this, and find ways to build upon it, instead of destroying it through wrong beliefs and ignorance, in the name of so-called science and modernity.

Small businesses, who often operate organically and purposefully by design, should be studied and celebrated much more for their grounded and contented attitudes to finance. The domination of 'corporate' finance as the principal ideology is shown to be damaging and distracting from lasting wisdom. Family-owned businesses are often prudent and factor quality products and services as primary drivers, rather than profit alone. Subsistence farmers who are in direct contact with the land, and know how to feed society, should be given much more respect and knowledge support, for they are protecting rural communities. Organic finance is based on a much deeper understanding of the nature and limits of money, than the fictions and falsehoods promoted by modern education. It also embraces the variety of influences which make for a sustainable enterprise, and does not privilege money and profits unnecessarily.

What this book has revealed is that finance has increasingly become more and more distant from truth, fact, people, animals and nature. Abstractions have become the reality, and now they are the only world that finance experts know and live by. The discipline is unable to admit the depth and breadth of the paper pyramid it has built, and its deep underlying fragility and fiction. In spite of repeated financial scandals and crashes, the 'theory' keeps on surviving, and real-world contexts like forests, animals, communities, cultures and even air and water systems are eschewed and deemed unworthy against the higher power and importance of protecting capitalism for its own sake. This book has demonstrated the deep flaws of this foundation and structure, and also shown how good positive examples of sustainable finance are hiding in plain sight, and ignored in the textbooks and the classrooms of finance, to the peril of society.

The ungovernable multi-national corporation is exposed as an extension of the fictions of finance, with our theories legitimating it, when in reality it is at the forefront of planetary violence and injustice. Our science and education need to be reframed from the bottom up rather than top down. Undemocratic corporate power, combined with a materialist science, is shown to be unsustainable, making corporations combine harvesters of soul destruction. The exclusion of plants, animals, water and air quality from finance theory can no longer be justified. Even public services like schools, roads, education and utilities, are taken for granted, and taxes avoided and minimised by the science – we need to reinstate public finance as part of the wider training curriculum so students can see the broader context. Ideally, the world needs a finance *declaration of interdependence*, to ensure its knowledge framework is fundamentally reoriented.

Traditionally, trade shaped a meeting point between different groups of people, where they had to dialogue and communicate, understand one another, and try to seek win-win solutions. It brought cultures, languages and faiths together, leading to peace-building, as trade cannot be sustained through conflict. Modernity has transactionalised trade globally, where technology and contracts replace culture, dialogue and personal communication. This has resulted in big losses for society and allowed finance to overwhelm and dominate the decision-making process. In turn, trust has declined, and relationships have withered, with transactionalism becoming more dominant. Business is now being taught as an analytical science, rather than a cultural practice, which requires investment in trust and relationship-building. The sustainability that comes from deep and lasting relationships is being undermined by financialization. Similarly, the experiential learning that arises from personal meetings, travel and field visits to customers and suppliers also diminishes in importance. Organic finance requires a revival of relationship-based long-term trade and trust building.

There are serious and damaging consequences when we train students and professionals in a finance detached from animals, nature, community and society. They become de-cultured, materialistic and soul-less. Purpose and meaning have been sacrificed at the altar of abstract calculations, and once destroyed, it is very difficult for students to reignite their sense of spirit and soul-fulness. This damage has been ignored for far too long, and is continuously being perpetuated through the models and the equations which hide the assumptions. Students learn to become selfish and individualistic, and suppress their own culture, trust and relationships in the pursuit of a transactional and highly abstract profession and workplace. If instead, the education is framed from the soil and soul upwards, encouraging the diverse meanings and practices of finance, it has the potential to transform future professionals and leaders toward a much more grounded and respectful plural approach. The detachment of belief, pedagogy and reflexivity from the science is unsustainable as has been amply demonstrated in this book.

The self-esteem that diverse cultures and traditions may possess is deliberately and actively undermined by the 'objectifying' science and its narrow research methods and agendas. It is critical that this damage is avoided in the finance classroom, by allowing different cultures to share their own stories and experiences. Indigenous wisdoms can help us out of our existential crisis, and students who come from diverse cultures should be encouraged to explore their own understandings and communal context. The spiritual and mental wellbeing of professionals can impact their leadership behaviour and decisions significantly, and needs to be core to finance science, instead of being ignored altogether. Cultural knowledge can integrate mind, body and spirit, and place money and finance within a much broader and more holistic perspective. The 'wholesome' framework introduced in this book could be adopted to encourage lecturers to research and write with confidence about the diversity of financial and belief systems all over the world, locally, regionally and nationally.

Culture and belief need to be urgently introduced into financial training programmes all over the world and made central to it. This means acknowledging belief, not necessarily accepting all beliefs or customs, but acknowledgement is the start of a deeper dialogue and denial is an abandonment of it. Ignorance or suppression of existing beliefs among the students will make matters worse when it comes to the encouragement of ethical behaviours. Basics about the nature of money and its different meanings and consequences for individuals, families and communities are important ingredients. They should be at the beginning of every textbook, instead of being ignored altogether. The diversity of cultures and beliefs around money and its significance could enrich the grounding of financial fundamentals. Such a course would be inter-disciplinary, and could also allow for debate and discussion about different customs and practices and their relevance to helping people find purpose and meaning in an increasingly turbulent and insecure world.

This approach is likely to empower diverse students to study finance and practice it with a clear conscience, enhancing meaning and purpose. Case studies and qualitative research which exposes different cultural nuances in finance can be particularly illuminating. A diversity of research methods and theories is critical if we wish to encourage pluralism. An understanding that while there may be global currencies like the US dollar or common languages like English, the variety of perspectives mean that the relationships of trust, attitudes to consumption and saving, and mutuality *vary* significantly across the world. Numbers do not alone explain the nuances of finance. Diverse perspectives also mean that the way people understand finance will vary from country to country and culture to culture. We should block attempts to homogenise students to suit the universalist ideology of finance.

For an introductory course, students could be encouraged to share their own personal and family finance stories, experiences, challenges and opportunities. Their beliefs around money and dialogues and narratives about 'success' and rich bankers or entrepreneurs can help frame an early discussion on the cultural impacts of money on people's lives and relationships. Different types of institutions, public and private, and their finance needs could also be explained at the early stages, leading to dialogues on the importance of public or charitable services, and their role in community building and cost-effective provision of public goods.

Financial literacy, a major challenge for modernity, could also be introduced earlier, to help students understand the fundamentals of saving, borrowing and investment at a personal level, and how basic needs can be fulfilled with a basic knowledge of finance. The social damage caused by financial complexity on society should also be taught to students, given the widespread evidence. Overall, if a multi-disciplinary personal and cultural foundation is laid in finance, rich with stories and case studies which students can relate to, it will make them much more curious and questioning in later years. It will awaken their sense of purpose and meaning in life, and improve their ethical commitments. The present approach throws them into the technical complexity, without even giving them the chance to question the fundamentals or even grow their personal passion for the subject.

Micro-finance and micro-enterprise, which have long been suppressed by corporate finance, is shown to have much more potential for hope and social construction of the sustainable kind. Patient capital is encouraged, and intergenerational equity is discussed to expose our flawed market logics. Investment is not just about return, but also about growth of community and the protection of our precious environment. Spirituality and belief, at the heart of finance customs and behaviours, is resurfaced and exposed, both of the flawed kind, and the positive shared customs and beliefs needed to heal our present world and reform its knowledge systems. Materialist obsession has spread fear and insecurity in society, and we cannot survive unless we address this corruption directly.

There is a gap in the training and certification of a trusted and locally sensitive financial field force all over the world which helps households deal with their basic financial needs in terms of working, saving, borrowing and spending, including major costs like housing and pensions. This is where most people all over the world live and cope with finance, including small businesses, market sellers or street hawkers, and many find it overwhelming and scary. Such advice could help revive rural communities and sensitise them to the basic needs for budgeting and accounting critical to surviving modernity. The income for such trained advisers can either be subsidised by governments or come from the customers, but should never be product or commission related to ensure objectivity. In the West, a lot of the household advice would be related to money habits and culture, and in the East, more to do with financial literacy and budgeting. Technological products like phone apps can support this work, but the personal coaching aspects relating to finance are important and need such trusted advisers. At times they will need to sit down with the whole family to give the cultural and behavioural advice relating to money which is so critical to a fulfilling life today.

This grounded meditation on finance also opens the possibility of new insights about macro-economic knowledge and analysis through going back to nature, and allowing it to speak to us on its own terms. Interest rates, exchange rates, stock prices are all numbers which abstract reality and have often been converted into hard facts and supreme gods, when they are symbols and representations imposed on society. Global capital flows and currency movements need to be traced back to their impacts on the ground, on whole communities and societies, and not left as abstractions to be suffered. Big questions about the causes and consequences of growth, about the types of economies and industries we desire, and the impacts of our laws, systems and production engines on planet earth are often avoided.

The human implications of economic policies in terms of health and well-being are often siloed – we need to reconnect the mind of economics with the body of the earth. The chapters in this book provide an alternative framework for looking at economics as an exercise in soul-nurturing and building communities and societies who care and share. They hope to encourage more grounded macro-economic thinking and recalibration of our markets and institutions to enable trust and community rather than usurp it. Economic strategies and policies need much deeper and firmer grounding and rootedness, with an understanding of the basic needs and strengths of different nations. History and context are important, and for deepening knowledge, we can no longer afford cultural and philosophical silos built and fenced by technocrats.

The future of finance knowledge is highly political. Its critique is already coming from the ground, who coined the phrase 'we are the 99%', the victims of the elites, kleptocrats and plutocrats of the world. Experts continue to be a big part of the problem. The required knowledge transformation is not a choice or an option, but an existential need. Hence the politics and history of finance need to be taught and debated in the training of experts, instead of being avoided and denied. The rebellion needs to embrace the content and teaching methods, and emancipate diverse cultures and traditions, especially in the so-called third world, to write their own case studies and textbooks in finance. Similarly, students from these countries and cultures should be able to hear their own case studies profiled in the elite Western classrooms, such that the knowledge and respect percolates more widely. Small is beautiful when it comes to finance, and the more micro stories we can discern and share, the more it will empower future leaders to think and act differently.

References

Fleming, P. (2014). *Resisting Work: The Corporatization of Life and Its Discontents*. Temple University Press.

Gerlach, P. (2017). The Games Economists Play: Why Economics Students Behave More Selfishly Than Other Students. *PloS One*, 12(9), e0183814.

Hawken, P. (1994). *The Ecology of Commerce: A Declaration of Sustainability*. Phoenix.

Klein, N. (1970). *On Fire: The Burning Case for a Green New Deal*. Allen Lane.

Ostendorf-Rodríguez, Y. (with González, R.). (2023). *Let's Become Fungal! Mycelium Teachings and the Arts: Based on Conversations with Indigenous Wisdom Keepers, Artists, Curators, Feminists and Mycologists*. Valiz.

Parker, M. (2018). Why We Should Bulldoze the Business School. *The Guardian*.

Shah, A. K. (2022). *Inclusive and Sustainable Finance: Leadership, Ethics and Culture*. Routledge.

Stiglitz, J. E. (2024). *The Road to Freedom: Economics and the Good Society*. Allen Lane.

Index

2008 Global Finance crisis 8, 12, 36n2, 57, 89, 102, 104, 146

academic journals 16–17, 23, 26–27, 36n1, 105, 112, 148, 164–165, 173
aesthetics of finance and nature 7, 170–171
Affluenza 5
agriculture, farming: agribusiness 73–75, 84; animal/nature trusteeship 14, 32, 67–68, 110, 134; animal keeping, industrialised factory production 14, 19, 55, 57, 66–67, 73–74, 118, 134, 146, 158; biodiversity removal, standardisation 81–82; de-chemicalisation 82; displacement of farmers vs holistic inclusion (soil, soul/faith, sentience) 51, 55, 56; farm banks 74, 78–89; finance and finance needs 69, 83–84, 85; industrialised, corporatised, chemicalised 14, 51, 65, 69, 74, 81–82, 96, 134; land owner- vs trusteeship 14, 61, 64, 67–68, 70, 144, 167; revival (local, organic, communal) 60, 65–66, 73; pre-agricultural nature connection 54; seasonality, natural life and indigenous tradition 32, 65, 76–78, 83, 86, 96, 134, 142–143, 145, 154, 170; seeding in forest, farms and finance 81–82 (*see also* seed/seeding); traditional, historical 73
Ahimsa 29, 36n3
American Finance Association 23, 104
animals: absence from economic models/financial science 3, 57, 66, 118; disrespect, violence, othering towards 1, 4, 13, 32, 66–67, 73–74, 103; industrialised factory agriculture 14, 19, 55, 57, 66–67, 73–74, 118, 134, 146, 158; natural ways of interacting 150; as property and income source 11, 14, 19, 22, 70, 146; soul, spiritual wisdom, social teaching 11, 66, 66–67, 70, 118, 150, 170; traditional land–people–animal interconnection 3, 9, 10–11, 14, 51
Anthropocentrism 1, 10, 13–16, 21–22, 32, 49, 135, 146–147, 158, 162

Bastiat, Frédéric 2, 14, 92–93
Bay, T. 16
Bedouin life 126–127
behavioural finance 7, 103, 106
beliefs *see* faith/religion and beliefs
Big 4 accounting firms 4, 116, 142
biodiversity 10, 29, 31–32, 33, 50, 69, 75, 76, 81, 88–89, 95
'biodiversity' in finance 88–89, 114–115, 149–150, 155
black intellectuality 36n5
Blackrock 58
border creation 103–105
boundary policing 103–105
Buffett, Warren 25

Çalışkan, Ahmet Selami 74
care and compassion finance and living 10, 13, 28, 33, 54–55, 81, 142, 153–154, 172
City of London, financial district 116
climate change / climate emergency 7, 13, 20, 21, 29–31, 49, 122, 171
commodification of all life / natural world 17, 20, 21, 22–23, 70, 171
communitarian finance 24–26, 165, 172
communities of souls 52–53
compassion and care finance and living 10, 13, 28, 33, 54–55, 81, 142, 153–154, 172
conscience: cognitive and emotional dissonance 6; collective 101; defining 166; faith and 23, 36n2, 110, 122; structural implementation 166–167; training, insight lack 22, 85

consciousness 30–31; animal 66; body–mind connected 30; eco 129; mind–universe connectedness 28; spiritual, transcendental 30, 87
context, nature and living ecosystem 59–60
corporate social responsibility 71, 169
corporation, multinational 5, 56–57, 89, 95, 116, 141–143
culture: 'cultural finance' 5, 106, 108, 174; cultural genocide / deculturation 15, 93–94, 106, 109, 115, 172, 127–129; cultural 'rain forests' 163; defining 8; indigenous, traditional (*see* indigenous cultures); superiority assumption 8, 9–10, 21, 36n5, 174
Cunningham, L. 25

The Dawn of Everything (Graeber and Wengrow) 4
declaration of interdependence 176
Declaration on Biodiversity, United Nations 63
deculturation / cultural genocide 15, 93–94, 105–107, 109, 115, 127–129, 172
deep control, surveillance 19–20
democracy and multinational corporations / shareholder concept 5–6, 7, 57, 58, 71, 187
democratic demands and failures 57–59
denial: conscience, emotions, intuitions 166–167; history, tradition, culture 13, 25, 74, 92, 111, 121–123, 164–165, 174; knowledge industry 161; money, constructive nature and effects 20; 'objective finance' 102, 161; responsibility and accountability 128; social needs and relationships 93–94; soul distance and 81–82
detachment, desensitisation: agriculture–farmer 51, 55, 56, 74; finance–virtue/morality 55, 119, 122, 136 (*see also* ethical finance, foundations); financial education–communities/cultures 92, 128, 176–177 (*see also* learning); *Homo Economicus* approach as 1, 3, 4, 6, 10, 74; meaning, purpose, responsibility 6–8; objectivity, neutrality assumption 26, 170–171; soul–soil and body / nature and life 19, 74, 81–82, 128, 154, 170–171, 171, 174; theory/science's outcome compassion 10, 26, 119, 122, 160
Dharmic wisdom, tradition 32, 110
The Dhandho Investor (Pabrai) 108
disconnect *see* detachment, desensitisation
displacement 55–56, 69, 70, 74, 106, 128, 134–135, 145

diversity 120–123; biodiversity 10, 29, 31–32, 33, 50, 69, 75, 76, 81, 88–89, 95; 'biodiversity' in finance 114–115, 149–150, 155; denial, destruction 15, 25, 71, 96, 125, 143, 163, 169 (*see also* standardisation; universalism vs cultural pluralism); growth mindset 150–151, 165; human, cultural, context 6, 10–11, 18, 21, 31, 50, 63–64, 81–82, 106–109, 112–114; plurality cultivation 120–123; practices, forces 23, 102–103, 111–112, 124–125; research methods and theories 129–130, 177–178; *see also* pluralism
Dockland London 119
Dodd, N. 61

earthly morality 60–61
ecosystem of finance beliefs 35, 101–130; boundary policing 103–105; chemistry 35; climate 35, 101; cultural diversity, cultivating plurality 120–123; de-culturation through finance 15, 93–94, 105–107, 109, 115, 115–117, 127–129, 172; elite finance networks of expropriation 116–117; finance culture documentation and mapping 112–114; finance knowledge 'environment' 104–105; financial reflexivity 101, 120–121, 123–124, 127–130; holistic/context-sensitive finance theories and methods 110–112; human diversity, ignorance and suppression 107–109; human health effect 102; inter-cultural trust and dialog 114–115; knowledge ecosystem 102, 103, 106, 130; knowledge framing, financial intimacy encouragement 126–127; nature's wisdom 117–119; owner-managed enterprise 123–124; plurality, cultural 121–123; plurality cultivation 121–123; power concentration effects, psychological 102; re-culturation of financial knowledge 109–110; rivers 101; small business finance 74, 87, 107, 108, 123–126, 137, 140–141, 145, 151, 175; social harmony 119–121; specialisation as border-creation 103–105; systems thinking science 102; Western environmental ignorance 101; wisdom and meaning wholeness 127–128
education *see* learning
empire / empire mindset, repercussions 3, 4, 8–10, 14–15, 21, 50, 54, 62, 171–175
empiricism 21, 28, 30, 173
The Enduring Value of Values (Cunningham) 25
environmental aesthetics 170–171

Index   183

epistemology 16, 21, 102
ESG 23, 25, 55, 91, 135, 163, 174
ethical finance, foundations 7, 34, 49–71; community 34; culture 34; earthly morality, soil–soul connection 60–63, 64; faith 34; knowledge and education/training 10, 12–13, 22, 78–79, 85–86, 92, 103–104, 127, 169–170; knowledge specialisation holistic finance prevention 103–104, 127; lack in finance (*Homo Economicus*) 1–2, 3, 4, 6, 10, 74; law and regulations 167; media 165; multinational corporations 55–56, 58; oxymoron assumption, positivism 3; relationships 34; and scientific 'objectivity' 12–13, 26–27, 28, 36, 36nn1~2, 55, 174; systemic hypocrisy 25; trust 34
ethics, ethical behaviour: Anthropocentrism impact 13, 15; knowledge system 2, 12–13; ontologies, ontological shifts 16
Euro-centrism 27, 34, 101, 115, 154, 171–172, 174; *see also* empire / empire mindset, repercussions
evil finance 1–36; Anthropocentrism 1, 10, 13–16, 21–22, 32, 49, 135, 146–147, 158, 162; climate change, environmental action failure 29–31; empire, mindset/policies of othering and subjugation 3, 4, 8–10, 14–15, 21, 50, 54, 62, 171–175; false pedagogy 6–8 (*see also* learning); finance fiction 4–6; vs holistic, communitarian finance 23, 24–26, 30, 32, 33, 91, 106, 111–112, 165, 172; *Homo Economicus* 1, 3, 4, 6, 10, 74; indigenous cultures, wisdom 10–13; life commodification, marketization 22–23; materialist 'science,' objectivity 16–19, 26–29; money concept, power reality 20–21; 'surveillance capitalism' 19–20
experiential learning 24, 62, 77, 137, 176
expropriation, nature / societies 3, 6–7, 22, 35, 53, 63, 115–117, 141–143, 168

faith/religion and beliefs 29–30, 86–87, 110, 169–170; climate change and nature consciousness 29–30, 118; communal/cultural function (protection, learning, identity) 52, 62, 86–87, 113, 155; conscience 36n2; death and seasonality acceptance 51 (*see also* seasonality); endangerment, modern transactional systems 96; exclusion from finance theory/science 3, 5, 7, 23, 150; faith networks 11, 122; faith–finance intertwinement 7, 10; finance and materialism as 16, 138, 169, 173; globalising 175; misinterpretation, faith illiteracy 29, 87, 169–170; and trust 79–81, 86–87, 113; wisdom source, tradition 10
false pedagogy 6–8; *see also* learning
farming, farmers *see* agriculture, farming
finance, evil, broken: Anthropocene, European imperialism consequences 1–3; culture, ethic loss 1–2; *Homo Economicus* 1, 3, 4, 6, 10, 74; language framing 2; monetary gain as end vs mean 1; science/knowledge system legitimisation 1–2; *see also* empire / empire mindset, repercussions
finance, holistic approach 23, 30, 32, 33, 91, 106, 111–112
finance, organic *see* soil and soul, organic finance fundamentals
finance fiction 4–6
Financial Times 6, 15
financialisaton 5, 14, 35, 56, 69, 78, 84, 122, 148
FinTech 20, 89
forests of hope institutions 35, 158–179; conscience and its implementation 166–167; cultural depth/wisdom as roots 162–164; defining 159; diversity/plurality acceptance 121, 142–143; environmental aesthetics 170–171; forest cultures 12; vs forest of materialistic finance 168–170; holistic learning 127–128, 169, 173; law and regulations 167–168; natural forest and finance organisation, metaphor applicability 157–159; natural/forest growth interdependence mechanisms 35–36, 90, 104, 118, 135, 140, 142–143, 145; as powers of tolerance and kindness 159–161; purpose and meaning 165–166; seasonality and natural circularity development 161–162; selflessness in nature/forests 35, 64–65, 71, 117, 142, 158, 162, 164–166
fossil fuel (extraction, emission, economy) 1, 4, 14, 57, 69, 118, 134
Freire, Paolo 12–13

Graeber, David 2, 6, 12, 16, 22, 27, 108, 112–113, 172
Green Finance 23, 168
greenwashing 174
groundedness: community, real world 15, 52–53, 59, 62, 83; financial 59, 63, 87, 90–91, 130, 171–172; nature (earth, soil) 55, 57, 83, 168, 174

growth 35, 134–155; anthropocentric measures, income and value 145–147; beyond money and finance 136–139; 'biodiversity' of finance knowledge 149–150; concept of indigenous cultures 11; corporate, human impact 143–147; corporate/anthropocentric, expropriation and offshore extraction 141–143; distribution, resilience 140; growth mindset 150–152; knowledge 'growth' consequences 147–149; limits and contentedness 166, 175; macro-spiritual growth vision 152–154; and materialistic culture 5; measurement 145–147; micro-enterprise 140–141; natural, sustainability limitations 34–35; nature of 135–136; organic growth 135; organic theory of finance 175; positivist paradigms 26; and seasonality acceptance 139; shared growth vs expropriation 3, 141–143; soul, ethics of 143–145

harmony: cultural–natural, inter-dependent ecosystem 2, 3, 21, 29, 32, 68, 76; social 27, 119–121, 136
high context cultures 63–64
Hoang, K. K. 116
holistic finance approach 23, 30–33, 91, 106, 111–112
Homo Economicus 1, 3, 4, 6, 10, 74
horticulture 32, 75, 78–79
hundi 63

identity, individual vs collective/shared 24, 62–63, 92, 103, 106
illiteracy and literacy, financial 77–78, 94, 104–105, 117, 152, 178–179
Indian culture, way of life 63, 108, 110, 118, 124, 169, 172
indigenous cultures: cultural–natural harmony, inter-dependent ecosystem 2, 3, 21, 29, 32, 68, 76; empire, subjugation and othering 10–12, 21, 54–55, 109–110 (*see also* empire / empire mindset, repercussions); growth concept 11; indigenous life–finance framework 28, 31–33, 122, 171; interdependence embracement, communities 12, 114, 122, 158, 160–162, 164; land trustee- vs ownership 14; local and micro-financing 109; rivers in 101; sacredness, consciousness and faith 14, 29–30, 31; social harmony 27, 119–121, 136; wisdom, traditional/non-colonialist, indigenous, traditional 2–4, 10–13, 21, 24, 31–32, 76–77, 83, 109, 162–163, 177; wisdom and respect, natural 33, 101, 117, 158, 159, 160–162, 162, 165
individualism 10, 24, 59–60, 62, 92–93, 101, 112
industrialisation 14, 19, 30, 73, 82, 95, 96, 134
inter-cultural trust and dialogue 24–25, 94–95, 113, 114–115
interdependence 64–65; animal commodification 66; climate crisis 24, 36; embracement, indigenous communities 12; encouragement 36, 153, 155; financial education 164–165, 171; natural growth mechanism 90, 104, 118, 135, 140, 145; soil–seed–society/culture wholeness 49, 73, 76–77, 82–84 (*see also* seed/seeding (culture, trust relationships)); soil–soul vs property/land ownership 68
'inter-temporal energy', finance as 78
investigative journalism 19, 104, 117

Jain culture and tradition, Janism 6, 12–13, 29, 31, 36nn3–4, 52–53, 78, 134, 172–173
journalists, investigative 19, 104, 117
journals 16–17, 23, 26–27, 36n1, 105, 112, 148, 164–165, 173

knowledge: biodiversity of finance knowledge 149–150; ecosystem 102, 103, 106, 130; and education/training 10, 12–13, 22, 78–79, 85–86, 92, 103–104, 127, 169–170 (*see also* learning/education); denials, knowledge industry 161; finance knowledge 'environment' 104–105; financial knowledge re-culturation 109–110, 129; knowledge framing, financial intimacy encouragement 126–127; knowledge 'growth' consequences 147–149; specialisation 103; knowledge system, nature 117–119; vs pedagogy/transformation segregation 7, 172; vs wisdom 21, 91; wisdom as wholesome, responsible, accountable knowledge 53–54
Kuhn, T. S. 26
Kumar, Satish 73

land owner- vs trusteeship 14, 61, 64, 67–68, 70, 144, 167
language, finance: control, empire 2, 9, 18, 33, 54, 81; English as dominant, impacts 9, 16, 113, 114, 178; environmental-oriented language, terminology

29, 30, 32–33; of groundedness and community/cultures 59, 61, 83, 108, 111, 112–113, 121–122, 153; plurality need 13; and thinking link 28
Latour, Bruno 3
law and regulations 35, 57, 58, 80, 93, 117, 122, 141–143, 167–168
leadership 91, 94, 115, 123–124, 127–128, 137, 161–162, 165, 177
learning: and adaptation 92–93; detachment from communities/cultures 6–8, 92, 176–177; ethical finance education 10, 12–13, 22, 78–79, 85–86, 92, 103–104, 127, 169–170; experiential 24, 62, 77, 137, 176; forest as laboratories of 160; group, communal 24; holistic, wisdom/life experience and meaning 12, 32, 127–128, 153; knowledge-vs-pedagogy/transformation segregation 7, 172; *Pedagogy of the Oppressed* (Freire) 12; research and teaching symbiose need 104–105; shared learning and identity 62–63; spirituality and 153
life commodification, marketization 17, 20, 22–23, 70, 171
literacy and illiteracy, financial 77–78, 94, 104–105, 117, 152, 178–179
local pooling 87–88

macro-spiritual growth vision 152–154
maximisation, value/profits 5, 11, 22, 28, 74, 88, 95, 103–104
McGoun, S. 16
meditation, mindfulness 30–31, 119, 121, 129–130, 152, 154, 155, 158–159, 165, 179
Meyer, Erin 24–25, 113
micro-economics 102, 147
micro-enterprises 140–141, 154, 178; *see also* small business finance
micro-finance 77–79, 87, 126
micro-normative approaches 103
micro-politics 126
money, function and effects 5; as construct 3–4, 5, 16–17, 2, 25, 56, 74, 104, 166; FinTech, money and finance 20, 53–54, 78, 94, 102, 120; wealth creation, maximisation effects 5
mono-culture 15, 89, 89–90; *see also* diversity
Monsanto 74, 95
morality, moral culture *see* ethical finance, foundations
morality and ethics *see under their own headings*

multinational corporation 5, 56–57, 89, 95, 116, 141–143
multiplication, multiplier effect 58, 73, 83–85, 90, 175

nature-based societies 50–52
nature's wisdom 76, 117–119
Net Zero 49, 82, 122, 163
networks, networking 7, 11, 24, 53, 78, 107, 115–117, 122, 141
nomadic life 52, 53, 54, 126–127, 138
non-violent life–finance framework 8, 31–33

ontology, ontological shifts 16, 18, 21, 28, 31, 32, 109, 154, 172, 175
organic finance *see* soil and soul, organic finance fundamentals
owner-managed enterprise 123–124
ownership, corporations 144
ownership vs trusteeship, land 14, 61, 64, 67–68, 70, 167

Pabrai, M. 108
paradigm shifts 26–27, 91, 103, 154
Pedagogy of the Oppressed (Freire) 12
pharma, big pharma 102
plants and soil–soul connection 65–66
pluralism 6, 15, 21, 31, 32, 106–109, 120–123, 129, 177–178
politicisation and critique resistance 102–103
positivism 3–4, 26, 28, 160, 168, 173
power concentration: psychological effects 102; technology and 102
Prahlad, C. K. 25
psychoanalytics 5, 102, 107, 120–121
purpose and meaning 128, 165–166; cultural, societal selectivity 11, 16; education and training 85, 166; learning, experience 12, 32, 127–128, 153; materialism and loss of 30; sense of, need and growing 61, 79, 121, 141, 165, 172, 177

racism 3, 21, 59, 174
re-culturation, financial knowledge 109–110, 129
reflexivity, financial 30–31, 101–102, 110, 120–121, 123–124, 127–130, 148, 154, 166–167, 173
religion *see* faith/religion and beliefs
Review of International Political Economy 27, 120
rivers: financial, neo-liberal/capitalistic 14; in indigenous cultures 101; and life, interdependence 51, 101;

pollution 66, 74; sacredness 11, 101; wisdom, truth of 33

Said, Edward W. 9, 36n5
Sanatana Dharma 110
Sartre, Jean-Paul 9
seasonality: finance, denial 76, 146; finance, respecting 139; natural life, farming 65, 76–78, 83, 86, 96, 134, 142–143, 145, 154
Sedgmore, Lynne 17
seed/seeding (culture, trust relationships) 34–35, 73–97; adaptation, learning needs 92–93; agribusiness as soil and soul attack 73–95; 'biodiversity' in finance 10, 88–90, 114–115, 149–150, 155; culturation and relationship needs 93–94; as education and training 85–86; as faith and beliefs 86–87; grounded seed finance 90–91; leadership, growing direction 91–92; local pooling 87–88; microfinance, seeding small entrepreneurs 77–79, 87, 126 (*see also* micro-enterprises; small business finance); multiplication 83–85; soil–seed–society interdependence and potential 73, 76–77, 82–84; soul–soil and body detachment 81–82 (*see also* detachment, desensitisation); spreading (travel, trade) 94–95; standardisation through wholesale finance 75–76 (*see also* standardisation); trust 74–76, 79–81, 86–87, 90, 95–96, 109, 112–115, 129, 161, 175–177
selfless science 160, 164–165
selflessness, nature/forests 35, 64–65, 71, 117, 142, 158, 162, 166
Seva 110
shared learning and identity 62–63
Shiller, R. J. 12, 36n2
silence of nature, indigenous wisdom 33, 159, 162, 165
silences, finance theories and practices 4–6, 7, 66, 117, 173
slavery 8, 21, 106, 149
small business finance 74, 87, 107, 108, 123–126, 137, 140–141, 145, 151, 175
Smith, Adam 29–30
social harmony 119–121, 136
soil and soul, organic finance fundamentals 34, 49–71; animal soul and spirit 66–67; care and compassion 54–55; communities of souls 52–53; context, nature and living ecosystem 59–60; democratic demands and failures 57–59; displacement effects 55–56; high context cultures 63–64; inter-dependence 64–65; land owner-vs trusteeship 67–68; morality and ethics (*see under their own headings*); multinational corporation and global destruction 56–57; nature-based societies 50–52; need for, Anthropocene impact 1–2; plants and soil–soul connection 65–66; shared learning and identity 62–63; soul–soil detachment 81–82; soil–soul–society trinity 73; source and aim 2–3; wisdom as wholesome, responsible, accountable knowledge 53–54
soul: and seed (*see* seed (culture, trust relationships)); and soil/body (*see* soil and soul, organic finance fundamentals);
spirituality, macro-spiritual growth vision 152–154
spreading, travel/world trade 94–95
standardisation 70, 75–76, 81–82, 84, 125, 145, 151, 167
State Street 58
Stein, M. 102
stewardship, environmental 22, 67, 71, 110, 134
Stiglitz, Joseph E. 101–102
Strevens, Michael 26
surveillance capitalism (deep control, technology) 19–20
systems thinking science 102

tax: Big 4 companies 4, 116, 142; history 49; land ownership 67; minimisation, avoidance 4, 7, 27, 57, 67–68, 117, 141–142, 170; multinational corporations 57, 141–142, 167; purpose, ethical dimension 4, 57, 68, 117, 176
technology: communication, interpersonal understanding 114, 115, 179; FinTech, money and finance 20, 53–54, 78, 94, 102, 120; Net Zero 49; suicidal / harmful use, Anthropocene 13–14, 30, 51–52, 55–56, 63, 82, 89, 118; surveillance capitalism 19–20
Tett, Gillian 6, 15
Thunberg, Greta 165
travel 52–53, 84, 94–95, 114
trust 74–76, 79–81, 86–87, 90, 95–96, 109, 112–115, 129, 161, 175–177
trusteeship, animal/nature 14, 32, 67–68, 110, 134

trusteeship vs ownership, land 14, 61, 64, 67–68, 70, 144, 167
TrustPilot 54

United Nations 63, 134, 165
universalism vs cultural pluralism 6, 8, 15, 69–70, 88, 91, 95, 102, 103, 107–109, 114, 121–123
urban vs rural finance 110–111; *see also* holistic finance
urbanisation, urban environments 15–16, 62, 69, 80, 95, 134

Wall Street 119
war, armament economy 4, 8, 51, 109
wealth creation, maximisation effects: capital globalisation effects 22; money as symbol 27; personal, psychological 5; sharing 6; surplus wealth and societal inequalities 5; wealth as disease 5; wealth transfer 7
WEIRD (Western, educated, industrialised, rich and democratic) subjects 17, 101
Wenger, Etienne 7

Wengrow, David 12, 27, 172
Whitehead, A. N. 27, 126
Whitley, R. 148
wholesale finance 75–76, 85
wisdom: biodiversity of finance wisdom 88–89, 114–115, 149–150, 155; defining 21, 91; Dharmic 32, 110; Jain 31–32; vs knowledge 21, 91; local wisdom and universal finance 78, 88; nature's 2, 32, 117–119; new economic 49; non-colonialist, indigenous, traditional 2–4, 10–13, 21, 24, 31–32, 76–77, 83, 109, 162–163, 177; scholarly ignorance vs wisdom sciences 16, 21, 28, 30–31; spirituality dimension of 29–30, 118; thirst for wisdom and meaning 127–128; as wholesome, responsible, accountable knowledge 53–54

yoga 53, 61, 101, 155
Yunus, Mohammed 77

Zingales, Luigi 104
Zuboff, P. S. 20, 56